Overdrive

T0122638

Also by James Wallace

*Hard Drive: Bill Gates and the Making
of the Microsoft Empire* (with Jim Erickson)

Overdrive

BILL GATES
and the
RACE TO CONTROL
CYBERSPACE

James Wallace

John Wiley & Sons, Inc.

New York • Chichester • Weinheim
Brisbane • Singapore • Toronto

Design by Jane Tenenbaum.

Copyright © 1997 by James Wallace.
Published by John Wiley & Sons, Inc.
All rights reserved. Published simultaneously in Canada.

Reproduction or translation of any part of this work beyond that permitted by Section 107 or 108 of the 1976 United States Copyright Act without the permission of the copyright owner is unlawful. Requests for permission or further information should be addressed to the Permissions Department, John Wiley & Sons, Inc.

This publication is designed to provide accurate and authoritative information in regard to the subject matter covered. It is sold with the understanding that the publisher is not engaged in rendering legal, accounting, or other professional services. If legal advice or other expert assistance is required, the services of a competent professional person should be sought.

Library of Congress Cataloging-in-Publication Data

Wallace, James
    Overdrive : Bill Gates and the race to control cyberspace / James
Wallace.
        p.   cm.
    Includes index.
    ISBN 978-1-62045-801-3
    1. Gates, Bill, 1956–   2. Microsoft Corporation—History.
3. Businessmen—United States—Biography.   4. Computer software
industry—United States—History.   I. Title.
HD9696.C62G3379   1997
338.7'610053'092—dc21   97-4464
    [B]

10 9 8 7 6 5 4 3 2 1

To Jackie Lincecum, for second chances, however brief.

Contents

Preface

This project began with a request in the spring of 1996 from publisher John Wiley & Sons to update my previous book *Hard Drive*, which I wrote with Jim Erickson. But it quickly became apparent that so much had happened since the publication of *Hard Drive* in 1992 that another book was needed to fully tell the incredible story of the rise of the Internet and how Microsoft responded.

As was the case with *Hard Drive*, Microsoft did not cooperate with research for this book. The company was not pleased with *Hard Drive*, which had been cited by U.S. District Court Judge Stanley Sporkin in rejecting the antitrust consent decree negotiated in 1994 between Microsoft and the U.S. Justice Department. As a result, Microsoft spent many more months in court before Sporkin's ruling was overturned.

While Microsoft officially refused any help with this book, some of its employees and executives agreed to off-the-record interviews. Their names are not used in this book, but they know who they are and I would like to thank them for helping me tell this story.

My most special thanks, though, goes to my editor, Hana Lane, at John Wiley & Sons, who offered hope and encouragement and whose life expectancy was probably shortened considerably because of the number of deadlines that I failed to meet.

This book would not have been possible without the tireless efforts of several others at John Wiley & Sons, including Marcia Samuels, managing editor, Elizabeth Doble, director of production, and, finally, Gerry Helferich, the publisher, who never lost his cool and gave the book his full support all along the way.

Many people outside of Microsoft were interviewed for this book, and I would like to single out a few for the hours they spent talking with me: Bill Joy, Eric Schmidt, Rob Glaser, Jeff Lill, Dave Thompson, Tim Krauskopf, and Mike Tyrrell.

I would also like to thank Jim Erickson, my co-author on *Hard Drive,* who provided help with interviews. Jim is now a reporter for *Asiaweek* in Hong Kong.

Thanks, too, goes to J. D. Alexander, publisher of the *Seattle Post-Intelligencer,* the newspaper where I work as a reporter. J. D. graciously allowed some of the newspaper's photos to be used in this book.

When I began *Overdrive,* I was doing research for a book about Philippe Kahn of Borland International. That project got sidetracked by this one but not before Philippe had given me about 50 hours of his time for interviews. Those interviews yielded invaluable insights and information about the computer industry, and relevant material from those interviews with Phillipe is included in this book. I am in his debt not only for his help but also for the kindness he showed me, especially when I had to tell him I was going to stop work on his book so I could write another book about his bitter rival, Bill Gates.

Finally, I would like to thank two very dear people in my life, Linda Moore and Jackie Lincecum. Linda helped me to survive a couple of very dark times during the writing of this book. And Jackie worked tirelessly to transcribe interviews, even though she had a full-time job. More important, she gave me her love, friendship, and support, without which I would have lost my way.

James Wallace
Seattle, February 1997

PROLOGUE
Prelude to War

Ringmaster Bill Gates was growing increasingly testy. Under the enormous white tent that had been erected on the lush green lawn of Microsoft's campus for this crazy circus known as the Windows 95 launch, a dress rehearsal for what was to be the greatest show on earth was going badly. After several weeks of unprecedented hype, the day that the entire planet seemed to be talking about was only hours away, and this was the last opportunity to work through the launch-day script.

The next morning, August 24, 1995, more than 2,500 journalists, industry big shots, and special guests, along with friends and family of Gates, would fill this cavernous tent to hear Microsoft's chairman deliver a now familiar sermon on why Windows 95 would change the world. Millions more in 42 U.S. cities and in major capitals around the world would watch on closed-circuit television from satellite feeds. Microsoft was spending more than a quarter of a billion dollars on the biggest and noisiest product launch in the history of the computer industry—hell, this was the biggest marketing extravaganza for a consumer product ever, outstripping the hoopla over New Coke or the first Super Bowl. But a series of minor technical glitches during the final run-through were making Gates nuts.

Probably the only person or thing Gates was not yelling at was comedian Jay Leno, who had been paid some of those marketing bucks to be the surprise guest at the Windows 95 party. Poor Leno. The square-jawed *Tonight Show* host was trying to learn how to use a computer before the next morning. At least Gates was showing some atypical patience with Leno, explaining where to position the mouse and how to click it.

But some troublesome equipment was not so fortunate. "C'mon!" Gates yelled in disgust at one point when the on-stage computer began to act up. He angrily picked up the mouse pad and threw it on the podium. Not far away, a reporter for *USA Today,* who had been given behind-the-scenes access to Gates during the pressure-packed hours before the launch, hurriedly scribbled notes.

"You've got the wrong screen set up here," Gates snapped at a technician.

By early evening Leno had had enough.

"I came illiterate," Leno quipped about computers as he walked out of the tent. "Now I'm leaving virtually retarded."

The others who remained in the tent did not escape Gates's wrath, especially when his TelePrompTer conked out. But it was not until he watched a special promotional video that had been prepared for the next day's show that his anger finally exploded.

"This video makes no sense!" Gates shouted at Brad Chase, the marketing manager for Windows 95.

Gates was especially upset about a scene in which an interviewer playfully asked an executive if Windows 95 would improve his sex life. Although the line in the video got a laugh from the sparse crowd in the tent, Gates was not amused. He was dumbfounded that anyone would try to link Windows 95 with people's sex lives. (No one dared tell Gates, of course, that the quarter billion dollars his company was spending to hype Windows 95 had already linked it with everything under the sun.)

"We are supposed to be making serious points here!" he heatedly told Chase.

Gates decided to watch the video one more time. Long before it was over, the dour expressions that washed across his face, which by now was beginning to show the strains of a very long day, gave the verdict away.

"I'd rather have nothing than have that!" Gates complained as he walked away for an interview with an anchorwoman from the BBC.

The interview was to be the last of his media appearances this day. They had started that morning, nearly 12 hours earlier, around 8:30 A.M., when Gates had done the first of what would be 14 television interviews over three hours. That brought his total for the week to 29, including *Today, Good Morning America,* and *Larry King Live.* After he had finished the last of those, Gates had explained their value to the reporter from *USA Today* as he walked back to his office for lunch, in Microsoft's Building 8.

"I have to ask," he told the reporter, "is it worth six minutes of my time? Well, each of those shows has 50,000 to 100,000 viewers. So it's time well leveraged."

Well-leveraged time. It was a concept of media relations that Gates had learned a year or so earlier from his pal Warren Buffett. The two were at a party thrown by mutual friend Meg Greenfield, editorial page editor of the *Washington Post* and, like Gates, a Seattle native. Gates was playing croquet on the lawn of Greenfield's house on Bainbridge Island, across Puget Sound from Seattle, when he overheard Buffett talking about how he had handled the media during the Salomon Brothers trading scandal. Croquet mallet in hand, Gates walked over to Buffett.

"Did you hire a media adviser?" Gates asked.

"No," Buffett told his friend. "You just call them all into a room and you go talk to them."

Later that week, for the first time, Gates invited the Seattle media to his office for one-on-one interviews.

For the Windows 95 launch, Gates had invited about 500 journalists and dozens of television crews from around the world to join the Microsoft party at its corporate campus in Redmond, a woodsy suburb east of Seattle. They had come from more than 30 countries: from Lativa and Turkmenistan, from Finland, France, and Australia. They had come from newspapers and the networks, from the trade press and the mainstream press, all to stoke the fires of Microsoft's relentless advertising hype with an incalculable amount of free publicity on what had become a worldwide "happening," a love feast straight out of the sixties, the computer industry's Woodstock.

All this for an imperfect software upgrade with 15 million lines of computer code that was more than two years late getting to market.

Microsoft had paid several million dollars for the rights to use the Rolling Stones song "Start Me Up" as the official soundtrack of its Windows 95 advertising campaign. In Great Britain, entire fields had been painted with the colorful Windows 95 logo to catch the attention of planes flying overhead. Microsoft had even bought the entire press run of the *Times* of London and on launch day planned to give away 1.5 million copies free, with an advertisement across the bottom of the front page that read: "Windows 95. So Good Even the Times Is Complimentary." In Australia, a four-story box covered with Windows 95 logos was to be towed into Sydney Harbor on a barge, as dancers performed in the streets. All babies born Down Under on launch day were to get a free copy of Windows 95. In Toronto, a 500-foot banner pitching Windows 95 was to be unfurled on one side of the government-owned 1,800-foot Canadian National Tower. In the Philippines, the very first copy of the new operating system to hit the country was to be hand-delivered to President Fidel Ramos. In Poland, Microsoft representatives planned to take reporters down in a submarine to show them what it would be like to live in a world without windows. In New York City, Microsoft, the 800-pound gorilla of the software industry, had paid to have the 102-story Empire State Building bathed in the logo colors of Windows 95. Even the "Doonesbury" comic strip was featuring the new computer operating system during the week of the launch.

And Microsoft's 270-acre corporate campus was the perfect setting for this media and advertising circus. It had been transformed, complete with Ferris wheel. The sweeping expanse of lawn had been decked with 15 large white tents, the biggest of which was to be used to accommodate the 2,500 people with special invitations. More than 10,000 others had received passes to take part in the event, but from outside. Those 14 other tents would be filled with software executives demonstrating their applications designed to run on Windows 95. More than 100 computer companies had signed up to participate.

Although The Launch was officially set for 11:00 A.M. on Thursday, August 24, the party had already started by the time Gates was blowing his top during the final rehearsal in the big tent with Leno.

As part of its savvy marketing campaign to convince customers that this was a must-have product, Microsoft had declared that Windows 95 could not go on sale until 12:01 A.M., local time, on August 24. Retail stores from coast to coast, their shelves stocked with boxes of Windows 95, had decided to open their doors at midnight to the hordes of customers who had bought into the marketing hype and couldn't wait to be among the first to buy what was billed as the greatest software product in the history of the universe. CompUSA, the computer chain, arranged to keep its 86 stores across the country open until past midnight for the first time, and offered free pizza to all customers as well as discounts on American Airlines tickets for buyers of Windows 95.

At the stroke of midnight in New Zealand, the first English-speaking country to greet the new day, the very first copy of Windows 95 was sold to a business student in Auckland. From there, the insanity spread west toward New York City, where hundreds of people pushed their way into computer stores at midnight.

Three hours away on the West Coast, Gates had finished his interview with the BBC anchorwoman and returned to his office alone to read his e-mail. He later returned to the big tent, where he and Chase and others discussed how to fix the promotional video. They finally agreed to take it out of the launch program altogether. Around 11:00 P.M., after a final review of the script, Gates left his office, got into his car, and headed for home. He was still hyped, but he looked beat.

A few years earlier, there might have been great concern among Microsoft's senior managers about the condition of the chairman when he showed up the next morning. After a restless night before the launch of Microsoft's Excel spreadsheet in New York City in May 1985, Gates had shown up for the big event without sleep, without a shave, and without a shower. He looked as bad as he smelled.

There was no need to worry this time. Gates was going home to his wife, not to some hotel room. Gates had been 29 years old that May day in New York City. Now, he was a couple months shy of his fortieth birthday. The computer geek once ridiculed for his personal appearance had cleaned up—literally. The personal changes in Gates had been as dramatic as the increase in his wealth, which was now approaching a staggering $20 billion. *Forbes* had recently named him the world's richest individual. He was also one of the world's most powerful. He was so well known internationally that he conducted his own foreign policy, calling on China's president and other world leaders during business trips abroad. He socialized with Buffett. He played golf with the president. Gates wanted to be taken seriously, as a visionary, as a statesman, as an adult.

But for all the changes, he was still very much that intense young college dropout who had founded Microsoft with buddy Paul Allen at age 19. Neither marriage nor fame nor fortune had diminished the white-hot competitive fire that consumed him. In the last few years, that fire had fueled the Microsoft juggernaut as it rolled inexorably across the computer industry, crushing all competitors and rearranging the landscape. Once-feared foes had been vanquished: Lotus was swallowed by IBM, and its chairman, Jim Manzi, one of Gates's most outspoken rivals, quit. Novell, which spent a fortune on what was expected to be Microsoft-killer WordPerfect, was instead losing market share and withering away. Borland International, once touted as the next Microsoft, was now a third-rate player whose flamboyant chairman, Philippe Kahn, had been knocked out of the game and off his board by his arch-enemy Gates. Microsoft had even taken on the U.S. government and won. When Gates and Justice Department trust-buster Anne Bingaman faced off in 1994, it was Bingaman who blinked. After investigating Microsoft's anticompetitive behavior and building what was thought to be a strong case against the company, the Justice Department backed down rather than risk a land war with Microsoft. Gates got off with a slap on the wrist.

Microsoft was entrenched on top, and Windows 95 was designed to keep it there. But for how long?

As a tired Gates left the Microsoft campus and drove home along Highway 520, he had far more on his mind than the launch of Windows 95, now just a few hours off. Old foes had been beaten back, and in some cases buried, but down the road was a new and even greater enemy than Microsoft had ever faced before. It was a Cold War relic called the Internet. And a bunch of wise-ass kids from an upstart company called

Netscape a thousand miles from Seattle in the Silicon Valley, a company that did not even exist two years earlier when Windows was initially supposed to be ready for market, had been keeping Gates up nights.

The Net, as the Internet had come to be known, represented a true paradigm shift in the computer industry. Remarkably, despite his prescience, Gates had missed the turnoff signs, and Microsoft now found itself far behind in the battle to create a new industry standard for tapping the unlimited resources of the Net. "We set the standard" had long been Microsoft's battle cry. First with DOS and then with Windows, Microsoft had become dominant because it controlled the operating system for most of the world's personal computers.

But while Microsoft's programmers were finishing Windows 95, the Netscape team had been creating a browser designed for cruising the Internet. By January 1995, seven months before the launch of Windows 95, when Microsoft had only a handful of people working on its own Internet browser, thousands of techno-hip computer users were downloading the Netscape Navigator. Netscape had set the standard, leaving Gates to face the very real possibility of Microsoft's demise unless the company could do a 180 and overtake Netscape's sizable lead.

Gates was all too aware of what had happened to once-mighty IBM during the last paradigm shift in the computer industry at the dawn of the personal computer revolution. Big Blue lost its dominance to another upstart company with a bunch of wise-ass kids in pizza-stained T-shirts. That company was Microsoft. Gates was not going to let someone else beat him at his own game. He had decided to reinvent the company. On May 26, three months before the launch of Windows 95, Gates had issued a lengthy memo to his executive staff titled "The Internet Tidal Wave," in which he announced: "Now I assign the Internet the highest level of importance. In this memo I want to make clear that our focus on the Internet is critical to every part of our business." Even as Microsoft readied for the biggest celebration in the company's history, it had already shifted into overdrive in the race to overtake Netscape. It was going to be a long, tough fight, but Microsoft had very deep pockets. And it also had Bill Gates.

If worries about Netscape had kept Gates up most of the night, it was not apparent when he arrived at his office the morning of The Launch. Dressed in slacks and a dark blue golf shirt emblazoned with the Windows 95 logo, Gates was pumped. After an 8:00 A.M. breakfast with a group of some 250 executives and managers of PC companies, Gates sped off in a golf cart to the big tent for a final rehearsal. This time, there were fewer glitches. The frustrations of the night before forgotten, Gates even danced onstage to the Windows theme song. Later, Gates retired to a nearby trailer for a touch of makeup and some rest.

By 11:00 A.M., the big, air-conditioned tent was filled. Among those seated up front was Gates's father, a prominent Seattle attorney. Next to him was Gates's wife, Melinda French, a product manager at Microsoft. Exactly on schedule, mystery guest Jay Leno walked onstage with Gates. The jokes started, with Gates playing the straight man.

"To give you an idea of how powerful Windows 95 is," Leno told the crowd, "it is able to keep track of all O.J.'s alibis at once."

Joking that Gates really wasn't so smart after all, Leno told how he had gone to Gates's home and found his VCR still flashing "12."

Leno was in fine form. Laughter filled the tent. Even Gates displayed a good sense of humor. At one point he asked Leno to demonstrate some of the features of Windows 95. When Leno paused and began making excuses, Gates quipped, "I think we paid you enough. You should do the demo."

Leno closed with a final joke that Windows 95 was like a good date: "Smart, user-friendly, and under $100."

Moments later, the Rolling Stones's "Start Me Up," the Windows 95 theme song, reverberated through the tent as a curtain fell away to reveal the product's development team, all of them wearing orange, blue, green, and yellow T-shirts that matched the product logo. The audience rose to its feet, cheering and applauding. Some danced to the music.

Outside, under a blue sky, the circus atmosphere prevailed. Balloons floated in the air. The Ferris wheel revolved. There was food, drink, and carnival games, along with tons of free merchandise. In tent after tent, technology companies promoted their Windows 95 products. Overhead, a plane towed a banner that read: "Windows 95, will you marry me? Texas Instruments."

After the opening presentation, Gates spent some time unwinding in a secure area of a nearby pavilion with some Microsoft employees. He was pleased. "It was the coolest thing I've ever been a part of," Gates said as he sipped from a can of Coke.

Nevertheless, it would be a long day for Gates. There would be more media interviews, more meetings. Later, when the launch-day party was finally over, Gates was scheduled to fly overseas to introduce versions of Windows 95 in several countries, including France. In Paris, he was to be picked up at the airport in a specially outfitted Citroen covered in Windows 95 logos. The Citroen was to take Gates to the Palais des Congrès, where he was to put on a Windows 95 presentation to several thousand people. From there, the Citroen was to take him to classrooms throughout the country where he would demonstrate Windows 95 to French schoolchildren.

Although Gates would be out of the country for days, his troops had their marching orders. Long before the tents and the Ferris wheel came down and the green lawn was cleaned of trash, programmers who had worked seven-day weeks for three years on Windows 95 were already attacking their new assignment: Netscape. The development of Windows 95 had been described by those who survived as a "death march." Now, once again, sleeping bags would hang from the doors of many Microsoft offices for the long days and nights ahead.

The party was over. But what a party it had been. Every soldier should have such fun before going to war.

1

The Road Ahead

At a formal dinner of the Churchill Club in the Silicon Valley in early 1990, Bill Joy, a tousle-haired programming genius and Silicon Valley legend known sometimes as "the other Bill," made what would prove to be a most remarkable prediction. Irrepressible Microsoft, Joy said, would continue to dominate for the next five to seven years, then everything would change. There would be an industry breakthrough unimagined at the time, and it would be made by a company that didn't yet exist.

The reclusive Joy, one of the fabulous four co-founders of Sun Microsystems, had been preaching the gospel of simplicity for some time. A year or so before his dinner talk that night at the Churchill Club, Joy had retreated to a mountain hideaway in Aspen, Colorado, to head a Sun research lab that he called Smallworks, dedicated to the proposition that successful software systems did not have to have 10 zillion lines of code. After all, successful large systems were once successful small systems.

Moore's Law, which was formulated by Intel founder Gordon Moore and which stated that the number of transistors that engineers could squeeze onto a silicon chip would double with machinelike regularity every 18 months, had been pushing the hardware envelope, but the software that ran personal computers, most of it designed by Microsoft, had become stagnant and overly complex, with layer upon layer of code. No one person could understand it; no one person could change it. Change one line somewhere, and it had repercussions somewhere else; ultimately, the whole system could crash. And it was not humanly possible to eliminate the complexity, because the software then would be even less compatible; it would be tantamount to trying to stir the sugar out of your coffee.

Joy felt Microsoft was "cruising for a bruising." They were big and arrogant and trying to take over everything. Worst of all, their software just wasn't very good. Joy compared Microsoft's software to the cars built by General Motors before the Japanese entered the market: they were breaking down all the time. Then Honda came along with quiet, reliable cars and changed the rules for success in the auto industry.

Likewise, Joy believed, Microsoft enjoyed its great success not because it had great software, but because people were stuck with it. Market domination, not innovation, drove the company's success, and it was this weakness that would eventually allow something else to emerge.

But what?

Disgusted by computer code complexity, Joy was convinced that something small and simple would generate the next great change in the computer industry. This breakthrough would come not from smart people working in a big company like Microsoft, or even Sun, but from a few unknowns working in a small company. Such companies didn't have meetings, they had lunch. Programmers got together and talked out their ideas. Decisions were made fast. They didn't have to try and turn the ship of state.

Joy understood what had happened to an industry being governed relentlessly by Moore's Law. He had a few of his own laws. One was that innovation would occur. And the corollary to this law was that innovation would occur elsewhere. Another corollary to Joy's Law of Innovation was that the number of bright people in any company went down as the size went up.

Even then it was clear to Joy that computers were boring because users could only look at their own files. Who wanted to use a computer just to see their own stuff? It was this realization that prompted the emergence of the Internet browsers. Joy knew something about the Internet. In the late seventies, as a graduate student at the University of California at Berkeley, he and his hacker pals had written some of the communication protocols for the Internet, which then was nothing but a crude Cold War link among universities, weapons research labs, and the Department of Defense.

Joy didn't talk about the Internet that night at the Churchill Club. He didn't reveal what would be the breakthrough that would eventually alter the fundamental power structure of the computer industry. What he did say was that Microsoft's size and dominance, like that of IBM at the dawn of the personal computer revolution, would spell its own demise. Mighty Microsoft would not be able to adapt and would be blocked out of new markets. Simplicity would win over complexity, small over big. As Apple founder Steve Jobs liked to say, when you are at simplicity, there ain't no complexity. Microsoft was too big, its software too complex. The next great innovation, Joy said, would make Microsoft's complex software irrelevant.

Later that same year, Joy visited Japan, where he made another prediction. The next great piece of software that he would be using all the time, Joy said, would come from a teenager.

The big blond kid with the baby face, lopsided smile, and hard-to-spell Scandinavian name was no teenager, but he had just come of age in December 1992 when, according to industry legend, he sat down one night with one of his programming buddies at the Espresso Royale Cafe at the University of Illinois at Urbana-Champaign. Before he left the cafe, 21-year-old Marc Andreessen had made up his mind that he and his friend would work around the clock for as long as it took to create that next great software program.

Andreessen was from Lisbon, Wisconsin. As a youngster he had dabbled in computer programming, but by high school the 6-foot-4 Andreessen was spending most of his time playing basketball. In college at Urbana-Champaign, Andreessen enrolled in the electrical engineering department, but—like Bill Gates, who attended college in the early 1970s—Andreessen often cut classes, and when he did go, he paid little attention. He dropped out of electrical engineering and transferred to the university's National Center for Supercomputing Applications (NCSA). He took a job for $6.85 an hour writing software for three-dimensional scientific visualization. Although he was surrounded by supercomputers, Andreessen found the work boring. It was in the physics lab that something finally caught his attention: the phenomenon of scientists sharing information around the globe over something called the Internet.

The Internet had its origin in 1969 in a Department of Defense project known as the Advanced Research Project Agency, or ARPANET. Its military planners had sought to design a computer network that could continue to function following a nuclear attack. Every computer on the network was able to communicate directly with every other computer on the network without having to go through a central point, so that in case any one site went down the remaining sites would still be able to communicate with each other.

But the Net did not begin to really open up to the world until Tim Berners-Lee, a researcher at the European Laboratory for Particle Physics in Geneva, Switzerland, designed a new kind of document description language known as Hyper-Text Markup Language, or HTML. The language, which consisted of a set of codes that were added to a document, was a way to format a document, to enable the embedding of graphics, sound clips, or other multimedia in a document, and to link a document with any other document on any other computer on the Internet. He distributed the HTML specifications free of charge over the Internet, and soon others were building HTML documents and linking them to each other. Thus was born the World Wide Web. Tapping into this wonderland of information, however, required a familiarity with UNIX code and its arcane commands. What the Web needed was a better way for the nontechnical computer user to navigate through this maze of information.

It was just such an easy-to-use Internet "browser" that Andreessen and his friend Eric Bina—and others at the NCSA, contrary to the legend of that night at the Espresso Royale Cafe—decided to design in late 1992. Over the next two months, Andreessen and Bina worked day and night, living on milk, chocolate chip cookies, Mountain Dew, and Skittles. A handful of other hungry, young, and super-smart programmers from the NCSA were recruited to help. Andreessen, the team leader, didn't tell anyone in management what they were up to. Larry Smarr, director of the NCSA, would not find out about what would be called Mosaic until later, after the work was done, when he was visiting the National Science Foundation in Washington, D.C., and a friend gave him a demonstration.

"This is going to be incredibly big," Smarr told his friend.

Nearly two decades earlier, in 1975 at Harvard, Bill Gates and his childhood pal Paul Allen had hunkered down in the Aiken Computer Center and spent eight weeks working day and night to develop a high-level computer language for the first microprocessing chip. Their software program, called BASIC, would become the foundation of a company called Microsoft, which they would soon found in the high desert of Albuquerque, New Mexico.

The Internet browser that Andreessen and his team designed in a similar eight-week marathon was christened Mosaic. Like HTML, it was distributed free of charge over the Internet, where it spread like a virus, unleashing the full potential of the World Wide Web. A year later, Andreessen and Jim Clark, former chairman of Silicon Graphics, would found a start-up company in Mountain View, California, called Mosaic Communications Corporation, later renamed Netscape.

Mosaic contained only 9,000 lines of computer code, thus validating Bill Joy's prediction that the next great innovation in software would be simple.

On a rainy winter day in early February 1993, at Microsoft's headquarters in Redmond, Washington, about the same time that Marc Andreessen and his pals at the National Center for Supercomputing Applications at Urbana-Champaign were getting ready to release the first version of Mosaic over the Internet, Bill Gates was sitting in his office across from Thomas Murphy, chairman of the board of Capital Cities/ABC. How would Gates like to be the next chairman of IBM, Murphy wanted to know.

It was no joke. William Henry Gates III, the 37-year-old hard-driving chairman of Microsoft, archenemy of Big Blue, was being recruited to take over for CEO John Akers, who had submitted his resignation. Murphy was on IBM's seven-member search committee, and Gates was at or near the top of their short list. In fact, he had been initially contacted by phone less than 48 hours after Akers announced he was stepping down.

The fact that Murphy was sitting in Gates's office that day spoke volumes about the sad state of affairs of the now-humbled computer giant whose name was once synonymous with American ingenuity. The previous year had been IBM's worst ever, ending with a loss of $5 billion, the biggest in American corporate history. About 40,000 IBM workers had left the company in 1992 after signing up for voluntary severance packages. Even so, IBM was still drowning in a sea of red ink. Its historic no-layoff policy was about to end. Morale among its workers was at an all-time low. Shareholders were not too happy, either. IBM's stock had collapsed—alarmingly. The bluest of Wall Street's blue-chip stocks had once traded at $175 a share, but by the end of 1992, it was selling for about $50 a share, a decline by half in less than a year. Shareholders were demanding that corporate heads roll, especially that of Akers, the former Navy fighter pilot who had been named CEO eight years earlier and had promised to lead America's greatest company to even greater heights.

It had been less than three years since Gates had met with some workers from Lotus in Boston after the Computer Bowl (the annual battle of wits for software execs) for what in industry lore became known as the "Gates Date" and had predicted that IBM would fold within seven years. Indeed, with each passing week, IBM was looking more like a house of cards.

Not only had IBM's stock collapsed, but—most humiliating of all—longtime foe Microsoft, the once tiny software company way out in the Pacific Northwest, which IBM had put on the map when it sought out Gates in 1980 to develop an operating system for the IBM PC, was now viewed as the industry's new leader. Microsoft had even supplanted Big Blue as Wall Street's favorite bellwether stock. Brokers who wanted to see what the market was likely to do over the next day or so looked at what was going on with Microsoft, one of the most liquid stocks around. About 400 million shares of Microsoft stock had changed hands during 1992, or about 1.7 million each day of trading on the stock exchange. In the jargon of the floor traders, Microsoft's stock was affectionately known as "Micky soft."

During the waning days of 1992, many analysts had predicted that it was only a matter of time before the unthinkable happened and Microsoft overtook IBM in total market value. That day came on January 20, 1993. With 303 million shares outstanding, and selling at a price of $88.375 a share, Microsoft's market value was $26.78 billion. IBM, meanwhile, saw its 571 million shares selling for $46.875 a share, giving it a market value of $26.76 billion. For Big Blue, whose shareholders had watched $77 billion in market value disappear since the company topped out in 1987, it was worse than any horror show.

Calculating a company's market value, also known as market capitalization, is not just a fun exercise with numbers. It can be a deciding factor when the market's biggest players select stock. By this one Wall Street measure, Microsoft was now the world's greatest computer industry company. It ranked fourteenth among all public companies, ahead of such giants as Ford, Boeing, General Motors, 3M, RJR Nabisco, and Eastman Kodak. Topping the charts was Exxon, with a market value of $72 billion. Coca-Cola was in sixth place, with a value of $55 billion. As IBM's stock rebounded, the company undoubtedly would again climb above Microsoft in value. But psychologically, Microsoft was now the undisputed industry leader. A generational shift had occurred, causing a sea change in a high-tech world.

"This is an unbelievable reversal of fortune," said one strategist for Salomon Brothers. "Microsoft was just a tiny company 15 years ago, and IBM ruled the world."

IBM's loss was Microsoft's gain in other ways, too. Résumés from Big Blue's top scientists were circulating in the industry. Some of the company's best brains were taking advantage of the company's early retirements. Nathan Myhrvold, head of Microsoft's advanced technology and one of the company's "Smart Guys," had hired entire groups of former Watson Lab researchers to move to Redmond and join Microsoft's small but growing research lab. IBM's Thomas J. Watson Laboratories, named after the company's founder, had been one of the country's largest and best private scientific and engineering research organizations.

IBM, some argued, had become a victim of its own success and its Soviet-style central planning. Either it didn't foresee the changing industry markets; or, when it did, the monolithic giant was so big and cumbersome that it couldn't get more advanced products to market quickly enough. All the while, powerful new personal computers in corporate networks were eating away at IBM's mainframe business. Mainframes had always been IBM's bread and butter, this argument went, and this infatuation with centralized computing was the root cause of its demise.

There were others, though, who argued that IBM was a victim of the microprocessor revolution that began with the world's first personal computer, the Altair, and that it had sown the seeds of its own destruction when it had handed the operating system contract for its first PC to a guy named Gates. Further, this argument went, giving the PC an "open" architecture was a critical mistake.

In fact, IBM had no choice, for in 1980, its engineers had to turn to outside companies like Microsoft and Intel in order to get a personal computer into the marketplace quickly. Designing a closed system would have required years of work.

A more convincing argument was one raised in the book *Computer Wars: How the West Can Win in a Post-IBM World* (Random House, 1993). Authors Charles Ferguson and Charles Moore held that the roots of IBM's decline began when it failed to demand the source code for DOS from Gates. Thus, each new upgrade had to be purchased from Microsoft, which maintained control of the most critical piece of software in the PC industry.

In the mid-1980s, industry talk said that Microsoft and IBM were about to split, but in August of 1985, they signed a long-term joint agreement that guaranteed the continuation of DOS and IBM. This followed months of speculation that

IBM was mobilizing to develop its own proprietary operating system for its PC line. According to industry insiders, there were internal discussions within IBM about going it alone, but in the end the company decided to stick with Microsoft. At the time, Gates said it was "the biggest contract" Microsoft had ever signed.

The reason Gates had won, though, was that he stubbornly refused to deliver the DOS source code to IBM. In a key meeting with the IBM brass at Armonk, New York, the young Microsoft chairman had refused to back down.

But perhaps IBM's decline was inevitable. Software, not hardware, now drove the computer industry. And by being smart, opportunistic, hard-working, aggressive, devious, and just plain lucky, Gates had cornered that market.

On January 26, 1993, one day less than a week after IBM's market value fell below that of Microsoft's, Big Blue's board of directors solemnly took their seats inside the company's glass skyscraper on Madison Avenue. Although the timing of the board meeting had nothing to do with the fall of IBM's market value, the end had come for Akers, and he knew it. But the old fighter pilot refused to be shot down. He proposed that he "retire" as chairman, then left the room while board members considered his offer. It was quickly accepted.

The search was then on for a new chairman, a Moses who could lead IBM out of the desert and into the Promised Land. Mitch Kapor, the founder of Lotus, was quoted as saying that Bill Gates would be the best choice to replace Akers as IBM chairman. Gates, his old rival said, had "the right combination of talent and ruthless ambition." That take-no-prisoners attitude had made Gates the most hated man in the industry and Microsoft the most feared competitor—some would say predator.

Gates, who had started out as only a low-level soldier in the information age revolution, now towered over the industry like a colossus. He had gained the kind of power and influence over an industry that John D. Rockefeller once held over America's oil industry at the turn of the century. Like a high-stakes player at a Vegas craps table, Gates was on a roll. Both his fame and his fortune were growing at an astronomical rate.

The title as America's richest person had officially been bestowed on Gates a few months earlier, in October 1992, when *Forbes* published its closely watched list of the 400 richest people in America. The magazine put Gates's net worth at $6.3 billion, or a billion or so dollars more than his closest challenger, Metromedia owner John Werner Kluge. Gates had at least $2 billion more than the third name on the *Forbes* list, that of his good friend Warren Buffett, who had made his fortune in the stock market. But not even *Forbes* really knew how much Gates was worth. The $6.3 billion figure was the result of a simple calculation, arrived at by multiplying the number of shares of Microsoft stock Gates held by the stock's selling price on Wall Street. Gates, however, was beginning to diversify, selling off nearly a half billion dollars of his stock each year, making investments that only a select few people knew about. And it was a pretty safe bet that Gates was making deals that were not losing him money.

Still, even the conservative $6.3 billion was an impressive figure, and writers and reporters who covered Gates and the computer industry did some calculating of their own to find new and colorful ways to express just how much money that was. One enterprising reporter for *Forbes* calculated that if Gates spent all his money on Rolls Royce Silver Spurs, they would stretch bumper to bumper from Seattle to Vancouver, British Columbia, a distance of some 130 miles. A writer for *Fortune* figured that Gates could buy an entire year's production of his 99 nearest competitors, burn it, and still be worth more than tabloid media mogul Rupert Murdoch or Ted Turner, owner of Turner Broadcasting.

Along with its leader, Microsoft was on a roll, too. The company's stock continued to rise toward Pluto. Its Windows program was selling a million copies a month. By early 1993, Windows had replaced DOS as the biggest-selling application of all time. Together, the programs brought in about $150 million a month for Microsoft. Its spreadsheet and word processing applications were also generating cash at record rates. Excel, first released for the Macintosh computer in 1985, was now the best-selling spreadsheet in the industry, well ahead of faltering spreadsheet pioneer Lotus. Sales of Microsoft Word for Windows were ahead of those for WordPerfect for Windows. Like a giant collapsing star, Microsoft was sucking in everything around it, including most of the software industry's money. It had become the Energizer Bunny on steroids, the company that kept going and going and going, hauling in money by the dump-truck load while others were laying off employees and watching profits shrink.

By the end of 1992, Microsoft had captured an astounding 44 percent share of the software market, while its closest competitors either held their position or lost ground. (Microsoft had 29 percent of the market at the end of 1991.) In second place at the end of 1992 was Lotus Development Corp., with 11.7 percent, down from 13 percent in 1991. WordPerfect remained in third place at 8 percent. Dataquest, the leading keeper of statistics for the software industry, put Microsoft's 1992 revenues at $3.4 billion. Lotus, producers of the popular Lotus 1-2-3, had revenues in 1992 of $894 million, according to Dataquest, which was the equivalent of just 26 percent of Microsoft's market share.

Neither Microsoft nor Gates was showing any signs of slowing down. Microsoft had hired 2,500 people in 1992 and planned to hire about the same number in 1993, which would bring its worldwide workforce to about 15,000. The company was now being called "Big Green" by some in the industry, not so much for the evergreen trees that dotted its sprawling Redmond campus, but for all the money the company was making, and because it was starting to act a lot like Big Blue of the 1970s.

"Microsoft is the IBM of the '90s and uses exactly the same marketing tactics IBM used to," Philippe Kahn, chairman of Borland International, told *Business Week* for a cover story on Gates that hit the newsstands in February. The cover asked, in large type, "Microsoft: Is It Too Powerful?"

As he talked about the IBM job with Thomas Murphy in his office that day, soon after Akers had submitted his resignation, Gates immediately made it clear he was committed to Microsoft and was not interested in the job. He then turned the job interview into a critique of IBM. Gates recalled that Akers had visited Microsoft several years earlier and they had talked about how difficult it was for IBM, because of its size, to keep up with the challenges presented by smaller, more focused competitors. Gates told Murphy that IBM had not kept pace with the fast-changing computer industry, and that in order to pull ahead, IBM needed to break up into several smaller firms.

Changes were coming fast, all right, so fast that some companies, unable to respond quickly enough to new markets, might never see the twenty-first century. Gates, always afraid of the fall, knew the pitfalls that lay ahead for Microsoft.

"We are scared all the time," he had told an audience celebrating the twenty-fifth anniversary of the University of Washington's computer science department. "We're always saying, 'Is this the day we've reached our peak?'"

For a clear and present reminder of what could go wrong when a great company didn't maintain the quick pace set by the industry, Gates needed to look no further than the headline of the day and troubled IBM.

Gates would later say that the phenomenon of the Internet had first shown up on his radar screen in April 1993 during one of his "Think Weeks." But he did not surf the Net for the first time until another one of these weeks later that year in October.

Gates spent these Think Weeks alone, using the time to read, write company memos, study the competition, and map out Microsoft strategy. It was a tradition that he had started in Albuquerque, when he would periodically fly home to Washington State to spend a week at his grandmother's house on the Hood Canal.

Although it took awhile before the Internet caught his attention, Gates had already started to focus on on-line services such as America Online (AOL) and CompuServe, where he believed Microsoft could gain an important foothold. In December 1992, Gates had called one of his product managers, Russ Siegelman, into his office and given him marching orders to find out everything he could about on-line services, come up with a strategy for what Microsoft should do, and report back. Siegelman was 30 years old. He had a degree in physics from MIT and an MBA from Harvard. Most recently, he had been working on Microsoft's Windows for Workgroups.

America Online was the early star of the on-line services, with its growth-at-any-cost strategy winning hundreds of new customers with each passing day. It had such a commanding lead that Siegelman considered a Microsoft gambit that had worked before when it needed to overtake the competition: if you can't beat 'em, buy 'em. Siegelman approached AOL Chairman Steve Case, but Case didn't want to sell. Microsoft would have no choice but to build its own service. Siegelman came up with a plan that he figured would eventually give Microsoft a huge advantage. He proposed that Microsoft create a rival service and include it as part of Chicago, the code name for what would become Windows 95. It seemed to be a brilliant strategy—all those millions of Windows customers hooking up to Microsoft's on-line service.

On May 11, Gates officially approved Siegelman's plan. The hush-hush project, code-named Marvel, would later be called the Microsoft Network, or MSN.

A few weeks later, a Microsoft executive who had met with Gates to talk about the on-line project found him angry and preoccupied with another pressing matter: the government's probe of Microsoft's supposedly anticompetitive practices.

"Is this goddamn crap ever going to end?!" Gates had exploded at the executive.

In fact, it was just heating up.

2

The Trustbuster

Microsoft's annual meeting with Wall Street analysts has become something of a predictable ritual of whistling past the graveyard, with the company posting phenomenal numbers, then parading out Gates and other executives who warn that such growth can't be sustained forever. The meeting with stock analysts in early August 1993 would be no exception.

The company was enjoying its eighteenth consecutive year of record profits and revenues. Quarterly revenues had topped $1 billion for the first time. For the fiscal year, profits were $953 million, up 35 percent from 1992 figures. Revenues had reached $3.75 billion, up 36 percent over the $2.76 billion the previous year. Such performance was being driven, for the most part, by the success of the company's operating systems, DOS and Windows, now installed on nearly 90 percent of the world's personal computers. Microsoft had shipped 30 million copies of Windows and continued to sell 1.5 million copies a month. Version 6.0 of MS-DOS, introduced earlier in the year, had sold 5 million copies. And as good as those numbers were, they could only get better. Just a few days before the meeting with the analysts, Microsoft had begun shipping Windows NT, its new-technology, 32-bit operating system aimed at more powerful computers.

Gates, still the poker player from his days at Harvard, was taking a huge gamble with NT, but if he pulled it off, Microsoft would control the operating system environment from the PC to mainframes. Said a report by First Boston of the NT development: "What Microsoft is trying to do is, in fact, the most aggressive piece of software ever written by mankind." Microsoft hoped that NT would not just eventually take the place of DOS, but would become a sort of universal interface between all computers, big and small. NT was Microsoft's industrial-strength operating system, or, more appropriately, its corporate-strength system. On a computer screen it looked nearly identical to Windows 3.1, but it had much more muscle. It was meant to run on more powerful workstation computers, those used in networks and in corporate America. In addition to being able to handle multitasking assignments, NT could also run on a variety of computer chips. NT had characteristics of a mainframe operating system, but it could use the wealth of software written for DOS and Windows. Users who already knew Windows and DOS would not have to learn a new operating system with NT. And Microsoft was already working on an improved version of NT, code-named Cairo, that was due out by early 1995.

"We Set the Standard," the company's motto since its early days on the eighth floor at Two Park Central Tower in downtown Albuquerque, New Mexico, was still at the heart of the company's strategy for staying on top. Gates knew that in the fast-changing computer industry, all it would take was just one slip, and in the blink of an eye some other company could come along, set a new standard, and leave Microsoft to play catch-up as a second-rate software company.

Gates had been prepared to put the usual spin on Microsoft's performance over the previous quarter when he addressed the analysts and reporters. But shortly before the meeting, he got word from Microsoft's general legal counsel, William Neukom, that the United States Department of Justice had decided to become involved in the investigation of Microsoft by the Federal Trade Commission. Less than two weeks earlier, the FTC had deadlocked in a 2–2 vote on whether to take action against Microsoft. Gates had flown to Washington, D.C., before the vote to personally lobby the commissioners. The deadlock represented a victory to Gates. Surely the FTC would not continue to waste taxpayer money on its probe, which now was nearly three years old? The commission also had deadlocked when it met to consider action against Microsoft in February.

There had been speculation in the media whether Anne Bingaman, the Clinton administration's new head of the Justice Department's Antitrust Division, might take over the case. But few lawyers familiar with the inside workings of Washington believed that would happen. It would be unprecedented for Justice to take a case that had already been investigated by the FTC. Art Amolsch, editor of the Washington-based newsletter *FTC Watch,* had told a reporter for the *New York Times* a few days before the FTC vote on July 21 that the odds against Justice getting involved were astronomical. "It's possible at some point an asteroid will hit the Earth," he said. "It's possible that this could get moved to Justice. We're looking at the same odds."

Thus, when Gates got the news in Redmond that the impossible had happened, the explosion there was nearly as great as an asteroid hitting the Earth. "Bill just went through the roof. He went ballistic. He was so mad he was actually throwing things," said one Microsoft manager.

Gates's publicist, Pam Edstrom, had advised him not to answer any questions about the FTC investigation at the meeting with analysts. But Gates was so upset at the intervention by Justice that he didn't even wait for questions before he launched into an angry attack on Novell and its chief executive, Raymond Noorda. Novell was the ringleader of a handful of disgruntled Microsoft competitors who had been complaining to the FTC and stoking the fires of its antitrust investigation. Gates put the blame squarely on the 69-year-old Noorda, whom Gates and other Microsoft executives had taken to calling the "grandfather from hell."

"Ray has a tremendous vendetta against us," Gates said, and accused Novell of mounting a "paranoid political attack" against Microsoft. "After dumping $110 million into an unpopular software product," Gates said, "Novell now asks, 'Government, can you help us?'" He was referring to DR DOS, a competing operating system to Microsoft's that Novell acquired when it bought Digital Research.

Not long after the meeting, according to Microsoft insiders, a still-angry Gates told several of his top executives that if the Justice Department wanted an all out war, it would damn well get one. Microsoft would never allow itself to be dismembered, Gates said, no matter how long the government's investigation lasted. He was not about to do what another Seattle magnate had done the last time a corporation in that city had come under attack from federal trustbusters: in the early 1930s, Boeing founder William Boeing had quit in disgust and sold his stock rather than watch as his company, United Aircraft & Transport, was split up.

But William Henry Gates III had much more in common with John D. Rockefeller than with William Boeing, and that's why the government's antitrust bloodhounds were on his trail. A century earlier, Rockefeller hooked America on oil and became one of the richest men in the world. Not content just to own most of the oil wells, Rockefeller had realized that he could get even richer if he also owned most of the filling stations that sold his gas. His fortune was estimated at $1 billion in 1911 before a trust-busting U.S. Supreme Court ruled that Standard Oil of New Jersey was an illegal monopoly. The oil baron was forced to break up his empire into 39 companies.

In less than two decades since its founding in the high desert of Albuquerque in 1975, Microsoft had become the computer industry's Standard Oil of the late twentieth century. And just as the government had moved against Rockefeller and again decades later against IBM, Gates's chief rivals wanted the government to move against Microsoft—if not to break it up then at least to level the playing field and slow down Microsoft's hard-driving leader.

Federal antitrust bloodhounds first began snooping around Microsoft in early 1990, a few months after the computer industry's biggest biannual shindig, known as Comdex, a trade show where more than 200,000 industry junkies gather in glitzy Las Vegas to schmooze, talk shop, and show off the latest software and technology. It was during the November 1989 Comdex that Microsoft and IBM had jointly issued a five-page, double-spaced news release, titled "IBM and Microsoft expand partnership; set future DOS and OS/2 directions."

DOS, an acronym for disk operating system, was developed by Microsoft for IBM's first personal computer in 1980. It became an industry standard and helped establish Microsoft as the most powerful software firm on the planet. OS/2 was a second-generation operating system, which in 1989 was under joint development by Microsoft and IBM.

FTC staff believed that the agreement between IBM and Microsoft smacked of anticompetitive collusion, and the investigation was on, run from an office on Pennsylvania Avenue across the street from the FTC building. It did not begin, as has been reported, because some of Microsoft's rivals complained about the IBM/Microsoft agreement. Instead, FTC attorney Norris Washington, who would become the lead investigator on the case, read about the agreement in *Byte* magazine and discussed it with Marc Schildkraut, an assistant director in the Bureau of Competition. But industry events soon overtook the investigation when the Comdex agreement fell apart.

Actually, the nine-year marriage between Microsoft and Big Blue was on the rocks months before they issued their "partnership" press release. The divorce was in the works a few months after Comdex, when Microsoft decided to abandon its role in the development of OS/2 in favor of Windows. Gates had chosen to bet the company on the future of Windows, and won, big time. IBM, on the other hand, stuck with OS/2, and lost.

Gates had made the smart move when he cut his ties with Big Blue, although the divorce papers would not be signed until mid-1992, after some legal fighting over what amounted to the prenuptial agreement—who got what. Microsoft agreed to pay IBM, in a lump payment, about $25 million for the use of various IBM patents. IBM relinquished all rights to the code for NT, and was allowed to use Windows code only until September 1993. In addition, IBM agreed to pay Microsoft royalties for each copy of OS/2 that it sold, since Microsoft had been part of the original development team. Neither IBM nor Microsoft would say publicly how much that royalty was, but it was believed to be about $23 per copy. The settlement brought down the final curtain on an historic relationship.

The split meant that the reasons for the initial FTC probe no longer existed. But the investigation had already taken on a life of its own, and it began to grow like mushrooms in the rainy Pacific Northwest, as competitor after competitor gave FTC staff an earful about the way Microsoft did business.

Despite the FTC "inquiry," as Microsoft liked to call it, Gates did not back off. Not only did he not take prisoners, but he shot the walking wounded. In early 1992, Microsoft had launched an all-out attack against Borland International for control of the database business. In December, Microsoft bought out Access, a database program aimed squarely at the $450-million-a-year market segment dominated by Borland,

and initially offered Access buyers an 86 percent discount from the product's normal price.

Microsoft also hired away from Apple a top executive, Roger Heinen, to run its database operations. At Apple, he had been in charge of about 1,000 of the company's most crucial programmers and engineers. The move took everyone at Apple by surprise. Heinen's defection came just days before he was supposed to deliver the keynote address at the MacWorld Exposition in San Francisco.

Access became Microsoft's first homegrown database program, although Microsoft had actually begun its move into Borland's turf with the acquisition, earlier in the year, of Fox Software, which sold a database product called FoxPro. Microsoft paid $173 million for Fox—its biggest acquisition ever—and moved Fox's entire 50-person technology team to the Redmond campus. At the time of the acquisition, Fox had about 10 percent of the database market; within a few months, thanks to Microsoft's killer sales force, Fox's unit sales increased 50 percent.

By buying Fox, Microsoft was able to go after some of Borland's customers immediately, essentially striking another blow against Gates's archenemy Philippe Kahn, Borland's flamboyant, French-born founder. The two industry pioneers were like matter and antimatter; bring them together and there was bound to be an explosion. In an interview in early 1992, Kahn had compared Microsoft's power to that of "Nazi Germany."

At Stewart Alsop's annual Agenda Conference that September in La Jolla, California, Gates had confronted Kahn over a comment he had made to an industry magazine that Microsoft used unfair tactics to maintain its stranglehold on the market. "What exactly did you mean by that?" Gates had demanded as he poked his finger at Borland's chairman.

Microsoft's move into the database market was extremely effective—and crippling for Borland. In December 1992, Borland reported a $61.3 million loss for the quarter. Kahn laid off 15 percent of his 2,200 employees, blaming Gates and Microsoft's heavy-handed business practices.

Kahn would later say: "Gates looks at everything as something that should be his. He acts in any way he can to make it his. It can be an idea, market share, or a contract. There is not an ounce of conscientiousness or compassion in him. The notion of fairness means nothing to him. The only thing he understands is leverage."

And it was leverage that had become a growing concern to lawyers with the FTC's Bureau of Competition throughout 1992 as they zeroed in on Microsoft's questionable business practices. In December, the bureau's staff filed with the five-member commission a 250-page report on Microsoft, which recommended that the commission seek a court injunction against Microsoft. The purpose of the report was to get Gates's attention and to bring his company to the negotiating table. Typically, antitrust charges brought by the FTC are heard by an administrative law judge, who decides after a trial whether the company did indeed break the law. But the FTC staff wanted the commission to take a quicker route, and a court injunction would bar Microsoft from what the commission considered illegal practices. This would force the company to change its business practices before the case worked its way through administrative proceedings.

The staff report on Microsoft spelled out action to be taken against Microsoft in several different areas. One involved the company's packaging of DOS with each computer, what Microsoft called its "per-processor" licensing. For some 10 years, Microsoft had been offering computer makers a huge discount on DOS, provided they paid a royalty for each computer shipped, even if DOS was not installed on the machine. The computer makers had a choice: they could pay Microsoft for each copy of DOS they bought, or they could simply pay a royalty to Microsoft and get the discount. The per-copy cost of

DOS was about $90, compared with about a $30 royalty per machine. The biggest computer makers might pay as little as a $7 royalty per machine. FTC staff pushing for action against Microsoft believed the arrangement dissuaded PC makers from offering competing operating system software since they were already paying for DOS with each machine they shipped.

Complaints about this practice were being raised not only in the United States, because in November 1992, Microsoft Ltd. began offering a per-processor licensing arrangement with computer makers in Britain, which prompted a probe there by the Office of Fair Trading. But the British review was not expected to turn into a full-blown investigation unless the FTC moved against Microsoft.

"It's like an old-fashioned monopolist. I'm afraid we're dealing with classic smoothies," Labor Party MP Nigel Griffiths, often considered Britain's answer to American consumer advocate Ralph Nader, had told *Business Week*.

The FTC's case against Microsoft was not limited to the licensing arrangement. Microsoft's tactic of "tying" application and operating systems had also come under examination. Competitors complained to the FTC that Microsoft offered cut-rate prices on DOS or Windows to a customer, provided that the customer bought large quantities of other applications, such as Word or Excel.

FTC staff had also spent many hours investigating allegations that Microsoft had not imposed a barrier between its applications and operating systems divisions. Competitors had long complained that they received critical information about operating systems such as DOS for Windows long after Microsoft's application people. Thus, Microsoft gained an advantage over them in developing applications that ran with Windows, for example. Over the years, Microsoft executives had made conflicting statements about whether this so-called Chinese Wall between the two divisions actually existed. In 1983, Microsoft Vice President Steve Ballmer had told *Business Week*,

"There is a very clear separation between our operating system business and our applications software. It's like the separation of church and state." Eight years later, in 1991, Microsoft executive Mike Maples gave a very much different answer in an interview with *InfoWorld:* "We didn't want there to be a Chinese Wall, and I don't think we've ever claimed that there was a Chinese Wall."

The Chinese Wall was always just a myth, according to Tim Paterson, the Microsoft programmer known as the father of DOS. "It doesn't exist; it never did," he said. "I remember Bill Gates saying many times, 'There is no Chinese Wall.' Somebody got this idea that there was this wall between systems and applications so we couldn't talk to each other. There's no such thing. We don't have any separation here, just one big company. . . . We don't have any limits to our cooperation across those boundaries. We never did. And there's no reason to. That doesn't make sense."

At the same Agenda Conference in September 1992 at which an angry Gates had confronted Kahn, Gates, too, had proclaimed there was no Chinese Wall. Eric Schmidt, chief technology officer for Sun Microsystems, was at the conference and took notes on what Gates said about the alleged separation between Microsoft's applications and operating systems divisions. "He denied there was a Chinese Wall at Microsoft," Schmidt wrote in his notebook, "and clearly stated that the software groups throughout all of Microsoft Corporation talked to all others. He claimed that the use of hidden APIs was an error by the team."

Sun was among the Microsoft competitors that had been talking to FTC investigators. "We had felt for a long time that Microsoft went beyond the bounds of proper behavior," said Schmidt, "and to the degree that we were aware of this, we pointed it out to them [the FTC]."

The hidden APIs referred to by Schmidt are applications programming interfaces, or "calls," programming codes integrated into an operating system such as Windows to allow it to respond to commands from an application program. If competitors don't know about these hidden or undocumented calls, their applications will not work as well as Microsoft's. During its investigation, the FTC had received numerous complaints from software companies that these undocumented calls prevented their applications for DOS or Windows from performing as well as Microsoft's Word and Excel, for example. Microsoft had long denied that it deliberately designed hidden calls into its operating systems, but in the summer of 1992, Andrew Schulman, a programming expert living in Cambridge, Massachusetts, published his book *Undocumented Windows*, which confirmed that Microsoft had lied. Microsoft later acknowledged that Excel and Word used at least 16 APIs that had been hidden in Windows.

Although some staff lawyers with the FTC's Bureau of Competition favored breaking up Microsoft into two companies, one for applications and one for operating systems, this argument never got very far. Microsoft would have regarded any such move as an assault on its very existence and would have waged an all-out legal battle to defend itself.

Much of the 250-page staff report on Microsoft by the FTC's Bureau of Competition focused on complaints leveled by Novell, complaints that investigators believed had merit. Novell, headquartered in Provo, Utah, had mounted an intense lobbying campaign to bring down Microsoft and its chairman.

Although Microsoft and Novell had long been fierce rivals, the open hostility that surfaced during the FTC investigation had its roots in two overtures by Gates to buy Novell, overtures that Ray Noorda had regarded as highly suspicious. Microsoft wanted a beachhead in a market that it did not control—the software that linked computers in networks, which was Novell's turf. When it came to networking software, Novell, not Microsoft, set the standard, capturing nearly 70 percent of the market.

Microsoft's network software lagged far behind. Given Microsoft's deep pockets, Gates once again played the if-you-can't-beat-'em-buy-'em card.

At the Comdex show in 1989, even while Microsoft and IBM were doing their partnership dance, Gates had quietly approached Noorda about a possible merger. Noorda, though surprised at the overture, said he was willing to talk. Later that month, Gates sent Ballmer, his most trusted lieutenant, to meet with Noorda at a hotel restaurant in Houston, Texas.

"Bill wanted Novell," said one Microsoft executive. "It was no ruse. We understood even then that networking was going to become very important to this industry. We saw Novell as our number-one competitor and this was a way to take them out of the picture."

Microsoft offered to buy Novell for about $2 billion, and Gates met with Noorda in late November to work out the details. But Gates soon had second thoughts. When Noorda did not hear anything more from Microsoft, he called Gates in January 1990 to find out whether the merger was still on. It wasn't. Noorda was told it was not practical to merge the companies; there were too many technical problems. Ballmer would later explain to Noorda in a letter that Gates was worried about potential antitrust problems. Noorda, however, didn't accept Microsoft's spin on the merger breakdown. He believed the merger had been a ruse all along and that Microsoft had used the talks to gain access to confidential information about the company's networking business.

There was no more talk about a merger until July 19, 1991, when Gates called Noorda out of the blue to talk merger once again. Noorda would later say he thought the call was a "joke." It wasn't. But the poker player Gates was keeping his cards close to the vest. Although Microsoft would later deny it, Gates had another reason for calling Noorda. A couple of days earlier, Novell had announced that it planned to buy Digital Research, a software company in scenic Pacific Grove, California, whose main product was an operating system called DR DOS. It was the only significant competition to Microsoft's DOS, and it had received good reviews in trade publications. Many users said it had features superior to Microsoft's operating system. Although DR DOS had only about 5 percent of the operating system market, in the hands of an aggressive competitor like Novell, DR DOS would almost certainly gain a bigger share.

Supposedly Gates had dismissed DR DOS as little more than a bad "clone" of Microsoft's operating system. The irony of his attitude was not lost on those who knew the history of the development of Microsoft's DOS. When in 1980 IBM decided to join the personal computer revolution and build its own machine for the masses, it sent a representative to visit Gates to determine whether Microsoft wanted to develop an operating system for the new machine. Gates sent the IBM representative to his friend Gary Kildall, a software pioneer who had founded Digital Research and developed an operating system then widely in use—CP/M. Gates told Kildall by phone that the IBM rep was coming down to the Monterey Peninsula to visit Digital Research. The story that became part of computer industry lore was that Kildall was on a business trip when the representative arrived, so no deal for CP/M was made. The IBM man returned to Microsoft and struck a deal with Gates and Paul Allen, and Kildall became known as the guy who blew the deal of the century. There wasn't time for Microsoft to develop an operating system from scratch, so Gates and Allen bought one, for $50,000, from a tiny company called Seattle Computer. The operating system, 86-DOS, had been designed by the company's programmer Tim Paterson, who soon went to work for Microsoft.

In time, CP/M evolved into DR DOS. Until his tragic and mysterious death from a head injury suffered in a fall in a Monterey restaurant in July 1994, Kildall maintained that Paterson had ripped off much of the code in CP/M when he designed the DOS that Microsoft bought for IBM's first personal computer. Not long before his death, Kildall self-published his memoirs, *Computer Connections*. Only a limited number of copies were printed and privately distributed to a handful of close friends and to Kildall's family. In this book Kildall described Microsoft's DOS as a "clone" of CP/M, and he wrote of Gates: "I have grown up in this industry with Gates. He is divisive. He is manipulative. He is a user. He has taken much from me and the industry." And about Microsoft's version of DOS he wrote: "To those who knew the industry, Gates's DOS was a blatant misappropriation of proprietary materials, and of my personal pride and achievements."

The weekend after Gates phoned Noorda on July 19, 1991, the two met briefly in San Francisco, at the American Airlines Admiral Club lounge to discuss the merger. Gates played his trump card. Before any merger could go forward, he said, Novell had to drop its plans to buy Digital Research. Noorda would later say that when he raised the possibility that the Justice Department might try to block a merger between the first and third biggest software companies on the planet, Gates responded: "Don't worry, we know how to handle the federal government." Gates denied ever saying such a thing, though he did acknowledge that Microsoft wanted Novell to drop its acquisition of Digital Research because clearly the antitrust folks at the Justice Department would not approve a merger if it appeared that Microsoft was buying out its only competition in the operating systems business.

In October 1991, Novell bought Digital Research for about $125 million in stock. Although the FTC staff at the Bureau of Competition had been spending a lot of time investigating Microsoft, they had heard nothing about a possible merger with Novell. It was not until December, when Washington, the lead investigator on the antitrust case, called Noorda to ask about the relationship between Microsoft and Novell that he learned

Gates wanted to acquire Novell. The news hit the FTC like a bombshell. It seemed clear evidence of Microsoft's predatory nature.

But discussion between Microsoft and Novell about a merger ended for good in early 1992 when Noorda found out that Gates planned to buy Fox Software, a database competitor. Gates had never said anything to Noorda about the Fox acquisition.

Noorda and others at Novell, including David Bradford, Novell's corporate counsel, later questioned whether Microsoft ever seriously wanted to merge the two companies. They figured Gates was up to his old business tricks and had engaged Novell in talks in an attempt to delay its purchase of DR DOS. With the merger talks over, and the distrust deeper than ever, Novell stepped up its anti-Microsoft crusade. Other Microsoft rivals, including Borland, Lotus, and WordPerfect, also were talking to FTC investigators. Microsoft now filled the bully role once played by IBM. Alan C. Ashton, president of WordPerfect Corporation, in Orem, Utah, summed up the feelings of many of Microsoft's competitors and victims: "Microsoft is a threat to everyone in the industry."

Novell had also been considering filing a civil suit against Microsoft. "If things get any worse, if Microsoft fails to make a level playing field, Novell would certainly have to consider legal action," Bradford, Novell's counsel, told the *Wall Street Journal.*

On September 29, three months before the FTC staff submitted its report to the commission, Novell gathered various legal representatives of Microsoft rivals at its office at Dulles Airport outside Washington to determine how serious they were about taking private legal action against Microsoft. Among those who came to trash-talk Microsoft were Bradford, Novell's counsel; Duff Thompson, WordPerfect's in-house counsel; and lawyers for Borland and Lotus.

Even Go Corporation sent a lawyer to the meeting. This tiny software company, which had developed an operating system for small, pen-based computers, had its own ax to grind. Microsoft had approached Go about writing applications for pen-based computers and had examined the company's operating system, then said it wasn't interested. Soon thereafter Microsoft developed its own operating system for pen-based computers, and some of the programmers who had examined Go's operating system helped design Microsoft's.

Although the roomful of lawyers agreed that there were grounds for a civil suit against Microsoft, they decided not to act immediately. It did not make good legal sense to take on Microsoft in the courtroom before the FTC acted, because any civil suit would become a costly legal battle, perhaps taking the rest of the century to resolve. It was better to let the government deal with Microsoft first, they felt.

Further, FTC investigators believed they had a strong case against Microsoft, especially in light of mounting evidence that the recalcitrant giant of the Silicon Forest in Redmond had tried to eliminate the market for DR DOS after it was purchased by Novell. The rival operating system had gradually gained acceptance since its release by Digital Research in 1988, especially in the retail market, as word spread that it was a superior product. Then, suddenly, by the end of 1992, the market for DR DOS all but disappeared, and many industry analysts were writing it off as a good but lost cause.

What happened? Initially, Microsoft upgraded its own version of DOS to include some of the features of Digital's operating system; then it cut prices. And when DR DOS 5.0 was introduced in April 1990, Microsoft announced that it was about to bring out DOS 5.0 with the same features, effectively freezing sales of DR DOS as customers eagerly awaited Microsoft's version of the product. In fact, it took another year before Microsoft's DOS 5.0 was released. There's a word for a product that is announced long before its time: vaporware. Although everyone in the industry plays the vaporware game from time to time, no one plays it as well, or as often, as Microsoft.

Microsoft's per-processor fee also helped doom DR DOS. Computer makers such as Dell, for example, could not afford to offer DR DOS on its machines since Dell had already agreed to pay Microsoft a licensing fee for DOS whether it shipped a computer with Microsoft's operating system or not. *Business Week* reported that one unnamed computer maker told Microsoft it planned to ship DR DOS on 10 percent of its machines, with the remaining 90 percent loaded with Microsoft's DOS. Microsoft responded by doubling the price the computer maker was paying for MS DOS. The computer maker quickly changed its plans and did not offer DR DOS on any of its machines.

To FTC investigators, these were troubling business practices by Microsoft, to be sure, but they paled in comparison to growing evidence that Microsoft had deliberately tried to sabotage the market for DR DOS by spreading the word that it would not work properly with Windows. This had become known to the antitrust investigators as the "incompatibility problem."

In fact, DR DOS *did* work with Windows. But Microsoft programmers had written some curious code into the beta version of Windows 3.1 that was distributed to tens of thousands of selected customers for testing in late 1991 and early 1992. When the beta version was used with DR DOS, an error message popped up on the computer screen, warning "nonfatal error detected." The user was directed to call Microsoft for assistance. This not only allowed Microsoft to determine who might be using the rival operating system, but it scared away DR DOS customers.

The FTC also heard from Andrew Schulman, a programmer and author who had written about hidden features in

DOS and Windows. He told investigators about a message that he had found in a Microsoft language compiler used to write programs for Windows. The message read, "Warning: This Microsoft product has been tested and certified for use only with the MS-DOS and PC-DOS operating systems. Your use of this product with another operating system may void valuable warranty protection by Microsoft on this product." Although the warning did not mention DR DOS by name, it was clearly the target.

In January 1993, a month after the FTC staff report on the findings of the 33-month Microsoft investigation had been given to the commission, Novell leveled a new charge against Microsoft, claiming that some of Novell's code was discovered in Microsoft's Access database product without Novell's authorization. Microsoft denied the charge but removed the code. Later that month, more evidence about Microsoft's questionable business practices suddenly fell into the laps of FTC investigators. Stac Electronics, a Carlsbad, California, maker of software that compressed files to save space on a computer's hard disks, filed suit against Microsoft for patent infringement. It also supplied information to the FTC.

The tiny company had tried to negotiate a deal with Microsoft in 1992 so that its award-winning data-compression software could be included in the upcoming version of DOS 6.0. Stac claimed Microsoft tried to leverage the smaller company into an unfavorable deal; and when it refused, Microsoft copied Stac's technology and built it into its own data-compression product.

On Friday, February 5, 1993, less than two weeks after Stac filed its lawsuit, the Federal Trade Commission finally met to consider whether to take action against Microsoft. In the final days before the hearing, the commissioners were heavily lobbied by attorneys and representatives of Novell, Lotus, Borland, WordPerfect, and other companies that for nearly three years had been complaining bitterly about Microsoft and providing the evidence the FTC staff needed to bring down Microsoft.

Novell, which had been working with an FTC legal team for up to 20 hours a day in the weeks before the scheduled hearing, had no fewer than seven representatives give presentations to FTC lawyers and economists, as well as to each of the commissioners.

When asked about the FTC investigation nearly a year earlier, Gates had remarked that the worst thing that could happen to him was that he would trip going up the steps of the FTC building. Now, given the number of times Gates and Microsoft lawyers called on the commissioners to make their case in private sessions in the last week before the February 5 meeting, it began to look not that far-fetched that Gates might indeed trip on the steps of the old FTC building on Pennsylvania Avenue.

Although Microsoft had long steered clear of politics, as a preventive measure the company had already begun to raise its profile in Washington. In the past, Microsoft had left the lobbying and legwork to the Business Software Alliance, the software industry's trade association that included Novell, Lotus, and WordPerfect. But in 1992, Microsoft began to use Bruce Heiman, an attorney with a Seattle law firm, to lobby in D.C., not so much to win special deals as to learn how to communicate with the government.

During the presidential campaign, Steve Ballmer, second in command to Gates, had publicly supported the Clinton-Gore ticket. Ballmer, who, together with Gore, serves on Harvard University's prestigious Board of Overseers, even led a group of software executives who endorsed Clinton.

Advisers to Clinton had said that if elected president, Clinton would review current antitrust investigations as part of a general examination of how antitrust laws affect the global competitiveness of U.S. firms. On October 20, 1992, Ballmer wrote a letter to software executives in the Pacific Northwest calling for them to support the Clinton-Gore ticket. Earlier in October, Ballmer had introduced Gore at a fund-raiser and written a $2,000 check to the campaign. He later felt compelled to deny that there was any connection between his support of the Democratic ticket and the FTC investigation.

Although Gates's parents had long been active in Republican Party politics, Gates had remained apolitical for much of his adult life, though he considered himself to be more liberal than his parents, and had voted for Clinton in the 1992 presidential election, according to a family friend.

In early January 1993, Microsoft co-sponsored a reception in Washington, D.C., for House Speaker Tom Foley, the Democrat from Spokane, on the other side of Washington State from Microsoft's Redmond campus. Two weeks earlier, Microsoft had hosted a reception for the state's new congressional delegation. This care and feeding of lawmakers was largely the work of Kimberly Ellwanger, who was hired in 1992 as the company's first lobbyist. Shortly after she was hired, Microsoft joined United for Washington, the political action arm of the Association of Washington Business.

By the beginning of 1993, Microsoft's political action committee (PAC) was five years old but still tiny compared to those of other companies half its size. Microsoft's PAC would disburse $7,541 in 1993, mostly to members of Congress. At the end of the year, it would have a meager $12,400 left in its coffers.

In part, the acknowledgment by Microsoft that it needed to become politically connected came with a greater maturity of the company, but it also came about because Gates and others realized that issues Microsoft faced, such as trade and software counterfeiting, were increasingly federal, and Microsoft needed a voice in D.C. Finally, it arose in response to the public criticism of Microsoft by Novell and other rivals.

Said William Neukom, Microsoft's general legal counsel: "When we learned our competitors were out to poison the well, we did make every effort to make sure Microsoft did not become viewed within the beltway as a one-issue company—a big software company with an antitrust problem."

Antitrust cases, despite all their legal trappings, are essentially political battles, and Democratic administrations have created a more favorable climate for antitrust action. It was on the last day of President Johnson's administration that Attorney General Ramsey Clark filed the government's antitrust suit against IBM, and it was on the first day of President Reagan's administration that the disastrous 12-year-long investigation was dropped.

The Federal Trade Commission was established in 1914, and over the years it occasionally had its funding cut when it took a position that was viewed as too extreme by the administration in power. Although Bill Clinton, a Democrat, was president in 1993, the five members of the FTC who would decide the fate of Microsoft had been appointed by Republican presidents, Bush and Reagan; three were Republicans, one was a Democrat, and one was an independent.

Commission chair Janet Steiger was new to the job, having been appointed by Bush in 1989. She was a Fulbright scholar, but she had no legal background. Before going to the FTC she was chair of the Postal Rate Commission, having been named to the job by President Reagan. Her late husband, Congressman William Steiger, had been good friends with Bush. Both came from Texas, and they had entered the U.S. House of Representatives together as freshmen in 1966.

Clinton could have replaced Steiger but chose not to, and it was Steiger who had persisted, despite some reservations from her fellow commissioners, in calling for the February 5 vote on the Microsoft case. "I don't have a lot of respect for the chairman," said a well-known Washington lawyer and fellow Republican who had worked in the Justice Department and the FTC and who knew Steiger. "She has never opposed the staff on anything. She's not even a lawyer. She votes for whatever the staff wants."

Of the five commissioners, Debra Owen, a conservative Republican, was by far the most colorful. Like Steiger, she had been appointed to the FTC by Bush in 1989. She had previously worked for a South Carolina law firm, which had an office in Washington, and was general counsel to that state's longtime senator, Strom Thurmond.

Dennis Yao, a soft-spoken professor of economics on leave from the Wharton business school, was the only Democrat on the commission. He, too, had been appointed by Bush.

Mary Azcuenaga had first been appointed to the commission by Reagan, then reappointed by Bush. Politically, she was more of an independent than a Republican. Azcuenaga was not highly regarded by the FTC staff, who considered her overly cautious because of what they considered her penchant for analyzing cases to death before taking action.

The fifth commissioner, Roscoe Starek III, recused himself because of a conflict of interest and did not take part in the Microsoft case. Starek had inherited a trust fund from his mother that included stock in some of the computer companies involved in the investigation. His recusal meant that an even number of commissioners would vote on whether to take action against Microsoft, and this factor set the stage for the eventual deadlock.

The Bureau of Competition thought it had built a strong antitrust case against Microsoft. While it is not illegal for a company under U.S. antitrust law to build a monopoly by offering a better product, it is illegal to abuse market position through predatory practices. And by that measure, Microsoft's competitors felt that Microsoft was clearly guilty, but it would not be easy to convince three of the four commissioners whose votes were needed for an injunction.

Shortly before the February meeting, Gates had said in an interview that the complaints of Microsoft's rivals were a case of sour grapes. "Our greatest success is due to one single fact . . . that I was willing to bet the whole company on the graphical interface," Gates said.

Although the FTC's Bureau of Competition saw him as Darth Vader, the agency's Bureau of Economics saw him as Luke Skywalker and was dead set against taking any action against Microsoft. Critics charged that Microsoft had grown so powerful that it dominated emerging new markets, stifling competition in a vibrant industry where entrepreneurship is considered the key to long-term health. But in the eyes of one FTC economist, Microsoft was a national treasure that needed to be preserved, and a drawn-out antitrust action could severely damage the company, not reform it. More than 500 companies had been formed to create software for Windows, and those companies employed about 18,000 people nationwide. The U.S. software industry, with Microsoft leading the way, held 90 percent of the worldwide market. Not only was Microsoft a significant job creator and a major exporter, but with the decline of Big Blue, Big Green had become the standard-bearer for American high technology. What would happen if the government pounced on Microsoft the way it had pounced on IBM?

A protracted court fight could damage Microsoft simply because of the expenses involved. This was an argument put forth by professor William Grimes of the Southwest School of Law in Los Angeles. Grimes worked on the FTC staff and had spent eight years as chief counsel to the House Judiciary Committee's Subcommittee on Monopolies and Commercial Law. He speculated that IBM's slide could be blamed, in part, on the antitrust action that was started against the company at the end of the Johnson Administration. Grimes noted that it cost IBM more than $100 million in legal fees. Even for a company as big as IBM, such costs can have a devastating impact on profits, Grimes said.

Of course, another reason for IBM's downfall was that in 1980 it needed an operating system for its first personal computer and turned for help to a young man named Bill Gates.

In their book, *Computer Wars: How the West Can Win in a Post-IBM World,* authors Charles Ferguson and Charles Moore argued that the nation's antitrust policies can destroy an asset like Microsoft. Given its past history, the U.S. Justice Department would simply harass Gates for the next decade, benefiting, in the end, not national policy but lawyers. "The best policy," they wrote, "is first, not to discourage the countervailing combinations that may be necessary to keep the industry competitive; and second—and far more important—to maintain a research and investment climate that ensures such a rapid generation of new technologies and new competitive entrants that no stakeholder, even one as powerful as Bill Gates, can stifle the industry's progress."

A few days before the February 5 FTC showdown, a senior official with the agency told *Business Week:* "Everybody here understands how important this industry is to us. We need to fix this thing without killing the goose that laid the golden egg."

With a pack of reporters, Wall Street analysts, and lawyers for Microsoft's competitors waiting outside the door of the FTC building, the four commissioners met for three hours, arguing the merits of a case that had been nearly three years in the making. Also present were Marc Schildkraut, the initial team leader in the FTC investigation, and Mary Lou Steptoe, director of the FTC's Bureau of Competition. The draft of the bureau's proposed federal injunction against Microsoft accused the company of illegal licensing practices, as well as "exclusionary tying practices: deliberate creation of . . . incompatibilities between its own and competitors' operating system software."

Although FTC rules prevented the commission from publicly acknowledging the investigation, the commissioners decided at the end of the meeting to issue a statement, a rare action that was meant to recognize the intense interest in the case while maintaining confidentiality rules by avoiding mention of Microsoft's name. The brief statement read: "At a closed commission meeting to discuss FTC staff recommendations regarding a nonpublic law-enforcement matter, the commission did not come to a final decision and will reconvene in the near future." No date for that next meeting was announced.

Microsoft's stock had gone on a roller-coaster ride on Wall Street that day. It plunged to $82.25 a share when the FTC began its meeting, then closed at $89, up $4 from the start of the day, which meant Gates was about a half billion dollars richer at the end of the day. The fluctuation of the stock showed just how central Microsoft was to the fate of the American computer industry.

Word soon leaked out that the commission had deadlocked on the vote to file a complaint against Microsoft. As expected, Yao and Steiger had voted to proceed over the strong objections of Owen. Azcuenaga, the swing vote, had sided with Owen, saying she needed more information, especially about the compatibility issue that had been raised by Novell.

The stalemate was demoralizing to the lawyers and staff of the Bureau of Competition. "We felt we had a strong case," said Schildkraut. Afterward, Steptoe ordered that a red pen be taken to the Microsoft case, telling the lawyers that worked for her that it needed to be narrowed and better focused. Over the next few months, the focus shifted more to the one issue of compatibility and what Microsoft had done to destroy the market for DR DOS.

Microsoft, meanwhile, continued to shoot itself in the foot. In May, when asked about Novell's competing operating system, Microsoft Vice President Brad Silverberg said, "Why take the risk with all the compatibility problems that DR DOS has had?"

That same month, Schulman, the programmer who had talked with FTC investigators about the undocumented calls in DOS and Windows, wrote to the agency, explaining that the hidden APIs were an "attempt to thwart discovery, and is more the sort of thing one expects from a teenager writing a virus than from a multibillion-dollar corporation."

By mid-summer, Microsoft had produced more than a half million pages of documents for the FTC since the probe had started, and had met nearly two dozen times with investigators to answer questions. As the investigation dragged on, and the verbal bashing of Microsoft by its competitors intensified, voices from outside the industry said that it was time for the FTC to back off and find some real scoundrels to pursue.

When syndicated computer columnists T. R. Reid and Brit Hume, who is also an ABC White House correspondent, wrote a rave review about Borland's new spreadsheet program Quattro Pro, hundreds of readers sent letters and faxes arguing that Microsoft's Excel was far better. In a subsequent column, they suggested that if President Clinton was looking for ways to eliminate 100,000 government jobs, he might start with the FTC.

"Any company could have written a program like Windows," they wrote in their column, "Computer Corner," "but Microsoft was the one that actually committed the huge investment and the thousands of person-years required to do the job. It doesn't seem right for the government to punish a company for hard work."

Gates said of his disgruntled competitors in a *Time* magazine interview in June: "Lotus lost ground because it was very late in catching the two biggest technology waves: the Macintosh and Windows. Borland International is too distracted with its bad merger with Ashton-Tate. Philippe Kahn is good at playing the saxophone and sailing, but he's not good at making money. WordPerfect is truly a one-product company. Our most successful software is for the Macintosh. We have a much higher market share on the Mac than anywhere else. How does Apple help us? Well, they sue us in court. In the future, maybe our competitors will decide to become more competent."

About the same time Gates was telling *Time* what he thought of some of his rivals, Novell was filing an official complaint against Microsoft in Europe with the Commission of the European Communities' Directorate General on Competition, the executive arm based in Brussels. "We find it disappointing that Novell chooses to compete with us in this manner instead of the marketplace," said Microsoft's Neukom.

By now, both Novell and Microsoft had assembled formidable lobbying teams, including some big-name legal guns, in anticipation of the second FTC meeting on the antitrust investigation, since scheduled for July 21, by which time Microsoft was prepared to match Novell lobbyist for lobbyist, lawyer for lawyer. Microsoft's legal phalanx included two attorneys from the New York firm of Sullivan & Cromwell and two from the Seattle firm of Preston Thorgrimson Shidler Gates & Ellis, where Gates's father was a partner. The Preston Thorgrimson firm also had an office in Washington, D.C., where Microsoft had tapped the talents of a couple of attorneys who had previously worked at the Justice Department. Microsoft had also hired the public relations firm of Edelman Worldwide to promote its Washington, D.C., interests. But perhaps the most important member of the Microsoft team was Patricia Bailey, a lawyer and lobbyist with Squires, Sanders & Dempsey, a prominent law firm in Cleveland that also had an office in the nation's capital. As a former FTC commissioner, Bailey knew her way around not only the hallways of the FTC building but also the corridors of power around Washington. And not to be overlooked on the Microsoft team was Lloyd Meeds, a former congressman from Washington State and partner in the D.C. office of Preston Thorgrimson. Meeds also knew his way around Congress and the White House.

The Novell team included lawyers with the Washington firm of Ablondi, Foster & Sobin. In May, Novell had hired its big gun, Michael N. Sohn, a partner in the Washington firm of Arnold and Porter. Sohn was FTC general counsel during the Jimmy Carter administration. The newsletter *FTC: Watch* had ranked Sohn as perhaps the most effective lawyer to have argued before the FTC, based on a poll of the FTC staff. After Novell hired Sohn, it also hired the well-connected Washington public relations firm of Fleishman Hillard Inc.

As the July commission meeting neared, Novell retained the services of another heavyweight attorney, Robert Pitofsky, a partner in the same firm as Sohn. Pitofsky, a professor at Georgetown University, was highly regarded in Washington legal circles, and was considered one of the country's foremost antitrust scholars. He had been a key Clinton antitrust adviser who served on the president's transition team. Previously, Pitofsky was director of the Bureau of Consumer Protection, from 1970 to 1973, and had served as an FTC commissioner, from 1978 to 1981.

Novell also had a powerful ally in its home-state senator, Orrin Hatch of Utah, the ranking Republican on the U.S. Senate's antitrust subcommittee.

In the weeks leading up to the July vote, Novell launched an intense and aggressive lobbying campaign, as did the rest of the anti-Microsoft crowd, including Lotus, Borland, and Sun, some of which had also bulked up their legal and lobbying teams. Lotus, for example, hired Andrew Barg, a senior adviser to former FTC commissioner Terry Calvani. Much of the lobbying was directed at Commissioner Azcuenaga, who was seen as the possible swing vote to break the February deadlock. Although appointed by Reagan and reappointed by Bush, Azcue-naga had since developed close ties within the Clinton administration.

Not to be outdone in the lobbying game, Gates made personal visits to each of the four commissioners in the week before July 21. Gates, however, was anything but the diplomat. During his meeting with Commissioner Yao, the easy-going economics professor told Gates that perhaps Microsoft could give advance copies of its software to Novell to prevent incompatibility problems. "Sure," an angry and incredulous Gates replied, "if you want to be a communist, we could do that!"

Of his meeting with Gates that day and the communist remark, Yao later recalled: "In my view, I didn't think that much about it. It was just a reaction to some of the lines of conversation and I didn't think anything of it."

Similarly, in the office of Mary Lou Steptoe, the director of the Bureau of Competition, Gates exploded when it was suggested that Microsoft had deliberately designed code in Windows so that it would not work with Novell's operating system, DR DOS. "You don't know what the hell you are talking about!" an upset Gates said before attorney Neukom stepped in to steer the conversation back to other issues.

As expected, the meeting between Gates and Commissioner Owen went well. One FTC official described it as a "love fest." Owen liked and respected Gates. "He struck me as a man who knew his business and was passionate about his business," she later recalled. "That is in marked contrast to a lot of corporate people whom I have seen while I have been here at the commission, and in marked contrast to some of the corporate people I spoke with on this matter who didn't seem to know their business at all. I was stunned at some of the representations that people came in here and made to me." She declined to be specific.

Even as Microsoft, Novell, and the other companies lobbied the commissioners, there was growing speculation whether the case would be handed off to the Justice Department should the FTC again deadlock on whether to take action against Microsoft. The division's newly appointed leader, Anne Bingaman, had been making a lot of noise about how the days of antitrust inaction were over.

On July 13, Senator Howard Metzenbaum, an Ohio Democrat, wrote to FTC chair Steiger, urging that the Microsoft case be turned over to the Justice Department should the commission not be able to reach a decision for the second time. Metzenbaum, an old-style trustbuster who headed the Senate's antitrust subcommittee, sent a copy of his letter to Bingaman. His office had called Bingaman beforehand to ask if she had a problem with the letter being sent to Steiger. Bingaman gave her consent.

In part, the Metzenbaum letter read:

> As you may recall, I contacted you almost two years ago to inquire about the investigation and, subsequently, my staff was briefed on it by FTC attorneys.
>
> I am concerned about possible anti-competitive conduct by Microsoft because I believe that robust domestic competition is vital to the strength of our economy. This is especially true in a high technology industry, such as personal computers and software, which has so much to contribute to our nation's economic prosperity. . . .
>
> I understand that the Commission has spent the past 36 months investigating allegations that Microsoft—the industry's leader in personal computer operating systems—may have engaged in anticompetitive conduct. However, last February, when the Commission considered bringing an antitrust action against Microsoft, it was unable to reach a decision. It deadlocked in a 2 to 2 vote because one of the Commissioners recused himself from participating. Consequently, a final resolution of the case was delayed, pending further review.
>
> I have been informed that the Commission intends to review the Microsoft case again later in July. I hope that the Commission will be able to decide what action to take at that time. However, if

the Commission remains deadlocked, I would strongly urge you to refer the case to the Department of Justice's Antitrust Division for an independent review.

As you know, the Commission has spent a great deal of time and taxpayer money in a legitimate effort to determine whether anticompetitive behavior is stifling growth and innovation in this important high technology sector. Therefore, I believe that the Commission should not abandon the case simply because it is deadlocked due to a recusal. Under such circumstances, it seems to me that referring the investigation to the Antitrust Division would be an appropriate way to bring the matter to a conclusion. . . . It would be regrettable if the Commission closed out the file on this investigation due to a deadlock.

It was not unusual in FTC investigations for political pressure to be applied by congressional lawmakers. Well-positioned members of Congress are often asked to do someone else's dirty work. But the Metzenbaum letter raised troubling questions about its authorship. Rumors, which were never reported by the press, said the letter was written by none other than Robert Pitofsky, the noted antitrust scholar who just happened to be representing Novell in the Microsoft case.

However, Mindy Hatton, an attorney on Metzenbaum's staff who advised the senator on antitrust issues, claimed she wrote the letter, and said the senator had been following the Microsoft case since its beginning with the IBM agreement at Comdex.

"When I first got to the staff, he [Metzenbaum] was very interested in allegations that there was price-fixing going on in the computer industry; that there might be some funny deals between IBM and Microsoft, and that Microsoft was leveraging its monopoly power," Hatton said. "We followed the Microsoft investigation closely. It seemed to us this was a young, dynamic industry, and we were concerned that someone that had an incredible lead like Microsoft might be tempted to abuse its power. We had the FTC in a couple of times to brief us on the progress of its investigation. When the commission first deadlocked, we were concerned. But when it got to the point [that] they were going to vote again, and finally there was this Justice Department that we had some confidence in, it seemed like a big fat waste of taxpayer money to let an investigation in an industry as important as this to go down the tubes because of a deadlock."

Before the July vote, the Novell reps came calling on the senator, as did Pitofsky. "But frankly, by that time, we had already decided to write the letter," said Hatton, who also met with Microsoft's representatives—twice. "It would have been unfair not to hear their side," she said.

Hatton strongly denied that the Metzenbaum letter was written by Pitofsky. "That's absolutely false," she said. "I wrote the letter. Would I ever let Bob Pitofsky draft a letter I gave to the senator? No. That would never happen. Bob Pitofsky did not dictate it to me, I assure you."

But two sources with independent knowledge of the letter insist it *was* crafted by Pitofsky. In an interview, Pitofsky, who would subsequently be picked by Clinton to replace Steiger as chairman of the FTC, first said he didn't remember whether he helped draft the Metzenbaum letter. Pressed on the matter, though, he eventually acknowledged that he and his law firm had indeed been involved. "I dealt with the senator and his staff," Pitofsky recalled. "I don't think I drafted the letter, but I'm not sure. . . ." Later in the same interview he said, "I don't want to mislead you. I'm sure we [his law firm] had something to do with drafting the letter. I'm not going to deny it. . . . Our conversation has reminded me. We did have a good deal to do with the first drafts of the letter; the firm did."

On July 20, one day before the scheduled vote on Microsoft, the commission received another letter, this one from Susan Braden, a nationally recognized antitrust lawyer with the Washington law firm of Ingersoll and Bloch. She had worked for the Justice Department's Antitrust Division from

1973 to 1980 and later was a staff lawyer for the FTC during the Reagan administration.

A Republican, Braden believed that Microsoft needed "behavior modification" but not restructuring. Her letter to the FTC, copies of which she sent to Senators Metzenbaum and Hatch, urged the commission not to vote on the Microsoft complaint, but simply to refer the matter to the Justice Department:

> [I]t is doubtful that injunctive relief in this case could be obtained and sustained on appeal. Moreover, as a practical matter, the Commission has a responsibility to recognize that an administrative trial unlikely would [sic] be completed by an administrative law judge and reviewed by the Commission any sooner than the end of the decade. Such a delay is unfair to the participants and too long for the software industry to wait to receive definitive guidance as to important competitive issues raised by this investigation.
>
> Under the informal liaison between the antitrust enforcement agencies, matters concerning the computer industry traditionally have been handled by the Antitrust Division since the initiation of the IBM case. There are, however . . . other important reasons why the public interest is best served by the Antitrust Division's review of this matter, which I believe have not been considered by the Commission. First, the Office of Science and Technology Policy in the White House now has a task force of industry and interagency experts working under the direction of the Vice President to promote interoperability throughout the industry. Since certain aspects of the Microsoft investigation concern that issue, any enforcement decision and proposed remedy should consider and reflect the overall goals of the task force effort. . . .
>
> Because of its unique status as an independent agency, the Commission does not have a role in these executive branch policy initiatives, even though they essentially are of a nonpartisan nature. Any proposed enforcement action and remedy in this critical industry to our economic health, however, surely must fully consider these efforts.

The procedural route suggested by Senator Metzenbaum is unsound as it would establish the precedent that deadlock commission votes . . . should be resolved by the Antitrust Division, rendering the Commission's independent authority subservient to the executive branch. . . .

Because Braden had worked at the FTC, she had been following the Microsoft case closely and knew all the commissioners. She had never understood why the FTC rather than Justice had taken the case in the first place. "I could not understand the rationale of companies like Novell wanting this to be investigated by the FTC," she said. "It was insane. The corporate guys didn't understand the difference between the two agencies—Justice and the FTC. I personally spoke to Novell's counsel, Bradford, kind of late in the game. My impression was that he just didn't understand why it would have been better to have had this case before Justice from the start."

Braden had a point. The FTC has only the authority to go to court to seek injunctive action, which is an extraordinary legal remedy. In order to get an injunction against Microsoft, the FTC would have to prove Microsoft would do irreparable harm, which is a very high legal standard, especially for the government.

"You are not going to get a judge to grant an injunction that will be sustained by any court of appeals of the type of conduct the FTC was looking at for Gates," Braden said. "The case did not lend itself to an injunction. The only other thing the commission could do was bring an administrative complaint. Well, they have not been able to get through an administrative complaint process in short of a decade. . . . So what did Novell think they were going to get? Even if they got the FTC to issue an injunction, the commission could never have sustained its burden of proof in court. Basically, the only time the government can get an injunction is if you have a merger going through and you are only going to court to block the merger because if the companies merge you can't unscramble the assets, so it's either now or never."

The FTC is an independent agency, a creation of Congress, essentially off on its own. It is not hooked into the rest of the government, whereas the Justice Department is. If the case were under the jurisdiction of Justice, its lawyers could have called the White House Office of Science and Technology or the Commerce Department and exchanged relevant information. FTC lawyers could not do that; they were out of the loop.

At one point, Braden called Novell's counsel to her office because she thought the company was handling the Microsoft case badly. "Frankly, I thought they should hire me. I knew more about what was going on than he did." Braden also thought Novell should have filed its own suit against Microsoft and not waited for the government to act. "File your own case," she said. "Be a master of your own destiny. They had the money to bankroll a plaintiff's case. It would have given the government a boost to do something. The government could have also stepped in in a case like that with little effort."

On July 21, the day of the long-awaited FTC meeting, the commissioners received yet another letter, this one from Utah's Senator Hatch. Even though the Hatch letter read like a shorter version of the Metzenbaum letter, it was significant. By writing his own letter first, Hatch had effectively blocked other Republicans, who might have sided with Microsoft, from turning the matter into a partisan political debate.

The Hatch letter, in part, read:

> I have written you earlier on the economic and anti-trust implications that flow from behavior that stifles competition in the computer hardware and software industry. I am therefore disappointed that the apparent barriers to market entry that lie at the heart of the earlier allegations continue to exist.
>
> In light of the continuing impediment to trade and commerce in this important sector, I am therefore requesting that the case be

referred to the Justice Department's Antitrust Division for an independent review, if the Commission is unable to break the current deadlock during this month's review. . . . The Commission's 2–2 vote in February suggests that Justice Department referral is a highly appropriate route for satisfying many lingering questions as to Microsoft's conduct.

According to aides of the senator, Novell's Ray Noorda phoned Hatch to thank him personally for writing the letter to the FTC. Noorda had contributed $1,000 to Hatch's 1988 reelection campaign, Federal Election Commission records showed. He also gave $5,000 to the Utah Republican Party in July 1992.

Bob Lockwood, legislative aide to Hatch, said he drafted the letter sent to the FTC. "All we cared about was a decisive vote one way or another," Lockwood said. "We had never been asked by Novell to write the letter. I had no contact with Novell."

But several sources confirmed that Pitofsky also had a hand in the Hatch letter. Pitofsky faxed Lockwood a copy of the Metzenbaum letter before it was sent, and urged Lockwood to rework the letter and send it to the FTC over Hatch's signature. These sources saw the fax that was sent to Lockwood.

The stage was now set for the climactic meeting of the FTC on the Microsoft case. It turned out to be anything but. Once again, it split 2–2 on whether to take action. The vote breakdown was the same as in February, with Steiger and Yao voting in favor of an injunction. A second vote at the end of the meeting again split 2–2 on a motion by Owen, Microsoft's strongest supporter on the commission, to close the Microsoft investigation.

Owen said later in an interview: "For me, a telling argument was this: This is an industry where people have to look over their shoulders all the time and be prepared to meet the competition on any day if they are to stay in business. I did a lot of personal research. It's a very different industry from a lot of others we see, and we must look at the case in that context."

The FTC staff would later put the following in the public record of that meeting:

> At a closed meeting on July 21, 1993, Chairman Steiger moved that the Commission—having reason to believe that Microsoft Corporation has violated Section 5 of the Federal Trade Commission Act and Section 3 of the Clayton Act—issue an administrative complaint against Microsoft Corporation. The motion failed for lack of a majority. For the record, Chairman Steiger and Commissioner Yao voted in the affirmative on the motion. Commissioner Owen and Commissioner Azcuenaga voted in the negative; and Commissioner Starek was recused.

A week after the FTC vote, the Justice Department's Antitrust Division filed a formal request with the FTC's Bureau of Competition to examine its Microsoft files. Bingaman made courtesy phone calls to each of the commissioners to explain why she wanted the files. Owen accused Bingaman of wanting the case for reasons of publicity. In a confidential memo to the other commissioners, Owen wrote that efforts to "second-guess the commission's decision should be resisted at all costs, as matter of institutional integrity."

Steptoe, director of the Bureau of Competition, was eager to hand off the case to Justice. On July 28, she sent a memo to the commissioners, advising them that she planned to turn the files over to Bingaman within 24 hours unless the commission voted to stop her. Commissioner Owen tried to force a vote but could not muster a second. On July 29, as Steptoe promised, the Bureau of Competition officially gave custody of the huge volume of Microsoft files to Justice Department lawyers. Except in price-fixing cases, the agency had never before surrendered a case to Justice.

The Clinton administration now had a sticky and sensitive problem on its hands. An antitrust action against Microsoft by the Justice Department trustbusters could damage one of the nation's high-tech stars, a key player in the global economy.

In an interview, Commissioner Owen was highly critical of Steptoe's actions. "At some point, one wonders if taxpayer money is being well spent by constantly looking and looking and looking and hoping you will one day find something. . . . This was gross abuse of government power. This business of duplicating what we did after 38 months of investigation was unheard of, absolutely unheard of."

Commissioner Starek would not say how he would have voted had he not recused himself from the case, but he was not surprised that the case ended up at the Justice Department after the second vote. "Perhaps even a Republican administration would have done the same thing," he said, "but I doubt it, because it was unprecedented. But we did have this 2–2 vote that folks on both sides felt strongly about; and there was a kind of clamor for some resolution. But I didn't view this as a deadlock. It was a decision not to take action. It was a refusal to vote out a law-enforcement action. I believe that if the vote of the commission had been 3–2 not to take action, then Justice would never have gotten involved. But because this was portrayed as a deadlock, there was this clamor that, 'Oh my God, there's been no resolution of this case.' I would argue that there was a resolution of the case. There was no consensus to take a law-enforcement action."

In an interview, Bingaman agreed that she would never have asked for the case had a majority of the commissioners voted to take enforcement action against Microsoft. "We viewed it as a deadlock at the FTC, a 2–2 vote in a very important case that appeared possibly to have merit; possibly not. It wasn't obvious where the facts were. It was obvious it was an important area of the economy. It seemed something that we should look at given this tie vote. If there had been a three-way vote, no way. We would have never touched it."

Novell and other companies that had been working with the FTC on the Microsoft case were, of course, delighted that the case had been moved to Justice. But most nationally recognized antitrust attorneys considered Bingaman's decision to be unfair to Microsoft. "It was unfortunate," said Phil Proger, an antitrust attorney in D.C. who knew Bingaman. "While there is no legal requirement that she not do it, if you are going to have two federal antitrust enforcement agencies with a procedure under which they clear to one or the other, once that clearance is done, that's it. If that agency fails to prosecute, it's a little unfair to the parties to have a second investigation by the second agency. It's not a question of due process. It's a question of fairness. It just wasn't fair to Microsoft."

That clearance procedure dates back to the 1940s, when a memorandum of understanding was issued on how the FTC and Justice Department should divide cases. When a potential case is brought to the attention of the two agencies, a committee with representatives from both agencies decides where it goes.

Bingaman's decision to take the Microsoft case came after a meeting with several people, including someone who worked for the Office of Science and Technology at the White House. Soon after the July 21 stalemate, Braden, the former Justice and FTC attorney who had urged the commissioners by letter not to vote but to give the Microsoft case to Justice instead, went to visit her friend Bingaman.

"You should use this [tie vote at FTC] to seize jurisdiction," Braden told Bingaman. "It's a disgrace that the commission has taken this much time, and the staff is recommending action."

Bingaman and Braden had known each other for years, since Braden's brother-in-law tried a famous uranium antitrust case in which Bingaman was involved. There are few female antitrust trial lawyers, so Braden and Bingaman had that unusual status in common. They also saw each other occasionally around Washington because of their husbands. Bingaman was married to a U.S. senator, and Braden's husband worked for many years for Senator Ted Kennedy. After she was nominated by Clinton, Bingaman met with a number of people, including Braden, to pick their brains about what she should do as head of the Antitrust Division.

"If the FTC did have a case, and staff said they did," said Braden, explaining why she went to see Bingaman to urge her to take the Microsoft case, "then it seemed to me that someone ought to look at this thing and either make a cut and say, 'There's nothing here, it can't be prosecuted,' and let Microsoft walk off. They are hard competitors, they may be a tough son of a bitch, we may not like them, but that's life, that's business. But at least belly up to the bar and make a cut. Bring in the resources of the people within Al Gore's task force and bring in the trade people and look at this in a multidimensional way and use your muscle."

In addition to talking to Bingaman about the Microsoft case, Braden talked with Robert Litan, who was a partner in the same Washington firm as Bingaman and had known her for about 10 years. A fellow with the Brookings Institute, Litan had a background in law and economics. Braden knew that he was about to go to work for Bingaman, even though the announcement had not yet been made. (When Litan did join the Antitrust Division, Bingaman placed him in charge of overseeing the Microsoft investigation.)

Braden knew Litan because he had worked for her brother-in-law years earlier. "I talked to him about what I saw in the Microsoft case," Braden said. "He's a policy guy. He would understand the policy implications of what I was suggesting. And he did."

Next, Braden called a friend of hers at the White House who worked in the Office of Science and Technology. "This is an atrocity," she told him. "It's government not being good government. To bring Microsoft in and go through all this and have the staff say there's a problem and the commission not be able to figure out what's on is ridiculous!"

The friend in the White House told Braden he didn't know much about the case. Braden told him to go talk with Bingaman and urge her to take the case because of the policy issues involved.

"I'm sure that's why she took the case," Braden said. "It was a confluence of events—Anne's instincts, Litan's influence, and this guy from the White House."

On Friday, August 20, the Justice Department officially notified Microsoft that it was proceeding with the case. This followed a 4–0 vote by the FTC not to pursue legal or administrative action against the company, clearing the way for the matter to be handed off to Justice and ending the commission's three-year investigation. The letter to Microsoft's Neukom stated:

> The Commission has conducted an investigation involving possible violations of the Federal Trade Commission Act by Microsoft Corporation. Upon further review of this matter, it now appears that no further action is warranted by the Commission at this time. Accordingly, the investigation has been closed. This action is not to be construed as a determination that a violation may not have occurred, just as the pendency of an investigation should not be construed as a determination that a violation has occurred.

Microsoft's fate was now in the hands of Bingaman, a 50-year-old trial lawyer and friend of Hillary Clinton, whose hero was one of history's most famous trustbusters.

No sooner had Anne Kovacovich Bingaman moved into her new office in the Antitrust Division on the third floor of the U.S. Department of Justice building than the office decor changed. It was hard to miss the symbolism. Down came 20-foot drapes; in came sunlight. On the wall of the hallway just outside her office, Bingaman hung a drawing of Teddy Roosevelt. The drawing, a gift, depicted Roosevelt in hunting garb complete with rifle, stalking the robber barons of the coal, cattle, and oil industries. The caption under the drawing said: "No Lack of Big Game." Among the big game Roosevelt bagged just after the turn of the century was John D. Rockefeller.

Roosevelt was one of Bingaman's heroes. Although he was called "the trustbuster," Roosevelt contended he wanted only to regulate and not "bust" the trusts. Nevertheless, during his presidency, the government filed suits against more than 40 corporations. It ended Rockefeller's oil trust, James B. Duke's tobacco trust, and J. P. Morgan's railroad trust.

Another of her heroes was Thurman Arnold, the legendary Depression-era trustbuster who was Franklin Roosevelt's assistant attorney general for antitrust. New Dealer Arnold took over the division when it had fewer than 35 lawyers and within five years had built it up to 144 lawyers in 1944. He was one of the founding partners in the Washington firm of Arnold and Porter, which was representing Novell in the Microsoft case.

Bingaman, the Clinton administration's antitrust gunslinger, was determined to take on a new gang of robber barons after 12 years of Republican laissez-faire inaction. She came to the job with a reputation as a skilled and tenacious litigator, a plaintiff's attorney who represented the people and companies that sue corporations for antitrust violations. Most big-time antitrust lawyers make their living defending large corporations against antitrust accusations. That she would take the Microsoft case after the FTC deadlock was very much the approach of a plaintiff's attorney.

The antitrust lawyer who had set her legal gunsights on one of the world's most powerful men was born out West, in Jerome, Arizona, a small mining town of a few thousand people. She grew up in Phoenix, the daughter of a grocer. One of her childhood heroes was Adlai Stevenson. Bingaman told the *New York Times* that she took it hard when Stevenson ran for president against Eisenhower and lost.

"Honest to God, I was nine years old when he lost and I cried for days. I didn't even know what a lawyer did, but I knew Adlai Stevenson was a lawyer so I wanted to be a lawyer."

She attended Stanford and went to law school there, graduating in 1968. One of her law professors was William Baxter, often called the intellectual father of President Reagan's antitrust policy. As his pupil would years later, Baxter headed the Antitrust Division at the Justice Department during the first three years of the Reagan administration. Baxter stressed economic analysis in developing antitrust policy.

Bingaman met her future husband, Jeff, in law school. After Stanford, they moved to Albuquerque, New Mexico, where she taught at the University of New Mexico, and Jeff Bingaman was elected the state's attorney general. Later, as a lawyer in private practice in New Mexico, she was involved in a lawsuit that would become well known outside of antitrust legal circles. She represented a uranium-processing company, United Nuclear Corporation, that alleged the existence of an international uranium cartel. When the defendants failed to produce witnesses and documents that were hidden abroad, a federal judge awarded Bingaman's clients $1 billion.

One of Bingaman's early political interests was women's rights, and she wrote one of the few books published on the Equal Rights Amendment. She led a coalition that successfully pushed for the adoption of New Mexico's Equal Rights Amendment, and she helped open the New Mexico Military Institute to female cadets. Bingaman also served as general counsel to Planned Parenthood.

When Jeff Bingaman was elected to the U.S. Senate in 1982, Bingaman and their son followed him to Washington, where she eventually became a partner in the Atlanta-based firm of Powell Goldstein Frazer & Murphy. Bingaman won a multimillion-dollar class action suit brought against Bell South Corporation by customers who complained that the company monopolized the business of installing and repairing telephone wiring.

As the wife of a senator, Bingaman raised millions of dollars for his campaign and hosted Washington parties. The outgoing Bingaman, known for her down-home style, was well connected in Democratic circles and among lawyers and lobbyists. She and Hillary Clinton had met three years before her appointment to the Justice Department while working for the Children's Defense Fund.

Bingaman was named by President Clinton to head the Justice Department's Antitrust Division in late April 1993. Following Senate confirmation, she moved into her office about a month before the FTC took its second vote on the Microsoft case. Her selection as the nation's top enforcer of antitrust law came as something of a surprise to Washington insiders. Her name first began circulating as a possible candidate during the winter after Clinton's election. But few knew much about her. She was not part of the old-boy network in Washington, and although she was a respected and tenacious litigator, she was not an antitrust expert. The favorite, at least among those inside the beltway, had been Robert Pitofsky. Like Pitofsky, Bingaman was a member of the Clinton transition team and lobbied for the antitrust post. Long before she was ever nominated for the job, Bingaman went so far as to send faxes denying rumors that she had employed an illegal alien—an issue that had sunk other Clinton appointees.

Once on the job, Bingaman soon became known within the Antitrust Division as a note-taker and hall-walker. She threw pool parties for her staff and gave her unlisted phone number to the division's lawyers.

But by the time Clinton was elected, the Antitrust Division was only a shadow of its former self. Bingaman described the division as having been "eviscerated" during the Reagan administrations, the years of free-market policies. Monopoly investigations fell from 20 to 5 from 1979 to 1991. The Antitrust Division had approximately 300 lawyers when Bingaman took over, some 100 fewer than in 1980 when Reagan was swept into office. Bingaman moved quickly to rebuild and reenergize the division. She brought on board a top legal team of deputies that drew praise even from her former professor, Baxter. Two key hires were deputies Litan and Richard Gilbert, both of whom were assigned to the Microsoft case. Gilbert was made deputy attorney general of economics in the division. He had a master's degree in electrical engineering from Cornell University and worked on semiconductor technology while in the Navy. At Stanford, Gilbert received his Ph.D. in engineering economic systems.

While Litan was to oversee the Microsoft investigation, Gilbert's job was to analyze the economic ramifications of the case. Those ramifications were many, and significant. The danger in taking action against Microsoft was that it could damage the highly competitive software industry, still in its infancy. When Clinton campaigned for president, he and Gore had promised to improve U.S. competitiveness by helping and promoting the country's high-tech industries, of which Microsoft was arguably the brightest star. Hardly a day went by after Clinton took office that someone in his administration was not preaching the gospel of high technology. When Justice took over the FTC's investigation of Microsoft, there were strong differences of opinion within the administration as to whether it made sense to go after Microsoft and possibly dim that light.

Not long after she began her new job at the Justice Department, Bingaman referred in an interview to the drawing that hung on the hallway wall outside her office. "I've got that cute little cartoon out there of Teddy Roosevelt in 1905 or 1908, shooting down three big cases. This division was started with the Standard Oil case, breaking up the Standard Oil trust. This division has a long and incredibly impressive history in major civil conduct cases that affect a major area of the economy." And Microsoft, she went on to say, certainly affected a major segment of the economy.

Bingaman said she intended to argue an occasional case in court herself, an unusual practice for someone in her position. No assistant attorney general for antitrust had appeared in court to argue a case since the late 1970s. Given her background as a litigator, however, her desire to be in the courtroom where the action was came as no surprise to those who knew her. Roger Marzulla, one of her colleagues at the law firm where she worked before coming to Justice, described Bingaman to the *National Journal* as a "bulldog." "Once she gets her teeth into something, she never lets go. The biggest temptation Anne will face is to go out and try these antitrust division cases herself."

Like her hero Teddy Roosevelt, Bingaman soon was talking tough about enforcing the nation's antitrust laws. Only a couple of months after taking office, in August, in her first major speech delivered to the antitrust section of the American Bar Association, she said: "Let me say at the outset that I am an unabashed and enthusiastic supporter of vigorous antitrust enforcement."

It was clear to those who knew Bingaman that if she were not serious about the possibility of bringing a lawsuit against Microsoft, she would never have asked for the case in the first place. So it did not bode well for Gates when Bingaman's troops began poring over the many boxes of files on the Microsoft investigation that it had received from the FTC's Bureau of Competition. If the Justice Department decided to take action against Microsoft, it would be the first monopolization suit by the government in over a decade. What Bingaman and her staff had to avoid at all cost, though, was another disaster like the IBM investigation, which had lasted 12 years and had left the division badly demoralized. Yale law professor Robert Bork called the lawsuit against IBM the "Antitrust Division's Vietnam." Bingaman's new team in the Antitrust Division didn't want to go into an antitrust war with Microsoft unless it was going to win decisively.

"It [the division] cannot afford to make the same mistake twice," said Braden, who had urged Bingaman to take the Microsoft case. "The division cannot afford to get involved in another debacle like they did with IBM. You can't litigate a case like that. There is no money for it. Courts don't have the stomach for it. You burn up staff. It's a loser." Braden knew something about the IBM debacle, because she had joined the Antitrust Division right out of law school and had immediately been assigned to do legwork in the field. She had spent more than a year running around with a team of lawyers taking depositions in the IBM case.

Braden and others had suggested to Bingaman that she focus on something Microsoft had done that didn't comply with antitrust laws and file a narrow lawsuit, then nail Microsoft as quickly as possible. If Gates was a big boy, the reasoning went, he'd come in to the Justice Department, say "mea culpa, mea culpa," and sign a consent degree and get on about his business.

But no one who understood the deep competitive fires that drove Bill Gates expected him to make it easy for Bingaman to get a win, however small. In the end, Gates did not lose, neither in business nor in the courtroom. He and Bingaman were like two very powerful locomotives speeding toward each other on the same track, and neither was going to move to a side track and let the other pass.

3

The Internet 101

The traffic jam on Interstate 4 a few miles north of Orlando, Florida, engulfed the rental car with total
indifference to the Very Important Person inside. Rivers of automobiles flowed or congested in disregard of social standing
and without consideration for wealth or power, so not even
Bill Gates was above this simple law of highway dynamics. Like
many others on the highway, the chairman of the greatest
computer company in the known universe was stuck in traffic,
already late for a speaking engagement at the Sheraton Hotel
in Maitland, a suburb of Orlando about 25 miles north of Walt
Disney World.

Tardiness had become a fashionable habit for Gates. He
was giving a lot more speeches nowadays, and more often than
not, he was arriving late. Gates had even been late for his talk
at the Comdex trade show in Las Vegas the year before, in November 1992. Showgoers and fans had lined up hours in advance to hear him talk, only to wait even longer for the computer industry's biggest name to take center stage.

On this Florida evening in March 1993, Gates was already
more than 30 minutes late for his talk at the Sheraton. And he

was going to be even later. Traffic was stalled as far as the eye could see in both directions along the interstate from the hotel. The pace was exasperating for Gates, who still loved to take his Porsche or his red Ferrari 348 out late at night and race at breakneck speed into the Cascade foothills east of Redmond. Now, his rental car inched haltingly toward the hotel as if consuming its last fumes of gas, bumper to bumper with other trapped motorists.

Usually, highway dynamics are influenced by random events like heavy rain and accidents. But on this evening, it was Gates himself who had created the traffic jam. All around him were kindred spirits, men and women who loved the PC, worked in the business, or did a little programming at home in their spare time. They subscribed to computer networks and computer magazines, and stayed up late too many nights, mouse in hand, wiggling a cursor across a green screen, and this night they were all on the road for the same reason, headed for the same destination. One of the pioneers of their industry was going to give a speech at the Sheraton. They were going to see their hero, Bill Gates.

Up the interstate in Maitland, the small security staff at the hotel already had been overwhelmed by the crush of fans who had come from all over central Florida to hear Gates. The Sheraton staff was accustomed to celebrity visits. Former President George Bush had stayed at the hotel. Vice President Dan Quayle had spoken there the previous year, in 1992, at a small Chamber of Commerce luncheon. Tommy Lasorda, the potbellied, legendary manager of the Los Angeles Dodgers baseball team had spoken there, too, and had even been able to fill a small meeting hall. But this was something totally different. The attention surrounding the visit by Gates rivaled that of a rock star. His appearance at the six-story, 400-room, salmon-colored hotel was hosted by the Central Florida Computer Society. Ever since the local paper had run a small item mentioning his scheduled appearance a few days earlier, the phones at the Sheraton had been ringing relentlessly, because his talk was open not just to those in the computer club, but to the public, who had come to the hotel by the hundreds, mostly out of curiosity, for a glimpse of the man who had more money than any other person in America.

To members of the computer club, though, Gates was one of their own. He shared their vision. He spoke their language. He was a rumpled, hyperkinetic nerd with oversize glasses who had become fascinated with computers as a seventh-grader in private school in Seattle, but now stood at the pinnacle of the industry, casting a giant shadow over even once-mighty IBM. He was the computer industry's grand master of chess, always looking ahead, plotting tens of moves in advance. And he had come to Orlando to share his vision of the future—a future that was unfolding right there in Orlando with the nation's most ambitious interactive television project under development by Time Warner.

When he wasn't spending valuable brain time on Microsoft's antitrust problems, much of Gates's attention had been focused on the role Microsoft would play when the cable and entertainment industries took advantage of interactive television and other cutting-edge technology to deliver information on demand into millions of homes across the land. It promised to be a dazzling multimedia future, and Gates was already positioning Microsoft to set up toll booths on the information highway. He wanted to move Microsoft beyond the desktop, exploiting the company's hegemony to shape the future that he had come to Orlando to talk about. So jazzed was Gates about the potential of the information highway to transform the industry, as the personal computer had, that he wanted to write the book on it—literally. Early in 1993, Gates and Microsoft's technology guru, Nathan Myhrvold, the driving force behind the company's push to develop interactive software, had started mapping out a book proposal about the information highway. (Their book, *The Road Ahead*, would not be published until late 1995. Like much of Microsoft's software, the book would be late.)

For many years, Gates had refused to even own a television, preferring instead to spend his time reading books and magazines. Now he saw in the future a marriage between television and the personal computer, a crossover between computer and consumer electronics. The television, he believed, would become the general-purpose entertainment and information device—a newspaper, a TV guide, a phone book, and a textbook for the kids.

Several months before his trip to Orlando, Gates had met secretly with Michael Ovitz, then chief of Creative Artists Agency and the most powerful man in Hollywood, to talk about interactive computing. Ovitz, a Hollywood power broker, had helped put together the purchase of MCA, the parent company of Universal Studios, by Matsushita. Apple's John Sculley had already talked with Ovitz. Apple had deals with Sony, the new owner of Columbia Pictures.

Before meeting with Ovitz, Gates read several articles about him, including a lengthy piece in the *New Yorker*. Gates liked to know everything he could about a competitor or a friend. When it came to business, he looked for every advantage. Gates and Ovitz had been brought together by Microsoft's Executive Vice President Steve Ballmer and CAA staffer Sandy Climan, who had been classmates at Harvard.

When word leaked out about the secret talks, there was rampant speculation in Tinseltown that perhaps Gates was getting into the movie-making business, that he would take over bankrupt Orion Pictures, the studio that brought *The Silence of the Lambs* to the silver screen. There was even talk that Gates was going to build his own movie studio in Seattle. Such speculation was ridiculous. Gates was just planning ahead, for that eventual marriage of the computer and the entertainment business. And most people in that business lived in Hollywood. "We're interested in getting together with anyone who might have thoughts about how technology will come together with content," Gates would say later in an interview with *Forbes.* "A lot of those people happen to be in Hollywood."

Gates had also been holding secret, face-to-face talks with John Malone, chairman of cable giant Tele-Communications Inc. (TCI), and with Gerald Levin, chief executive of Time Warner, the entertainment conglomerate, about experimental television services that could run flashy multimedia technology on Microsoft's Windows system. Gates was especially interested in Time Warner's pilot project to bring interactive television to approximately 5,000 Orlando homes sometime in 1994. That project was well under way when Gates flew to Orlando to speak to the computer club.

Gates was scheduled to speak at 8:00 P.M., and the line to enter the hotel's banquet hall had started to form two hours before. By 7:00 P.M., cars blocked Interstate 4 for two miles in both directions leading to the hotel. Maitland police were summoned to untangle a car accident outside the hotel and to keep the cars moving through the 500-space parking lot, which had filled quickly and was now clogged with motorists desperate for an empty place. Near pandemonium reigned in the hotel lobby, because although the hotel banquet hall could seat 800 people, four times that number were waiting to get in. Two Maitland fire marshals arrived after a guest complained. They ordered the lobby area outside the hall to be emptied. The hotel's beleaguered security staff enlisted the help of catering personnel to form a human Maginot Line to keep the software king's fans at bay. Shoving matches broke out among the pocket-protector crowd, some of whom had driven more than a hundred miles to hear Gates talk, only to be turned away. One woman in the crowd offered a security guard a sexual favor if he would let her boyfriend, who worked for a computer company, into the hall. Others, trying to bribe or bluff their way in, offered cash or flashed phony press credentials. "I've never seen so many nerdy-looking people in my life," said Jasmine Richards, the hotel's manager.

"In the 15 years I've been in the hotel business," said Steve Kleinberger, director of catering for the hotel, "I've never seen that kind of response to one person. It was remarkable. It was like we were dealing with some kind of rock star. There was enough of a surge of people that if it had gotten a little more hostile, we could have had some real serious problems on our hands."

When Gates finally appeared in the banquet hall, around 9:00 P.M., an hour late, he apologized to those he had kept waiting, and to the hundreds more who had waited in line but couldn't get in.

Gates talked for nearly two hours in his high-pitched, boyish voice. He talked about a coming mass market for information and about how communications technology would liberate computers from the desktop. Digital information, Gates said, would be available anywhere, anytime, beamed to devices that hardly resembled computers anymore. People would soon be able to talk back to their televisions, ending the era of passive entertainment. He predicted that a pocket-size computer would make the leather wallet obsolete. Microsoft, Gates told the packed banquet hall at the Sheraton, was working on software that would allow the holder of such a device to carry digitized credit cards, receive and transmit messages, and record appointments. It would be able to hold thousands of computerized photos and display maps that showed the owner's exact location. These pocket-size computers would be on the market within two years, Gates predicted, and cost about $500 each.

As Gates talked about the future that night, his attentive audience hung on every prophetic word. But not once in his two-hour talk did he ever discuss the Internet. Internet-savvy computer users around the country—perhaps some of them listening to Gates that night at the Sheraton—were by now discovering the wonders of the World Wide Web through the simplicity of the Mosaic browser. In homes and businesses, and especially on college campuses around the country, they were surfing the Net by the thousands, their numbers growing daily, techno-hip riders of a great wave of innovation that was about to wash across the land and transform the industry. Gates, meanwhile, was cruising along the information highway, focused on the promise of interactive television and other goodies. The Internet was still not much more than another blip on the clutter of his radar screen—little more than a curiosity, if that.

Fortunately for Microsoft, some very bright people who worked for Gates had started to take notice and were wide awake to the possibility that the Internet just might set the course of the industry for a long time to come. It was becoming apparent to them that the Internet, not the boob tube with set-top boxes running Microsoft software, would bring the information highway into the homes of millions of Americans.

The Internet flashed onto Rob Glaser's computer screen about the same time that Gates was attacking Novell and its chief executive Ray Noorda during his annual meeting with Wall Street analysts and reporters, accusing Noorda of launching a vendetta that spurred the antitrust suit. Glaser had dialed into the Net after downloading an early version of Mosaic for Windows from the National Center for Supercomputing Applications (NCSA) at the University of Illinois at Urbana-Champaign, where some six months or so earlier Marc Andreessen and his band of programmers had developed the software that would unlock the potential of the global Internet.

"It was amazing! Absolutely amazing!" remembered Glaser of the first time he used Mosaic, sounding like a teenager retelling the story of his first sexual experience. With Mosaic's point-and-click ease of exploring the Internet, Glaser realized just how powerful this new medium could be. "All the light-bulbs went on for me. I honestly thought, 'This is the future!' That was my epiphany, if you will."

A month or so later, in mid-September 1993, Gates called Glaser, who at the time was on a leave of absence, and arranged a meeting at which he asked Glaser to prepare an analysis of how the Internet might affect the Marvel project, Microsoft's fledgling effort headed by Russ Siegelman to develop an on-line service. Siegelman had recommended to Gates that the company build its own proprietary system like America On-line, Prodigy, and CompuServe. It would prove to be the wrong strategy—and a strategy that Glaser recommended against—that would end up costing Microsoft millions of dol-lars, as well as time it could not afford to lose.

Glaser was the perfect guy to review the relationship be-tween the Internet and Marvel. In a company staffed by smart people, he was one of the truly heavy thinkers. He had arrived at Microsoft in 1983, at age 21, when the company had fewer than 300 employees and annual sales of a paltry $50 million or so. He quickly became one of the key people in the organiza-tion who advised Gates, and was eventually named vice presi-dent of Microsoft's multimedia group, launched in 1985 to de-velop CD-ROM titles like Encarta. It was Glaser who pioneered Microsoft's push into multimedia and oversaw Microsoft's transformation from a software company focused primarily on Windows and DOS to one where content became increas-ingly important.

"One of my jobs at Microsoft was to be something of an advance scout," said Glaser. "And one of the reasons that I had so much fun at Microsoft was [that] there was a valuable role to play for being, not the only person, but one of the people who looked at the future and then figured out how to get there from here."

But after a decade at Microsoft, Glaser began to look at his own future and decided it might be time to do something else, so he took his millions in stock options and, despite repeated attempts by Gates to convince him to stay, walked away in the spring of 1993. "I really just wanted to put my periscope up and think very broadly about what the next chapter of my life would be like. So I figured the best thing for me to do was to just really disconnect, and I did it formally as a leave of absence."

He spent a couple of months traveling abroad, and when he got back, he decided to get involved in various civic and nonprofit projects. A year earlier, Glaser had felt a similar sense of civic duty when he dipped into those stock options to buy a multimillion-dollar percentage of the Mariners baseball team to keep it in Seattle under local ownership. After returning from his trip abroad, Glaser hooked up with the Electronic Frontier Foundation (EFF), a group focused on computer-related civil liberties issues. The EFF was begun by Mitch Kapor, founder of Lotus Development Corporation. The initial funding came from Kapor and Stephen Wozniak, co-founder of Apple Computer. Early on, the EFF came to the defense of hackers whose rights were under attack from the government. Given Glaser's leftist politics, it was not surprising that he would be drawn to the liberal foundation.

Glaser was born in Yonkers, New York. His father owned a small printing company, and his mother was a psychiatric social worker. By the time Glaser graduated from the Ethical Culture high school in Manhattan, he had already become an activist, helping to leaflet New York City during the United Farm Workers boycott. At Yale University, Glaser was involved in several anti-Reagan causes, including the Campaign against Militarism. He organized. He rallied. He helped out in soup kitchens and at homeless shelters. During the summer of 1981, he divided his time between working for IBM and the antinuke group Sane Freeze. The next year, he was in charge of fund-raising during a massive antinuke rally in Central Park. Somehow, Glaser still found time to study, earning a bachelor of science in computer science and a master's in economics, all within four years at Yale. When Microsoft recruiters came calling in 1983, Glaser was considering a $10-a-week job in California with the United Farm Workers. Instead, the friendly and unassuming young man from Yonkers headed for Redmond, not because of the money but because he was so impressed with the intelligence of the Microsoft people who recruited him. They asked good questions, off-the-wall brainteasers designed to test a potential employee's problem-solving ability, regardless of the answer he or she came up with. Why are manhole covers round? How many gas stations are there in the United States? If you were to put artificial turf on all the Major League ballfields, how many square yards would you need? If you were a product, how would you position yourself? Why do vending machines and jukeboxes have both letters and numbers?

When he left Microsoft 10 years later, Glaser had a few questions of his own, mostly about the future of interactive television. Would it ever amount to anything? Would interactive multimedia develop off the PC? Would the TV win by becoming intelligent, or would the PC win by adding video?

"I spent a lot of time thinking about this," Glaser said. "Okay, if PCs are going to be multimedia devices, now what? Would the multimedia revolution happen through cable boxes, or set-top boxes, or Sega machines? Or will it happen through PCs? And what will the bootstrap be? I mean, that was to me always the most interesting thing to ask in a new technology area. You get the vision of what could happen; how do you actually make it happen? And that's what I've always endeavored to focus on, and tried to be ahead of the curve on."

But it was the Internet, not interactive television, that soon caught Glaser's interest after he took his leave from Microsoft. Someone on the EFF board had mentioned to Glaser a "cool" new thing called Mosaic, so he set up an account to have direct access to the Net and downloaded Mosaic.

"I then joined the cult, drinking the Kool-Aid," said Glaser. "I really wanted to understand the phenomenon in much more detail. I spent all of my time thinking about the Internet." He also began thinking seriously about starting an Internet company and did a detailed analysis of the Net's business prospects. But Kapor, who had been there, gave Glaser a few words of advice about starting a company: "Don't jump back into the fray until you know what you want to do, and how. Once things start, they happen fast."

It was about this time, in mid-September 1991, that Gates phoned, and the two met at Gates's office to talk about Glaser doing some consulting work on the Marvel project headed by Siegelman. Gates said the work would be only for a few months and no more than 10 to 15 hours a week. Glaser accepted the assignment, even though at the time he was busy preparing a business plan for his own company. He had helped recruit the strong-willed Siegelman to Microsoft and respected his intelligence.

"I knew Russ well, and I thought highly of him, and I thought it would be fun to work with him on this project, particularly because I was already thinking about those issues anyway," said Glaser. "This was something I was very interested in."

But Gates had another assignment for Glaser in addition to the consulting work on what would become the Microsoft Network. He wanted Glaser to work directly for him, helping evaluate whether Microsoft should create an alliance with cable-TV titans Time Warner and Tele-Communications Inc. The high-stakes negotiations involved the formation of a company tentatively called Cablesoft, which would bring interactive television to millions of homes across the country, with Microsoft supplying the software. When they had formed Microsoft in 1975, Gates and Paul Allen had dreamed of the day when there would be computers in every home, all running Microsoft software. Now, Gates's vision of Microsoft's dominance included the home television using Microsoft's software, too. He wanted it all.

"There was a concrete business proposal on the table, but the deal was extremely complicated," said Glaser. "It was going to be a very, very sweeping relationship, and Bill wanted somebody who was not directly trying to close the deal to analyze whether it would make sense. Bill wanted an objective, independent assessment. He wanted me to help him understand the details of this alliance with Time Warner and TCI and make recommendations, based on my understanding of the agreement itself, and based on my analysis of the market dynamics, whether it made sense for Microsoft to do it."

Some 15 million or more computer users were roaming around the Net with Rob Glaser in the fall of 1993. Once the private, arcane world of scientists, engineers, computer programmers, hackers, and military planners holed up in the dusty bowels of the Pentagon, the Internet had exploded into the mainstream. It was now being used by the masses to send and receive e-mail, to search vast databases, and as the world's biggest bulletin board. At the National Center for Supercomputing Applications in Champaign, Illinois, the birthplace of Mosaic, a new service had been set up to answer queries to the World Wide Web, and it was getting upward of 400,000 hits a day by October, up from 100,000 just a few months before. The center was considering diverting one of its $15 million supercomputers from scientific-research duties just to handle the growing volume of World Wide Web requests.

But other than an occasional story that usually ended up being buried inside the local paper, the national media in 1993 took little notice of the Internet. Like Gates, the media were focused on the information highway, interactive television, and the much ballyhooed prospect of 500-channel cable systems.

There was so much hype that the information highway had become hyperactive.

For its April 12, 1993, issue, *Time* ran a cover story on the information highway. The subtitle on the cover read: "Coming Soon to Your TV Screen." Not to be outdone, *Newsweek* ran a cover story the following month was about interactive television and the zillion-dollar industry that would change the way we shop, play, and learn. Both the *New York Times Magazine* and the *Los Angeles Times Magazine* also ran cover stories in May about the information highway. According to the reports, millions of Americans would soon be sitting in their La-Z-Boy recliners, pointing a remote control at a box on top of the television and being transported along the information highway at the speed of light into a brave new world where they could order movies or music CDs, tap into on-line information, make travel plans, play video games, watch sports events or concerts, pay bills, make a deposit at their bank, or just watch television the old-fashioned way. The unbounded optimism ran fast and deep, as did the hyperbole and euphoria.

"All this talk about interactive TV—I really think right now it's a triumph of technological hype over good sense," Sheelagh Whittaker, president of Cancom, a Canadian national satellite communications company, told the *Toronto Star* in July 1993. Microsoft's advanced technology guru Nathan Myhrvold told *USA Today:* "The level of hype is truly astounding."

With the exception of a few technology beat writers like John Markoff of the *New York Times,* it would be well into 1994 before the media discovered the Internet, and the feeding frenzy shifted from the information highway. Microsoft, meanwhile, had its engines going at warp speed to stay ahead of the curve in developing futuristic technology for the information highway. It could not afford not to. If Microsoft hoped to maintain its industry dominance and its phenomenal double-digit growth, the company had to look beyond the desktop, where the revenue stream would eventually dry up. It had to keep pushing its software business into the leading edge of technology, and that was the information highway. Whoever controlled the pipelines through which the digital future flowed along the information highway would be rich, very rich.

Even though Microsoft's Myhrvold didn't much care for all the hype, he certainly understood the importance of the information highway to Microsoft's future. Later in 1993, he told *Fortune* writer Alan Deutschman: "We believe the notion of the information highway is the future of Microsoft. It's the future of computing. It's the future of communications. And it's the future of software, because software will bind computing and communications together. . . . It is very important to us."

And to others. Hardly a week went by in 1993 without a giant merger or technological advance being announced. It was a modern-day gold rush, with cable, software, media, telephone, and telecommunication companies all scurrying to stake their claims. Even Hollywood movie studios had joined the stampede. This made for a cast of characters different from the usual computer industry roundup. Strange alliances formed in order to cash in on the information highway. In early 1993, appearing for a conference on interactivity in California were Gates, John Malone of TCI, Barry Diller of QVC, and John Sculley of Apple.

Diller had visited Gates at Redmond a couple of times before he hooked up with QVC. Gates was impressed with his smarts and the questions that he asked. "Not everyone loves him, but they all respect the hell out of him," Gates said in an interview with *Playboy*. "Apparently he's a tough manager."

Throughout 1993, Gates would meet with Diller, Malone, Fox owner Rupert Murdoch, and Gerald Levin of Time Warner. And after the first secret meeting he also had a lot of dinners with superagent Michael Ovitz. During his Hollywood visits with Ovitz, Gates met several movie stars, including Barbra

Streisand and Kevin Costner. He also spent time with writer Michael Crichton. But Gates was more famous than most of the stars he met, so he was not impressed. "Bill found most Hollywood celebrities to be rather boring," said a Microsoft executive. In other words, movie stars did not have the high-bandwidth intelligence that Gates most prized in those he liked and got along with.

A more interesting outcome of the possibility of forming new partnerships in the coming digital revolution was that Gates visited an old friend turned adversary—IBM. In late May 1993, Gates met with new Chairman Lou Gerstner at IBM headquarters. This was more than an opportunity to discuss detente between the two powerful rivals. IBM had recently announced a joint deal with Blockbuster Entertainment to produce customized video, music, and multimedia on demand with a "jukebox" mechanism. The companies would develop the technology to transmit recorded music over optical fibers to retail stores, where CDs would be manufactured on the spot.

When Gates showed up at IBM headquarters, he was greeted by a woman who obviously didn't know him. "Thanks for coming, Mr. Manzi," she said. The reference was to then Lotus Chairman Jim Manzi, a bitter rival. Gates was somewhat taken aback by the remark. But the meeting with Gerstner went well, even though the new chairman insisted on showing Gates the famous Thomas Watson Library. Gates had been in the library before, but he kept his patience and said nothing as Gerstner told him the history that he knew better than Gerstner. Eventually, the two men got down to business. Gerstner chided Gates about having talked to the IBM board during the search for a new CEO, but the two seemed to get along, though no deals were struck.

Earlier that month, John Malone, chairman of Tele-Communications Inc., had announced that his company would spend $2 billion to build a nationwide fiber-optic network for interactive television in 37 states over the next four years. Microsoft was only a software company. It was not going to dig up streets and put down fiber-optic cable. But it had to work with the companies that did.

Gates, the most powerful man in the computer industry, had been meeting as often as twice a month with Malone, the most powerful man in the cable industry. Gates respected Malone. They had similar backgrounds; both understood both business and the technology. TCI's employees were a lot like those at Microsoft. They came to work in jeans and didn't worry about titles.

A gifted science student, Malone had started working for AT&T at its prestigious Bell Labs in 1963. He later earned a master's in industrial management from Johns Hopkins and a doctorate from the same university in operations research. Malone, often called Dr. Malone by his employees, was comfortable talking either business or the bits and bytes of computers. Like Gates, he was fiercely driven, blunt, and ruthless. He had built his company from next to nothing. A few years earlier, before Gates and Malone hooked up, Congressman Al Gore had called Malone "Darth Vader, the godfather of the cable industry." It was a description that could just as easily have been applied to Gates in the computer industry.

It was Malone who had inadvertently coined the term "500 channels" that the media had fixed on and repeated with each story about interactive television and the information highway. In an announcement by Malone on December 2, 1992, to reveal that TCI was going to build digital-compression technology into its cable operations, Malone had picked the hypothetical number out of thin air. But it was a good round number and it stuck.

All the talking between Gates and Malone had proved productive. Microsoft and TCI were considering several interactive ventures, including an unprecedented and eye-opening alliance with Time Warner that could dramatically alter the digital landscape. It was this joint venture, called Cablesoft, which would set the industry standard for interactive television, that Gates asked Rob Glaser to analyze later in 1993 to determine whether it made good business sense for Microsoft.

On paper, at least, the deal seemed to make sense. TCI, based in Englewood, Colorado, was the nation's biggest cable company. Time Warner, based in New York, was second. Together they provided service to 30 percent of the nation's 57 million households. TCI had 10 million customers in 49 states, and Time Warner had 7 million customers in 36 states. Time Warner also had a vast film library that could be transmitted to homes through interactive television. And the company's cable and entertainment divisions were already involved in the ambitious interactive project in Orlando, Florida.

The project was known as the Full Service Network, and its goal was to test the system with about 4,000 customers in the Orlando area by late 1994 or early 1995. Those involved in the pilot project would be able to order movies, shop from home, or choose from a full range of services simply by pointing a remote control device at the set-top box and pushing buttons on the remote. Time Warner had announced in May 1993 that Silicon Graphics would supply the hardware and software for the Orlando project.

The Silicon Valley company had been founded in 1982 by Jim Clark to make 3-D graphics for computer workstations used by engineers and scientists. But the movie industry's special effects folks had also discovered Silicon Graphics and had used the company's technology to make the water creature in the movie *The Abyss* and the morphing cop in *Terminator 2*. The company's big break came in 1993 with the release of *Jurassic Park*. Clark would leave the company in early 1994 to team up with Marc Andreessen for a new venture—Netscape.

For the Orlando project, Silicon Graphics was providing a $2 million supercomputer system and video servers—multimedia libraries that store, retrieve, and manage several forms of information. AT&T would supply the switching devices needed for the Full Service Network. The set-top boxes would come from Scientific-Atlanta. Customers would be able to make their interactive selections from a three-dimensional on-screen menu.

None of this came cheap. The cable, media, telephone, and software companies that had decided to embark on the information highway into an uncertain future were prepared to spend billions of dollars for a payday that could be years away. The potential consumer market was estimated at a trillion dollars a year.

There were no fewer than five dozen other experiments under way by mid-1993 to test consumer interest in various services that would be available on the information highway. In Sacramento, California, some 150 households were testing a system that allowed viewers to play along with quiz shows such as *Jeopardy* and *Wheel of Fortune* using small computer terminals.

But the question was, how many people really wanted to interact with their television beyond the usual channel surfing? In Cerritos, California, in mid-1993, GTE was offering airline reservations, bill paying, stock quotes, business news, an encyclopedia, children's stories and games, and other services in a pioneering interactive TV project. But out of 7,200 cable TV customers, only 350 had signed up for this two-way TV service, which was called Main Street.

At Microsoft, Gates was making a significant bet that the information highway would become a major growth sector for the company, and he had approved spending more than $100 million in 1993 on research and development of technology that would give it control of that pipeline through which digital information would flow.

"At Microsoft, we have hundreds of people whose job it is to create the software that will make the information highway an idea worth having," Gates said in an interview in the summer of 1993. "The way in which you find and interact with information will change. It's not going to change tomorrow. It takes time. . . . But when that day comes, we will be a major player in delivering the software that makes it go."

In five years, Gates said, it would be hard to recognize Microsoft because of the revolutionary technological changes that were coming as the planet rushed toward the twenty-first century along the information highway. Microsoft, he said, would either be different or it would be out of business. Gates was clearly counting on the former. And the person he was most counting on at Microsoft to make that difference was his intellectual sidekick Nathan Myhrvold, Microsoft's number-one propeller head with the wire-rim glasses, frizzy beard, wild curly hair, and exuberant laugh, who was constantly cooking up futuristic business opportunities for the boss.

Nathan Myhrvold was raised by his mother, a schoolteacher in Santa Monica, California, who would recall years later that he was 2 years old when he proudly announced that he was going to be a scientist.

A child prodigy who taught himself programming, the gifted Myhrvold graduated from high school at age 14, and from UCLA five years later with a bachelor of science in mathematics and a master's in geophysics and space physics. From UCLA he went on to Princeton, where the great Albert Einstein had taught. By age 23, Myhrvold had a master's in mathematical economics to go with his doctorate in theoretical physics. His thesis, titled "Vistas in Curved Space Quantum Field Theory," dealt with some of the problems confronting scientists in their search for the origins of the universe. After Princeton, the young Myhrvold crossed the ocean to England, where he had accepted a postdoctoral fellowship at Cambridge to work with the great theoretical physicist Stephen Hawking, who held the prestigious Isaac Newton chair and was generally regarded as having the best mind since Einstein when it came to understanding the concepts of time, space, quantum physics, and the origins of the universe.

Inevitably, Microsoft's immense gravitational field finally attracted Myhrvold. In 1986, he was head of his own small software company in Berkeley that he had started with a handful of his Princeton physicist pals. The company, called Dynamical Systems Research, had recently launched a graphical user interface, and Microsoft became interested in licensing the technology for Windows. Instead, it bought the company and hired its six programmers, including Myhrvold, then 27, and his brother Cameron. For the next several years, Myhrvold worked for Steve Ballmer on Windows, and later on the joint effort with IBM to develop what would become Big Blue's operating system known as OS/2.

In Microspeak, Myhrvold had super-high bandwidth, just like the boss, who, before Comdex, named Myhrvold the company's chief technologist. Other than Gates, no one at Microsoft would have a greater impact on its long-term strategy than Myhrvold. A prolific writer, Myhrvold was soon knocking out long memos about future strategy and technology. It was not unusual for him to write a dozen or more single-spaced, 30-page memos in a single month. Some went on for 100 pages. Myhrvold was passionate about many subjects, and his mind raced along like the Formula I car he occasionally took for a spin around the track at a driving school in Blakeslee, Pennsylvania.

One lengthy memo in 1990 explained to Gates why Microsoft needed to be developing new technology for the coming information highway. Myhrvold saw the highway as much more than just movies on demand. He foresaw a highway rich in computer networks over which hundreds of services would be offered, and through which people, businesses, and government would freely interact. Discount warehouses such as Wal-Mart and Costco had succeeded by eliminating many of the distribution points in the retailing food chain. Myhrvold believed the information highway would do the same thing. "After being at Costco a few times, I've concluded many of the things you'd be willing to do there, you'd be willing to do remotely," he would later say in an interview.

That 1990 memo had led to the formation the following year of Microsoft's research think tank, known as the Advanced Technology Group. Gates put Myhrvold in charge. For the first time in its history, Microsoft had a true R&D effort. For years, Gates had been criticized by his peers within the industry for taking innovations that had been developed elsewhere and simply improving on them. It was a sore point with Gates, who would go to great lengths to argue that Microsoft created innovative software. But the fact was that Microsoft bought its cash cow, DOS, for $50,000 in 1981, when IBM needed an operating system. And Microsoft's graphical user interface that became Windows was so similar to what Apple had developed for its Macintosh computer that Apple sued Microsoft. Of course, the idea had not originated with Apple. The graphical user interface was the work of a team of brilliant scientists at Xerox's Palo Alto Research Center, or PARC. Apple's Steve Jobs had taken one look at the interface technology during a visit to PARC and realized its commercial potential. PARC was known for its innovative technology, but it didn't know how to bring that technology to the marketplace. Gates and Myhrvold were determined that Microsoft's Advanced Technology Group would not make the same mistakes as PARC, and leave its best work in the lab.

They divided the Advanced Technology Group into three subgroups. The basic research fell to the Advanced Research group. It was dedicated to developing "smart" software that would make computers easier to use, and was headed by Rick Rashid, who had been recruited by Microsoft from Carnegie

Mellon University, where he had been a computer science professor for a dozen years. Rashid had developed Mach, a version of the UNIX operating system.

Another subdivision was an unnamed special projects group within the Advanced Technology Group, but by far the largest of the three subgroups was the Advanced Consumer Technology group.

Gates was well aware that no high-tech company had ever made the transition from one technological era to the next. IBM had once ruled the industry with its "big iron" mainframes, only to stumble when the personal computer came along. If Microsoft was going to make that transition, it would do so because of the ideas and work coming out of the various divisions within the Advanced Research Group. As Myhrvold was the heavyweight thinker of the bunch, it was his job to peek into the future, identify trends, and help position Microsoft so it could capitalize on those trends. His philosophy was simple. The future, he said, belonged to those willing to make fundamental investments in technology.

In a memo to Microsoft's board when the Advanced Technology Group was formed, Myhrvold proposed that the company spend about $10 million a year on research. In fact, it would quickly spend more than 40 times that amount. But for a company with some $2.5 billion in cash reserves, spending $400 million a year on research hardly seemed exorbitant.

As Microsoft's elite technology shock troops, the Advanced Technology Group had a twofold mission: to coordinate various technology strategies across business lines, and to conduct basic research for software likely to be needed in the future. The group's goal was to develop products that would become important to Microsoft as future business and technology markets opened up. One of those products was the software to make interactive television a reality. In 1993, U.S. consumers were spending about $12 billion a year on movie rentals and videocassettes. With a full-scale interactive system, they could become true couch potatoes and never leave their homes. Gates was banking on the next DOS being the software that would be used to run those millions of television set-top boxes.

But Myhrvold did not believe that video on demand was the be-all and end-all application. Instead, he thought Microsoft should develop a new class of applications that mixed communications and data storage and computing. "If all you want to do is watch movies, then 500 channels may be good enough," he said in a 1993 interview. "But I don't think that's what it's all about. It's not the thing that really restructures our economy. That's not what creates an information highway where goods and services are marketed. That's not what allows us to reach out with video telephony and e-mail and other rich forms of communication. It's not what brings distance learning to people, or remote medical diagnosis, or any of those other wild and exciting applications. Our belief at Microsoft is that all of the stuff I mentioned, as well as many other things we can't even guess at today, [comprise] the exciting things."

Myhrvold had become an oft-quoted and high-profile figure as the media hyped the information highway. After Clinton took office, Myhrvold was invited to join Secretary of Commerce Ron Brown's industry advisory group on the formation of infrastructure for the information highway. The position gave Myhrvold an opportunity to lobby for an open and competitive marketplace. As Myhrvold liked to point out, the information highway was illegal, strictly speaking, because the various players, like cable and phone companies, were prevented by the Communications Act of 1934 from offering the same services.

While Myhrvold was shuttling back and forth between Redmond and Washington, D.C., the job of developing Microsoft's interactive television software fell to Craig Mundie of the Advanced Consumer Technology group. Despite the name, the group was totally separate from the company's consumer products division, which was developing multimedia and PC software titles.

Mundie was the former chief executive officer of Alliant, a supercomputer company that he had co-founded in 1982 and that had gone belly-up. He was hired by Microsoft in 1992. That he had headed a failed company was not an issue. In fact, as far as Gates was concerned, it counted in Mundie's favor, because he had learned from failure—a rare experience around Microsoft.

The Advanced Consumer Technology group had been started with about two dozen people, but after Mundie arrived it quickly expanded into the biggest division within Myhrvold's Advanced Technology Group. Mundie said it was the largest start-up in Microsoft's history. He would need all the smart troops he could get. Like Gates, Mundie was convinced that interactive television would drive the digital revolution and foster the creation of the information highway. Microsoft would have to spend a lot of money to develop not just the software to run in the box that would be on top of the television, but the much bigger and more complex software at the other end of the fiber-optic cable, the program that would run on the computers that stored the movie database, the directory, and everything else.

In April 1993, Microsoft, Intel, and General Instrument Corporation announced a deal to develop a set-top box for managing all the games, shopping, movies, and other options that would be available to homes through interactive television. General Instrument was a major supplier of hardware for the cable industry.

At the heart of Microsoft's interactive software strategy was a hush-hush project code-named Tiger, which would permit the sending of digitized video streams over advanced cable and telephone networks. Tiger would be able to store massive libraries of digital information such as movies on laser disks or on hard drives; powerful PCs would deliver the information to a set-top box. Tiger was being designed by Mundie's group to work with Microsoft's powerful new operating system, Windows NT. Rashid's research group was building and testing models of the complex tools Tiger would need.

Microsoft's chief competition to develop interactive software was an old adversary, Oracle Systems Corporation, the industry's number-one producer of software for corporate databases. The battle promised to be fierce, with the industry's two biggest and most aggressive companies going head-to-head in the race to set the industry standard for interactive software. Oracle's flamboyant founder, Lawrence Ellison, was the software industry's "other" billionaire, after the Microsoft triumvirate of Gates, Paul Allen, and Steve Ballmer. Ellison had committed Oracle to an interactive strategy that was the opposite of that being pushed by Microsoft. It was, as Microsoft's Craig Mundie, the onetime creator of supercomputers, liked to say, the "big iron approach." Oracle would use lots of supercomputers working together—massively parallel supercomputers in industry terms—to handle the overwhelming amounts of video data that would be sent to set-top boxes. The hardware would come from a 10-year-old supercomputer company in Foster City, California, called nCube Corporation, in which Ellison had a controlling interest. nCube was perfectly suited for the interactive job. And with a little rewriting, Oracle's database software, originally designed to run on high-end computers, seemed ready-made to work as the operating system for the processors from nCube.

At this point in 1993, Oracle had the early lead over Microsoft. It already had a project under way to test video on demand through Bell Atlantic, British Tele-Communications, and nCube. And Bell Atlantic and US West were eyeing Oracle's system for an interactive test scheduled in late 1994.

Ellison was slamming Gates and Microsoft in the media, insisting that Microsoft would be the Johnny-come-lately of interactive technology. In the fall of 1993, he said publicly that there was no need to wait for Microsoft; that Oracle was ready for a serious rollout of its technology by the next year. Gates, meanwhile, was saying that video on demand and other services would not hit the market for at least two more years, and that companies that came out early with inadequate technology would just end up being embarrassed. Gates would prove to be right. The challenges were daunting; video on demand had to overcome major technological hurdles.

At Microsoft, figuring out the best way to store the huge amount of video and sound and serve it up to hundreds of thousands of users at peak demand times would test the high-bandwidth types being hired to work with the Advanced Technology Group. Gates and Myhrvold were hiring the best and the brightest. Mundie was just one. Others included Bob Frankston, who years earlier had developed the industry's first PC spreadsheet, known as VisiCalc. When he was hired by Microsoft in 1993, Frankston's mission was to research the infrastructure of the information highway. There were many such "big think" projects under way within the Advanced Technology Group, which would double in size to about 400 people in 1993. But only a handful were working on a project that would soon become far more important to Microsoft than the work being done to develop interactive television software. That project was Marvel.

Like many important talks at Microsoft, this one took place outside, on one of those postcard-perfect spring days in Seattle when the rain stops and the low-hanging cover of gunmetal gray clouds gives way to sunshine and deep blue sky. It was on such a day that a songwriter must have come up with the line: "The bluest skies you've ever seen are in Seattle."

All over Microsoft's sprawling campus, Microserfs in jeans, sport shirts, and tennis shoes were enjoying the weather. Some, like the two men walking slowly between Buildings 8 and 10 near the fountain in the huge courtyard at the core of the campus, were engaged in serious talk. Others played Frisbee or soccer on the acres of grass that gave the campus a parklike setting, with its explosion of color from the springtime flowers in bloom. Everywhere they looked, the lush green landscape was rich in hues of deep purple and electric pink.

"I'm going to recommend to Bill that we build our own," said Russ Siegelman, one of the two men having the serious business discussion. "Boy, that's great! I'd sure like to be involved if you get the okay," said the other man, Jeff Lill. "Well," said Siegelman, "I'm not sure I'll be running things, but if I am, you will be the first guy I come looking for to help manage the project."

A few weeks later, on May 11, 1993, after Siegelman made his recommendations, Bill Gates gave the go-ahead for work to begin on the yet-unnamed project to build an on-line service to compete with the existing big three—America Online (AOL), Prodigy, and CompuServe. Even though he had no previous experience managing such a large, critically important development effort, Siegelman, 33, was put in charge.

As he had promised, Siegelman tapped Lill to be his number-two guy, the overall technical manager for the new project. Lill was finally getting the opportunity to do what he had wanted for some time—help take Microsoft into the wired world.

"That was real cool," said Lill, who would remain with the project until shortly before he left Microsoft in January 1996 to form his own Internet company in Seattle. "We didn't really know where we were going with the project, what it was going to look like, but at least something had finally been approved that would have direction from the top."

Lill had joined Microsoft four years earlier. He and a friend had been running a very small software company when Microsoft came calling and wanted to hire them. They said no. "We kind of liked being on our own," said Lill. But they did begin making a Windows product, which they sold to Microsoft on a royalty basis. Eventually, though, Microsoft bought them out, and Lill and his friend joined the growing ranks of Microserfs in Redmond.

"I really wanted to get into the on-line world," said Lill, who in 1992 transferred to Myhrvold's Advanced Technology Group, where there were several projects under way related to on-line services.

"These were pretty much ill-defined projects," said Lill. "Typically, Nathan would say, 'Here are some guys. Go do something really cool.' " Lill went to work on a project that would be called RIP, for remote information protocol. Their marching orders from Myhrvold: come up with the ultimate, patentable protocol. It was one of Myhrvold's many nonsanctioned projects within the Advanced Technology Group, and that was just fine with Lill. It meant they would have less direct supervision and more freedom to figure out what, exactly, they were supposed to come up with.

"Once we got into this thing," recalled Lill, "we quickly realized that without a customer base and not really knowing what the heck we were trying to do, we couldn't just write it. We weren't being watched very closely, so we decided why not just do an on-line service? So we went to work on lower-level protocol things." Soon Lill took over as leader of the project, reporting to Craig Mundie in the Advanced Consumer Technology group.

Lill visited bank executives and other potential customers to tell them: "You should do on-line banking through our protocol." Of course, he didn't tell them that the protocol didn't exist. At about the same time, Siegelman, under orders from Gates to find out all he could about the on-line world and report back on what Microsoft should do, was making the rounds within Microsoft to get a handle on what internal efforts were under way. He found several, all going in different directions with no central oversight. In Microspeak, they were "random."

One of these random efforts was an Internet-related project under the direction of James Allard, and known by the acronym TCP/IP, for Transmission Control Protocol/Internet Protocol. For years, Bill Joy of Sun Microsystems had been putting TCP/IP into his company's UNIX-based computers. Allard's job was to develop TCP/IP for Microsoft's Windows platform. His orders had come directly from Steve Ballmer, who had discovered during an out-of-town sales trip that some of Microsoft's best Fortune 500 customers were better connected to the Internet than was Microsoft. The nontechnical Ballmer didn't know what TCP/IP was, but he knew he wanted Microsoft to have it.

Allard, who would become one of the first within Microsoft to beat the drum for the Internet, said the message he got from Ballmer about TCP/IP was: "I don't know what it is. I don't want to know what it is. [But] my customers are screaming about it. Make the pain go away." So in early 1993, Allard took charge of the development of Microsoft's first Internet server, which would connect Microsoft to the Internet and distribute test copies of its TCP/IP to customers.

In addition to Allard's project, Microsoft had a business arrangement with CompuServe, which sponsored an on-line forum where customers could get technical support for Microsoft products, for which Microsoft received about $1 million a year in fees. And Microsoft's Exchange group, which was developing an e-mail and groupware product, was talking about an on-line deal with AT&T. Even the folks working on what would become BOB, the ill-fated project to develop a social interface using cartoon characters to help make applications easier to use, were talking with MCI and others about an e-mail server. (That group of managers included Gates's wife-to-be, Melinda French.) And, of course, there was Jeff Lill's random on-line effort, which would become the nucleus of Siegelman's project once it got the okay from Gates.

"Russ was really doing two levels of things for Bill," said Lill. "He was reporting on all these random efforts that were going on within Microsoft, and he was going outside the company and meeting with CompuServe and others to get a feel for what was out there before going back to Bill with his recommendations. Once Russ determined that Microsoft would not be able to buy off the big services like America Online, it was clear we would have to build our own."

In early 1993, AOL had only about 350,000 subscribers, which made it less than a third the size of rivals Prodigy and CompuServe. But AOL boss Steve Case had decided to put the pedal to the metal to overtake his competitors. AOL began flooding the mail with free sign-up software specially designed for Microsoft's Windows, and it went to work signing up content providers, including magazines and TV networks. New material was added almost weekly.

AOL was not the only on-line company Microsoft tried to buy as a way to jump-start its entry into the market. It also was interested in a buyout of Sierra On-Line, which was headquartered in nearby Bellevue. But that deal didn't pan out either.

"If we could have bought something, we would have," said Lill. "The AOL thing was for a significant amount of money. I don't know how much, but it was significant. The initial idea was that we would just go out and buy a company and get into the service that way."

But even though it had to start from scratch, Microsoft believed it would gain the advantage later by bundling its on-line service with Windows 95. The promise of millions of customers signing up for Microsoft's service when they bought Windows 95 convinced Gates to give the green light. But it meant that Siegelman and his team would face a daunting schedule, because the service would have to be finished in time to ship with Windows 95, whose coming-out party was scheduled for June 1994. (That launch date would later slip to December, and finally to August 1995.)

Once Gates had given the okay, the next decision was where in the organization to put Siegelman's development team. "Bill realized there was no real good place to put this," said one Microsoft executive. "And there was no real division that wanted it, because it just didn't fit with any of the existing divisions. So Bill just plunked it under Nathan. The Advanced Technology Group's job was to provide a sort of nurturing for new stuff that wasn't well defined enough to be in a real product unit with hard-core goals and things. So it was actually a fairly appropriate place to put this."

After the project had been officially launched, it was time to come up with a code name, as for most Microsoft products under development. Windows 95, for example, was known in 1993 only as Chicago.

The story of how the Windows team chose to nickname Windows 95 Chicago began with a spur-of-the-moment decision in early 1992, when Jon Lazarus, then Microsoft's vice president for strategic relations, was preparing to give a confidential briefing to software developers about an exciting new operating system that would be a successor to Windows NT. He decided to invoke an exotic locale—Cairo. The city theme immediately caught on, so when Microsoft began developing a successor to Windows 3.1 and needed a code name, a number of cities, foreign and domestic, were kicked around. "We wanted something between Seattle and Cairo in terms of functionality," said Microsoft Vice President Brad Silverberg. "The less ambitious picked names closer to Seattle—like Spokane for a minor upgrade, all the way to London for something closer to Cairo." Eventually, the name Cleveland was chosen. But that didn't stick for long. "We knew Cleveland wouldn't fly too well as a code name," said Silverberg. A few hundred miles due west of Cleveland was that city of big shoulders, Chicago. That name stuck. Microsoft had good memories of Chicago, which had been the launch site of Windows 3.1. It was just co-incidence, though a nice one, that some 375 miles south of Chicago was a city named Cairo. (Microsoft would continue the city theme when it needed a code name for the successor to Windows 95 and settled on Memphis because that was where Elvis lived. A minor upgrade was to be called Nashville, because it is near Memphis.)

Finding a code name for Microsoft's on-line service wasn't so complicated and had nothing to do with geography. Siegelman's team came up with Marvel by doing an on-line search of Prodigy's thesaurus. The Marvel Comics name immediately fired up the team because of the prospect of naming servers and other components of the project after some of America's superheroes, like Batman.

No Microsoft code name remains a secret for long, however; nor is it supposed to. Microsoft executives use project code names when giving confidential briefings to outsiders, and they eventually make their way into the public domain through media reports. Thus, Marvel became known outside of Microsoft early in its development. Consequently, the company received a letter from a lawyer representing Marvel Comics, who explained that the name was a trademark and Microsoft could not use it. But as far as Microsoft was concerned, the Marvel name was for internal use only and was not going to be the name of the on-line service when it came to market. The letter was ignored.

At the beginning, the Marvel team consisted of fewer than 10 people, including Siegelman and Lill. The team took over an office area in Building 8, where Gates himself worked. The team's first mission was to come up with a plan for the kind of service they were going to build.

"We did some market research to get a feel for what the hell we were doing, for what the goal was," said Lill. "We were going into this with the goal that it was going to be a computer user–oriented service, rather than a general-purpose service.

So, we were looking at our CompuServe traffic and saying 'Hey, we've got a lot to offer a computer user. A lot of users are going to CompuServe to visit Microsoft support areas. We know something about that. So we, as Microsoft, have something to offer computer users.' We were originally going to focus on being a very targeted product. And we did some very early prototypes that we showed some of these market research folks down in Los Angeles."

Lill and Siegelman also flew out to Washington, D.C., to visit a tiny company that had developed some on-line technology that they thought might be useful in starting Microsoft's service. The company was providing on-line support for software companies, with bulletin boards, e-mail, and a lot of the services that the Microsoft team thought they might want to include in their own, even though it was all UNIX-based.

Siegelman, who had a reputation around Microsoft as a first-rate negotiator, reached an agreement with the company for Microsoft to license its product, pending a technical review by Lill. But Lill recommended they pass on the license deal, even though he found it to be a very good product. He decided it just didn't fit with the Marvel plan.

The initial design for Marvel looked a lot like Prodigy, which Lill soon realized was the wrong approach. "It was not very Windows-like," he said. "We were trying to go for a very, very easy-to-use thing in the prototype. And just after that, I realized that we were reinventing the wheel. We would have had to create new user interfaces, and we were not a user interface group, and our overall goal was to ship something with Windows 95. And so we just didn't have the time to be monkeying around and inventing things. And I had seen the BOB effort, and it was a black hole of changes and changes and changes and changes. So I basically told the team, 'We are going to make this just be Windows.' "

The group was under the gun. Gates was supposed to be briefed on the project in late September. And he wanted more than a report; he wanted a demonstration, proof that it could actually work if the company invested further time and resources. True, Gates had approved the project in May, but it would be the September meeting at which he would decide whether to go forward or scrap the effort. Thus the team had to be able to convince Gates at that meeting that they could do this. But could they?

A number of technical problems had to be resolved before the fateful meeting, the most important of which was to decide the underlying infrastructure for using an X-25 network. This was an older technology, but very similar to the TCP/IP that Allard was working on. AOL, Prodigy, and CompuServe all used the X-25 network for their on-line services.

The team by now was also thinking about content. What would the service offer customers? Because it was being designed primarily for computer users, the initial intent was to follow the model of CompuServe and make various computer-oriented publications available. The service would also, of course, need a traditional e-mail function and bulletin boards. The plan was to use Exchange for both these capabilities. "All that was pretty much the core technology of what we were looking at to deliver with the initial service," said Lill. "We figured that since it was mostly for computer-oriented users, they'd be a little bit more forgiving."

It was Lill who gave the crucial briefing to Gates at the end of September. The team managed to get a simple demo functioning on an X-25 network. They even had some image-compression technology working, and downloaded an image using a 9600 baud modem. "We were really just trying to show Bill that we had the technology figured out," said Lill. "We had the scary modem figured out and the scary network figured out, and we actually had a server running and making this thing work."

As he always does at such briefings, Gates asked some tough technical questions. But overall, the presentation went well. Not once did Gates scream at anyone—as he had been known to do at these briefings—or throw something, or shout his familiar phrase, "This is the stupidest thing I've ever heard of!"

Nevertheless, Gates was highly skeptical that the team would be able to meet the June 1994 shipping date for Windows 95. He didn't think it could be done. He also had some nontechnical questions. "How much is all this going to cost?" he wanted to know. "Can we really make any money?"

Lill did not have ready answers for those questions, but Gates gave his approval anyway and authorized the hiring of some 30 more people for Marvel.

Which raised the question of where to put them. There wasn't enough room in the team's small office area in Building 8. Microsoft had been growing so fast that not only was there a shortage of big buildings on campus, but all the existing buildings were having space-crunch problems. Lill got on the phone and called a Seattle real estate company, figuring there had to be some office space available somewhere near the campus. If Marvel was going to fly, the team had to have the space in which to set up a large lab and to accommodate future growth.

Lill called Coldwell Banker, which unbeknownst to him was Microsoft's outside realtor. Microsoft employees, even managers working on hot projects, are not supposed to look for office space on their own. A representative from Coldwell Banker phoned Microsoft's property department, and word of what Lill had done soon filtered up to Gates. Lill got a scolding, but he also got his office space—way out on the far northeast part of the campus, in something called the East Tech building, near the company store and the executive briefing center. They took over the space left vacant when the PC repair folks moved off campus.

Lill went over to check out the building, a one-story structure with a concrete floor, a plus because of all the heavy computer equipment the Marvel lab would need. (The floor in the Windows NT lab had collapsed under the weight of the equipment, so Lill wanted the Marvel lab on the ground floor.)

"It was perfect," said Lill. "It was off by itself. Nobody was going to bug us. There was great space for labs. We managed to get that whole building. I called it the Microsoft Enterprise Zone because it was this little sort of crappy place, but great because we had the room we needed; and frankly, I liked being away from the rest of the campus. I wanted to avoid a big political situation, where everybody wanted a finger in our pie and needed to know our plans. I really wanted to be way out there on the side so we could get this thing done and get it launched."

Siegelman and Lill began hiring like crazy, and started setting up a lab with six server computers. In keeping with the comic-book motif, it became known as the Manga Lab because the man who ran it had spent a lot of time in Japan, where a manga is an erotic comic book.

Among the new influx of bodies was Bill Miller, the project's marketing director. Several others came from a Seattle company called the Daily Planet, which was developing software tools for multimedia on-line content. Although the Daily Planet had initially told Siegelman it did not want to do business with Microsoft, it eventually agreed to a friendly buyout, and Microsoft hired its technical staff to work on Marvel (where else would characters from Superman's building work?). The staff from the Daily Planet formed the core of what would become the Blackbird group, the code name for a project to develop a set of proprietary software tools for exclusive use by companies creating content for Microsoft's on-line service. It allowed content developers a simpler way to create a unique look and feel for their services, with better graphics and interactive capabilities.

The idea for Blackbird—the code name came from the high-tech, superfast, high-flying Cold War spy plane—had grown out of a conversation that Lill and Siegelman had before the Marvel team moved into Building 8. They wanted Marvel to contain something similar to Microsoft Publisher, with some easy-to-use features that would let organizations post on-line content, enabling a school district, for instance, to post its PTA minutes.

By November, though, the Marvel design had begun to shift away from its computer-user focus and toward consumers. As technical manager of the project, Lill saw some risks in this change in strategy. Although a consumer-oriented service certainly would have a wider audience, it also meant that a significantly larger database center would have to be designed into Marvel's infrastructure. And there were continuing problems lining up publishers to post content. In those days, everyone who was anyone in the publishing business, from the *Wall Street Journal* to Ziff-Davis, was passing through Microsoft, usually to talk with the Exchange folks or with Craig Mundie's group working on interactive television. They also stopped off to visit with Siegelman.

"It was pretty clear," said one member of the Marvel team, "that we were not going to be able to provide them with really sophisticated and ready tools they could use to publish sophisticated stuff on-line anytime soon."

Meanwhile, the marketing team was trying to come up with a name for the on-line service. A number of trade names already had been rejected. Finally, an expensive name-search firm was hired, which came up with the name ONVO. "None of us knew what the hell it meant," said Lill. "I still don't know what it was supposed to mean."

ONVO didn't mean anything, and that was the point, said a member of the project's marketing team. "It was a word like Kodak or Xerox," he said. "It didn't mean anything but what you put into it with marketing and product. We liked the 'on' part, and the letters seemed great for logos."

When the marketing staff met with Ballmer to pitch the ONVO name, he threw them out of his office. "Fuck, no! We are not going to call this ONVO!" he screamed. Gates had a similar response, as did a lot of others. In time, everyone agreed just to call it the Microsoft Network. (After the Microsoft Network was redesigned for the Internet in 1995, "on MSN" was used in marketing.)

New digs, new lab, more people, and now a name. The Microsoft Network was finally getting up to speed. Then, one night in early November, Russ Siegelman's brain exploded—literally. He was at the opera when his head started to hurt. But it was no ordinary headache. He had suffered a brain aneurysm. The next morning, Siegelman's administrative assistant called the management team together and through tears told them that Russ was in the hospital. A short staff meeting with Myhrvold followed. Within days, Siegelman had surgery. He would not return to work until the last week of December. Lill, second in command, was due to leave on a vacation to the Caribbean with his family when Siegelman fell ill. His wife and two young daughters went on without him.

The team motored on without Siegelman, almost on autopilot. They were facing a difficult, perhaps impossible schedule that required that Marvel be ready to ship with Windows 95 in June 1994. That meant beta testing would have to begin in the early part of the year. What became known as the death march had started. Members of the development team were working all hours of the day and night. Lill had meals catered in every night.

"It really was a death march," he said, "but what was fun about it was that we were doing something big. At one of the meetings, I told the guys that this was really a unique chance to create something that maybe their grandkids would recognize. I don't know how true that was, but it rang, it really did ring with people that they were creating something very, very big, very, very exciting. In a lot of ways—and this is somewhat ironic—we were building a big mainframe. We ended up with a couple hundred servers over in the lab; and in some ways, it was just a giant mainframe that happened to be in separate boxes."

But something for the grandkids was not to be. Little did they know that they were creating a product that would be obsolete before it was finished. Rob Glaser tried to tell them that, when he came over to make his Internet pitch in December, about a month after Siegelman had his aneurysm. Change your strategy, Glaser told the team leaders; the Internet has arrived, and you'd better get with it. No one was listening.

A month or so before he met with the Marvel team, Glaser had given his recommendations to Gates on Cablesoft, Microsoft's proposed venture with Time Warner and Tele-Communications. By then, talks among the three companies had pretty much broken down. The two cable giants were concerned that Microsoft was making unreasonable demands, such as wanting to limit the use of software by other companies for set-top boxes. Microsoft had many problems with the proposal, too. For one, Time Warner was insisting on a joint venture partnership that gave it half ownership. Gates did not want to give away that kind of control.

Glaser made two rounds of recommendations to Gates. The first, in October, led to a resumption of the talks with TCI and Time Warner. "Bill decided he would either try and get the deal back on track, or not do it," said Glaser. "Bill and John Malone met several more times in December. Then Bill asked me to review one more draft. It was different, but still had big issues that needed to be resolved, so I passed along a second recommendation for substantial changes, absent which I didn't think Microsoft should proceed. I ended up recommending that Microsoft not proceed on it for a very specific set of reasons, and Microsoft ended up not proceeding on it."

At Microsoft's insistence, Glaser would not be more specific in an interview about his recommendations or what changes he thought Microsoft should make in the draft contract. "I can tell you," he said, "that it was not clear to me that the cable companies were going to be the inheritors of the information highway, and I made my recommendations to Bill accordingly."

What was clear to Glaser was that the Internet had produced a radical change in the computer industry. The last such change had occurred in the late 1970s, when the development of the personal computer triggered a revolution that gave rise to companies like Microsoft, and altered the fundamental power structure of the industry. Glaser believed the same thing was about to happen because of the Internet, and he was beating the drum loudly.

Even though Glaser was no longer working at Microsoft, he and Siegelman had talked several times since that day in mid-September when Gates had asked Glaser to evaluate Microsoft's on-line service and how it fit with the Internet. Glaser was convinced the Internet was going to be the leading platform for distributing information in the future. And having become convinced of that, it was simply a matter of deciding what Microsoft should do.

In the pre-Internet world, each of the on-line services had its own architecture, its own way of browsing information, its own way of transmitting information, its own infrastructure of servers and clients. Other than through the most minimal form of interchange through e-mail gateways, nothing could connect to anything else. And that was precisely what Microsoft was buying into with its on-line service. The alternative was a standard architecture. But where would it come from? Did it already exist? Glaser believed it did, in the form of the Internet. And Microsoft needed to embrace and extend that architecture.

"I became convinced that Microsoft was building the last minicomputer," said Glaser, "that the Microsoft Network was based on the notion that your competitors were the model—proprietary on-line services like America Online—and that the reality was that the Internet was going to be such a fundamental paradigm shift, or sea change, that you needed to think about your strategies fundamentally differently."

Glaser was prepared to make some very radical proposals to Siegelman regarding Marvel. He was going to tell Siegelman that he had to totally change his strategy and build a nonproprietary on-line service that anyone could access through the Internet. But fate stepped in. About a week before the two men were to meet, Siegelman suffered the brain aneurysm. Glaser considered giving his recommendations directly to Gates, but he worried what that might do to the Marvel team while Siegelman was out. Instead, he requested a meeting of all the Marvel managers. He had decided to play schoolteacher, and give a slide-show presentation about the Internet in the conference room of the East Tech building.

"I did not want to randomize the team while Russ was out getting well," said Glaser. "So I decided to basically teach his staff Internet 101. I explained to them what the Internet was; that it was a fundamental architecture, a fundamental platform and they needed to design their system in light of it. I told them, 'You guys need to get over to the Internet as soon as possible.' But what I didn't say was, 'If you don't do this, you're going to fail.' Their leader had just taken ill. I had the view that if I just basically educated them on the Internet, they ultimately would reach the right conclusion. Of course, at that point, they were planning to ship MSN with Chicago. But I got the sense that everybody basically bought into my recommendations for the long term. But they were all so busy on their short-term priorities that no one was willing to say, 'Hey, the emperor has no clothes, we have to change strategy.' "

What some members of the Marvel management team remembered most about the meeting that December day with Glaser was that he had one hell of a time hooking up to the Internet with Mosaic. And they wondered what that coffeepot thing was all about. The coffeepot was just one of the many "cool" things on the World Wide Web that Glaser had wanted to show the Marvel team. In England, someone had rigged a camera to take pictures of a coffeepot, and the live image was transmitted to a Web site. Glaser wanted to use Mosaic to connect to the Web site, but he kept losing his Internet connection, and eventually gave up.

Glaser might have hoped the Marvel team was buying into his vision of the Internet, at least for the long term, but he might as well have been shouting into the wind. "We were not thinking about the Internet at all," said one Marvel manager. "At the time, our competition was Prodigy and CompuServe and America Online, and that's what we were focused on, a proprietary on-line service. After that Internet talk, it was like, 'Okay. Great. Now let's all get back to work.' There just wasn't any sense at all at that point that the Internet was an alternative way of providing information."

Lill, as technical manager of the project, was determined to keep things on track. A debate within the team about going in a new direction would mean that the deadline for shipping with Windows 95 would not be met. "My attitude was, 'This is great, but we'll worry about it later.' My goal for the whole effort was not so much to come out with a glorious technology that was going to live on for 40 years. It was more to develop an organization that understood what it meant to build an on-line service and run it. We needed to get our foot in the door with a product that could ship with Windows and start getting significant users. My goal was just to learn and get a foot in the door. In my mind, it was, 'Yeah, great. We're going to rewrite this thing in two or three years anyway.' It ended up being sooner than that. But the primary goal was just to get something out so we could start learning. And frankly, that is Microsoft's forte: A competitor comes in and does something interesting, then we come in and basically clone it; do it marginally better and throw some marketing clout behind it, then relentlessly make it better over the years. That's our strategy. And it has worked damn well."

Siegelman returned to work just after Christmas. The surgeons had shaved his head before they operated, and his hair was just beginning to grow out, and his speech was slightly impaired. His doctors had told him to take it easy, but he didn't. Other than taking time off for speech therapy, he worked as hard as anyone on the team. "The rate at which he recovered and how soon he jumped back into things was exceedingly courageous," said Glaser. "This was a serious, life-threatening situation. What Russ did was just amazing."

Even though he didn't succeed in talking the Marvel team into changing its strategy, Glaser himself embraced the Internet. He formed his own company, called ProgressiveNetworks. Several of his Microsoft pals, as well as Mitch Kapor, became investors. One of its first products was RealAudio, which allowed Internet users to pluck sound off the World Wide Web and play it through a computer's speakers immediately, without the long wait for data to download to the computer's memory bank.

Although Glaser didn't talk to Gates about his recommendations for Microsoft's on-line project, he gave the material he had used for his slide-show presentation to Steve Sinofsky, Gates's technical assistant.

"At the time," said Glaser, "there were only a few people at Microsoft who were true Internet believers. Steve was one." James Allard was another. Early in 1994, the two would play important roles in dragging the company, at times kicking and screaming, toward the Internet. It would be the beginning of a remarkable 180-degree change of direction for Microsoft, unprecedented in the history of American business. But change was imminent and not just for the company. Its still-boyish, 38-year-old leader was about to undergo a transformation of his own. Before the sun had set on the first day of the new year in 1994, the country's richest bachelor would be a married man.

4

Bachelor Tycoon Takes a Wife

A lone on a bluff high above the Pacific Ocean, the two old friends walked back and forth over the lush green golf course fairway, occasionally stopping near natural lava outcroppings to look at the cobalt-blue waters below. Anticipating another glorious Hawaiian sunset, the cirrus-streaked sky to the west already had started to turn shades of gold and pink, nature's signal that the wedding ceremony was about to begin. But there was still time for Bill Gates to spend his final moments as a bachelor walking and talking with his best man, Steve Ballmer.

Their friendship went back nearly two decades, to their days together at Harvard. Later, after Gates had dropped out of school in his sophomore year to found Microsoft with Paul Allen, he had called on Ballmer to become one of his most trusted advisers. It was to Ballmer that Gates had turned in 1984 to lead what would become a death march to develop Microsoft's first Windows program after it fell far behind schedule and threatened to sink the company. Now, here they were 10 years later, on the first day of the new year, with the sun about to set into the Pacific and Gates about to be married.

Gates had long felt the pressure to marry; he had watched as other Microsoft executives, many of whom he had known practically since they were fresh out of college, settle down into family life. Microsoft had even been sued by a couple who claimed that the company's relentless demands on its employees amounted to discrimination against married people. Even Ballmer, as committed to the cause as Gates, had exchanged vows with a Microsoft consultant a couple of years earlier and now had a son. Finally, Chairman Bill, at age 38, was about to tie the knot.

After about 15 minutes together on the bluff, Gates and Ballmer got into a golf cart and drove several hundred yards to where the wedding guests were seated on the tee box of the twelfth hole of the golf course at the Manele Bay Hotel on the tiny Hawaiian island of Lanai. Gates, wearing a white dinner jacket and black trousers, walked to a white wooden lectern that had been positioned off to the side in front of the 130 seated guests, who included four other billionaires. The lectern was to be used by Father William Sullivan, an old Gates family friend who was to officiate at the wedding. Ballmer, wearing a black tuxedo, stood near Gates. Gates's parents were seated in the first row. Mary Gates, fatally ill with cancer, had summoned all her strength to be there. Moments after Gates took his place, the wedding guests who had been seated in white chairs facing the ocean stood and turned around. The bride was coming.

Melinda French, dressed in a traditional white gown, walked down the aisle through the gathering of guests on the arm of her father and stood next to the man she was about to marry. The guests sat down. Five bridesmaids, dressed in pink, stood in attendance. The wedding ceremony began. It was 5:25 P.M., Hawaiian time. Fifteen minutes later it was over. Gates and his bride kissed. The sun had set, leaving a golden pink glow across the evening sky. America's richest bachelor was a married man.

It was a day that many of Microsoft's rivals had long waited for as they speculated how a change in marital status would affect Gates's first love—Microsoft. Perhaps marriage and a nursery full of children would slow down the workaholic Gates, distract his focus from business, and at last give them a competitive edge. Few in the industry, though, had actually believed Gates would ever marry.

His life as a bachelor had been the subject of much media humor. Syndicated cartoonist Berkeley Breathed modeled his comic strip antihero Bachelor Tycoon after Gates. Appearing in more than 400 newspapers across America, Bachelor Tycoon, the founder of Micro-Squish Inc., has bad skin, bad clothes, thick glasses, and a microchip tattooed on his stomach. The nerdy character looks a lot like Gates. In one strip, Bachelor Tycoon, the "richest guy on the planet," has a hard time getting a date until he offers to buy Norway for the girl. But "no kissing," she tells Bachelor Tycoon.

Borrowing from a standard routine of late-night TV talk show host and funnyman David Letterman, *NewMedia* magazine had listed 10 reasons why a woman would want to marry Gates, and 10 reasons why one wouldn't. The 10 reasons to marry Gates: Money; he works late at the office; money; necking in the Porsche; money; career advancement; money; a household of gadgets; money; Steve Jobs is taken. The 10 reasons not to marry him: Too much rain in Seattle; those pre-bed DOS quizzes; having to address him as Sir William; the Porsche is grounded; no college degree; premarital agreement will take too long to read; he works late at the office; legal bills from the inevitable lawsuits; wedding vows in BASIC; Pee Wee Herman is still available.

During his two years at Harvard before he dropped out to run Microsoft, Gates rarely dated. But he did like to frequent Boston's notorious Combat Zone, with its porn shows, strip joints, and prostitutes. His first serious girlfriend was Jill Bennett, a tall blonde who sold computer equipment in Seattle.

They met in the early 1980s. Bennett found a sensitive side in Gates.

"Although he hides it well with his hard-core exterior, and certainly will not admit it, Bill's feelings get hurt easily," she recalled.

Gates and Bennett broke up in the mid-1980s, in part because Gates could not make time for the relationship.

"In the end," said Bennett, "it was difficult to sustain a relationship with someone who could boast a 'seven-hour turnaround'—meaning that from the time he left Microsoft to the time he returned in the morning was a mere seven hours."

Melinda French is nine years younger than Gates. They met at a company function soon after she went to work for Microsoft in 1987. At the time, he was dating Ann Winblad since his breakup with Bennett. Like Gates, Winblad was a company industry junkie. A former college cheerleader, the daughter of a Minnesota high-school football coach, Winblad had founded a Minneapolis software company for $500 and sold it several years later for $15.5 million. But she was nearly 10 years older than Gates and wanted to marry and have children. Gates was not yet ready to settle down with one woman. They broke up in December 1987, at the wedding of Gates's sister, Kristi. Winblad remained one of Gates's closest friends, however, and he kept her picture in his office even after their romance ended. Gates and Winblad also continued to see each other as vacation buddies. Their week-long spring breaks together had become something of a ritual, one they did not want to stop even if they were no longer romantically involved. They liked to assign motifs to these times together. On one vacation trip, they each read as many physics books as they could and listened to tapes of noted physicist Richard Feynman lecturing at Cornell.

Gates and Winblad had such a special friendship that he sought her approval before he married French. "When I was off on my own thinking about marrying Melinda," Gates would later tell *Time* magazine, "I called Ann and asked her approval."

And before French and Gates married, French gave her approval for him to continue to take a week's vacation with Winblad at her beach cottage on the Outer Banks of North Carolina. "We can play putt-putt while discussing biotechnology," Gates told *Time*. Or as Winblad put it: "We can share our thoughts about the world and ourselves."

Whether such an arrangement, even if platonic, bothers French is not known. She has never spoken publicly about her personal life with Gates.

At first glance, it might have seemed that Gates and French had little in common. She was an avid runner and hiker who also enjoyed the theater. Gates had never exhibited interest in any activity that smacked of drudgery. In contrast to his "nerdy" dress and manners, she was poised and gracious and looked like the girl next door. She was also smart, well-read, and extremely driven, just like Gates. They hit it off.

Though Gates began dating French in 1988, he continued to play the field for awhile, especially when he was out of town on business, when he would frequently hit on female journalists who covered Microsoft and the company industry. His womanizing was well known, although not well reported, because Gates and Microsoft spoon-fed stories to industry writers for such papers as the *New York Times,* and none of them wanted the flow of information to stop. They also didn't report on the wild bachelor parties that Microsoft's boyish chairman would throw in his Seattle home, for which Gates would visit one of Seattle's all-nude nightclubs and hire dancers to come to his home and swim naked with his friends in his indoor pool.

French was well aware of Gates's womanizing, and consequently their relationship ran hot and cold. At one point, they broke up for nearly a year, reportedly because Gates refused to make any kind of commitment. When they got back together again in 1992, however, the relationship grew closer and stronger. They were often seen together at Seattle restaurants and the movies, and they vacationed in Australia, Thailand, and the Dominican Republic. But they never appeared together socially at industry functions. Gates, worried that publicity about their romance would cause French to have to leave Microsoft, had requested that computer industry writers and newspaper reporters who knew about the romance not mention her name. They didn't.

"She has very much her own life," said Ida Cole, a former Microsoft executive who has worked with both. "She has her own set of friends, and hasn't been totally wrapped up with him. . . . It's a fine match."

Along with several other Microsoft employees, French served as a board member of the Village Theater in the Seattle suburb of Issaquah. She and Gates donated $100,000 toward the theater's capital campaign. "She's a strong woman who knows what she's about, and makes her opinions known," said Robb Hunter, the theater's executive producer.

In June 1992, French looked on as President George Bush, in a ceremony in the Rose Garden, presented Gates with the National Medal of Technology. Only Steve Jobs and Steve Wozniak had won the award at a younger age. Later that year, at Christmas, Mary Gates asked her son when he was going to get an engagement ring for French. His mother had often expressed disappointment to friends that her only son had deferred marriage for so long. His father had even told the *Wall Street Journal* that he believed young Bill was in danger of defaulting on a part of life's purpose. Philippe Kahn, Borland's chief, had remarked that he had little to discuss with Gates socially because he, Kahn, had a rich family life, while Gates could talk only business.

Gates himself was worried that he would be too old to enjoy his children if he waited much longer to marry. It had been clear for some time that he was thinking about marriage and children. The $50 million high-tech home he was building on Lake Washington included a children's wing, complete with an extra room for a nanny. And Gates had sought reassurances from friends that he was doing the right thing in contemplating marriage. In an e-mail note to Microsoft executive Jonathan Lazarus, Gates wrote: "You seem to like married life, so that's a good sign that independent types like you can make it work." By early 1993, Gates had confided to close male friends that he was very much in love with French, and planned to ask her to marry him. He had finally found someone with whom he wanted to spend his life and raise a family.

The woman who would one day marry the king of software grew up with two brothers and a sister on a street called Princess in a middle-class neighborhood of Dallas, Texas. She was born there, in 1964, the daughter of Elaine and Raymond French. Her father was an engineer in the aerospace business. At St. Monica grade school, math was her favorite subject.

"I had parents who told me every step of the way, 'You can get what you want,' " French would later tell a Catholic newspaper.

After St. Monica, French attended an exclusive private school, the all-girls Ursuline Academy in Dallas. Susan Bauer, French's computer teacher at Ursuline, remembered her as one of her brightest pupils, and definitely not a high-school computer nerd. French was also a member of the Academy's drill team.

"She was hard-working and personable," recalled Bauer. "She was one of the best students I ever had."

French was valedictorian of Ursuline's class of 1982. After graduating, she was accepted into an accelerated program for computer science undergraduates at Duke University in Durham, North Carolina. She joined the Kappa Alpha Theta sorority and gave guided tours to prospective students. French, an attractive woman who usually kept her long, sandy-colored hair pulled back with barrettes, dated a few men, among them William Wrigley, the heir to the chewing-gum fortune.

She spent three years getting her undergraduate degree in computer science, and in her fourth year enrolled at Duke's Fuqua School of Business for a two-year MBA program. She graduated cum laude. Because French went into the Master's program after her third year of college—most students spend four years working in the corporate world after graduating from college before they enter Fuqua—she was much younger than the other students in her class. Lee Junkans, director of career services and placement for the business school, said French was very mature for her age.

"She was just one of three or four students in the [fast-track] program. It can be tough when your classmates are 26, 27, 28 years old. She was well respected by her classmates, and certainly by me."

French was also one of the most "marketable" women in the class as far as attracting the attention of companies interested in recruiting Fuqua grads, Junkans said. One of those companies was Microsoft. The company interviewed her during a recruiting trip to the campus, and she went to work in Redmond as soon as she earned her MBA in 1987. This was a year after Microsoft had gone public (turning Gates into the nation's youngest billionaire), and French received stock options that would eventually be worth more than a million dollars.

Her rise to a midlevel management position at Microsoft was steady. Even though she was soon known around the company as the chairman's girlfriend, she received no special treatment. Early on she told Ruth Warren, a former Microsoft manager and friend, that she had two goals: to run in a marathon and to be assigned responsibility for Microsoft Word for MS-DOS. She succeeded at both goals. By 1993, she oversaw the work of about 50 people as product unit manager for Microsoft Publisher, a desktop publishing software program.

Although she was serious about her work, French also had a fun side that appealed to Gates and brought out the little boy in him. At one company party, when Gates was challenged to jump over a table—a feat that he had enjoyed performing in female company for many years—French placed a lighted candle on the table and challenged him to try again. He did. Another and another candle was placed on the table as Gates took longer and longer running starts.

"Even though Bill's mother had urged him to marry Melinda, he was not going to be pressured, even by his mother, until he was sure she was the one," said a Gates family friend. "Bill and Melinda talked often about how being married would change her life. She was very concerned about being in the public spotlight. She and Bill came to an agreement that once they were married, her life would stay private. He would never talk about her to the press or discuss their relationship. That was the agreement, that she stay private."

Gates finally proposed over the weekend of March 20, 1993. As a surprise he had cooked up with his pal Warren Buffett, Gates and French boarded a private jet and flew to Omaha, where on Sunday morning, Buffett had arranged to open Borsheim's, the famous jewelry store owned by Berkshire Hathaway, so that French could pick out her engagement ring. Buffett had joked to Gates that when he first got engaged, he spent 6 percent of his net worth on the ring and that Gates should do the same as a sign of true love. (Gates never publicly said how much the ring cost, but the diamond was so big that French would place one hand over the ring to hide it at public speaking outings after the engagement. On one occasion when she was talking to a reporter, French placed a coffee cup on her hand to hide the ring.)

News of their engagement quickly spread through Microsoft after the couple returned to work on Monday morning, March 21. Gates told a friend about the engagement, and French sent an e-mail message to an associate, who in turn sent the message to a friend. This became the hottest e-mail ever at Microsoft. By the end of the day, electronic messages being sent around the company by employees contained little jokes: Did French do Windows? What about offspring—would they name their kids Bill 2.3, Melinda 3.1, and so on? Around Microsoft's campus, French quickly became known as the "E-Mail Bride." Word of the engagement even went to e-mail systems outside the company.

On Tuesday, Microsoft's public relations department notified the media that Gates was engaged to be married. It became front-page news in papers around the world, from London to Hong Kong. The *Wall Street Journal* proclaimed that the engagement was a "Marriage Made at Microsoft."

Gates took French to a professional basketball game that Tuesday night. The Portland Trail Blazers, owned by Paul Allen, were in town to play the Seattle SuperSonics. Gates and French had front-row seats. Photographers from both Seattle newspapers assigned to cover the game spotted the happy couple sitting side by side, clapping their hands and urging the local team on, and took their pictures, which ran on the front page of both papers the next day. Soon, newspaper editors from around the world were calling the two Seattle papers, asking to buy the pictures of Gates and French. Most hungry for the photos were the British papers on Fleet Street.

The same night as the basketball game, Gates was part of Jay Leno's monologue on the *Tonight Show*.

"What's Bill Gates like after sex?" asked Leno of his live studio audience.

"Micro soft," came his answer.

The joke was an old one in the industry, but it got a good laugh from the *Tonight Show* audience, and probably from millions of others watching on television. Gates's fame had transcended the computer industry. He was now a favorite subject of jokes on late-night talk shows, elevated to the status usually reserved for movie stars, the president, and the royal family. Newspaper columnists around the country had fun with the news, too. Some suggested wedding gifts: How about gold-plated pocket protectors? Instead of a Nintendo game, what about Nintendo itself? Mary Ann Calvin, managing editor of *Modern Bride,* told one newspaper columnist she thought an appropriate wedding gift would be either a Waterford crystal computer or arranging with Dan Rather to document Gates's final two days as a bachelor on *48 Hours.*

Friends were very much in favor of the engagement, and thought it good, and inevitable, that Gates chose a "Microsoftie" for a walk down the aisle.

"Melinda is a very good companion for Bill," said Vern Raburn, a longtime friend of Gates and former Microsoft executive who now manages Paul Allen's multimedia empire. "She's funny, very engaging in conversation, intelligent, and super-intense."

Raburn visited with Gates in Seattle the day after the engagement story broke. Gates appeared happier than Raburn had seen him in a long time. Other than the normal prewedding trepidation, Gates appeared ready for that walk down the aisle. "I think Bill sees this as a great step in his life; in some sense, simplifying his life," said Raburn. "Now there is just one person, instead of dozens. . . . In many ways, it was almost inevitable he would end up marrying someone at Microsoft. If you are going to be Bill Gates's wife, you are going to be part of Microsoft, or you are only going to participate in a very small segment of his life."

Old flame Winblad was happy for the man she, too, had wanted to marry. "This is not just a serendipitous choice," she said. "A relationship with Bill early on is a test. Are you smart enough? Do you have enough common sense? Can you make the grade? Are you athletic enough? Melinda is Bill's pick. He could have chosen any woman as a wife for life. He has chosen her, and that means she is an exceptional woman."

Microsoft officials would not say whether the couple had signed a prenuptial agreement. Friends said Gates is, despite his pragmatism, too much of a romantic to ask his bride to sign such an agreement limiting her claims to his fortune should they divorce. More than a year before the engagement, Gates had told an industry journalist he would never ask a future spouse to sign a prenuptial agreement. "It would not be necessary," he said.

"I don't think Bill views marriage as a legal agreement," said Winblad. "He views it as more of a long-term commitment of love."

According to knowledgeable sources, however, Gates did, in fact, sign a prenuptial agreement with French. Gates could not ask French himself, so he talked his pal Ballmer into convincing her to sign. Ballmer, according to those sources, explained to French that the agreement was for the good of the company.

Another of Gates's old loves, Bennett, wondered about French's expectations of married life with the hard-driving Gates. "It's going to be hard for her," Bennett predicted. "There are expectations when you finally get married. And I think there might be some expectation that he won't work as hard."

That certainly was the hope, at least, of Microsoft's competitors. "If the rest of the industry is lucky," Pete Peterson, former executive vice president of WordPerfect Corporation, said upon hearing the news that Gates was engaged, "he'll have a couple of kids soon." But Gates himself had told Raburn during their meeting in Seattle that he would now be more focused than ever since the matter of his marital status was no longer something that would consume his time or his thoughts. "If anybody thinks being married is going to lessen my intensity," Gates told his old friend, "they are in for a surprise!"

Although she was now engaged to the chairman, French continued her job as a Microsoft manager. She told her bosses that she wanted no special treatment. But there was no way she could prevent it. Microsoft employees who worked for her said they were always very much aware that she was going to be the wife of Bill Gates. They wondered if what they said to her helped or hurt them. One Microsoft manager recalled being in a department meeting with French when someone told a not-so-nice story about Gates. French kept her cool and her professionalism. She said nothing about the joke, but directed the talk away from Gates and back to the subject.

There was one significant change in French after the engagement. She became almost obsessive about her privacy. She wrote to her former neighbors in Seattle's Leschi neighborhood, asking them not to talk about her to the press. Her family contacted the Ursuline Academy and requested that no one at the school give any further interviews about their daughter. The school complied. Residents of the Dallas neighborhood where French grew up were also asked by the family to say nothing about French. When reporters called her mother or father, they were told to call Microsoft's public relations department.

One of those Dallas residents contacted by the family said she was told that Melinda was worried not only about her privacy but also about her safety. "After all, she was going to marry one of the richest men in the world, and there are a lot of crazy people out there."

Long before the engagement, security had been beefed up at French's $350,000 home in Leschi, and a Microsoft security officer would occasionally park on the street and watch the house. Gates, too, was concerned about his future wife's safety. He would later talk about it in a court deposition for a lawsuit brought by a television news reporter who was arrested for trespassing when he tried to cover Gates's wedding.

"The visibility that I've had, including the visibility of wealth, does create a situation where sometimes security is necessary; and a few years [ago] my mother was kidnapped, and our seriousness about security increased because of that," Gates said in the sealed deposition. "I've had problems where people . . . a guy came up to me and pulled a hunting knife. People have made various threats from time to time."

Although it was never publicly reported, there was an "incident" involving Gates's younger sister Libby when she was in college in the late 1980s, around the same time that Gates was beginning to garner considerable attention in the national press. No one knows what the incident was. No police report was ever filed, and the family kept the matter quiet, even from friends. The kidnapping of Gates's mother occurred in December 1984, when she was accosted by a man outside her Laurelhurst home. The masked man had jumped out of the shadows of her carport and demanded her keys as she parked her car. She agreed to give the man her keys if he let her go. But the man told her, "I want you." After he grabbed her, Mary Gates broke free and ran across the street to a neighbor's house, where she banged repeatedly on the door until she was let in. The man fled and was never caught. A few months later, Mary Gates happened to mention the incident to friend John Akers, then chief executive of IBM. Akers arranged for IBM's corporate security experts to contact Microsoft, and a new high-tech security system was soon in place at the homes of several Microsoft executives, including Gates, who lived in the same Laurelhurst neighborhood as his parents.

Gates was living in Laurelhurst for much of the time he was dating French, but after they became engaged, he bought a home less than a half mile away from his $50 million high-tech dream home that was under construction. This temporary home had been owned by Jack Sikma, an all-star basketball center who had played for the Seattle SuperSonics. Sikma had paid $2 million for the four-bedroom, 6,000-square-foot waterfront home in 1986. Although the property was assessed at $4.3 million, Gates paid $8 million for it in July 1993. Gates told friends he wanted to be closer to the construction of his mansion, which was already a couple of years behind schedule and falling further behind, in part because French had taken over supervision of the project and was demanding many architectural changes before she was willing to live there.

In August, five months after their engagement, French and Gates took a three-week vacation in Africa with 10 friends, including Winblad and her pal Heidi Roizen, another computer industry executive and a "Friend of Bill." It was a milestone for the hard-working Gates, who had never before taken more than one week's vacation at a time. During the photo safari, the group traveled by Land Rover through Kenya, Tanzania, and Zaire, sleeping in tents around roaring campfires as guards patrolled the perimeter to keep wild animals away from the computer industry's most vicious predator and his party.

When they returned from vacation, Gates and French began finalizing their marriage plans. There was a growing sense of urgency because Mary Gates was by now seriously ill with breast cancer, and her doctors had told the family they did not expect her to live more than a year. But what kind of wedding? Gates was not religious, but French was a devout Roman Catholic.

"At the time that Melinda and young Bill decided to get married, she expressed the fact that it was very important to her personally that the wedding be a Catholic ceremony," said a close friend of the Gates family. "So Melinda talked with Mary Gates and told her she wanted a Catholic wedding. Mary told her if that's what she wanted, then she needed to talk with Father Sullivan."

With his wavy white hair and imposing physique, Father William Sullivan had become one of the better-known figures in the Seattle community since he arrived in 1976 to become president of Seattle University, an institution steeped in the Jesuit tradition, but one that had been struggling financially. Since Sullivan took the reins, it has operated in the black. He and Mary Gates became close friends while working together for the United Way and various civic projects. Mary loved Sullivan's spirit of adventure. In 1990, Sullivan had participated in the International Peace Climb of Mount Everest, and celebrated mass at 20,000 feet.

At Mary's suggestion, French contacted Sullivan, and the two met for breakfast to visit and talk about her wedding plans. French later wrote a note to Sullivan saying she and Gates would be very pleased if he could officiate at their wedding.

By this time, they had decided to have their wedding in Hawaii, on the island of Lanai. Once known as the "Pineapple Island" and more recently as the "Private Island," Lanai is as beautiful as it is secluded, which is why it has become a favorite of A-list celebrities such as Richard Gere, Gene Hackman, Kevin Costner, and Oprah Winfrey. At the island's two resorts, Hollywood celebrities can escape the usual tourist crowd and autograph seekers who hound them at other luxury Hawaiian resorts. Here, the twentieth century is left behind. There are no hula dancers or high-rise hotels with revolving restaurants; instead, flat pineapple fields stretch to the horizon, mountains are wrapped in mist, and cliffs plunge into the dark blue waters of the Pacific.

Only 18 miles long and 13 miles wide, Lanai is the sixth largest island in the Hawaiian chain. Reachable by air or via an hour-long boat ride from the old whaling town of Lahaina on the leeward side of Maui, it has only two paved roads, traversing fewer than 30 miles. Most of the island's 3,000 residents live in Lanai City, a village of 1920s-era plantation homes and Hawaiian bungalows with washboardlike tin roofs. Boston businessman James Dole bought the island from missionaries for $1.1 million in 1922, imported workers from the Philippines, and turned it into the world's largest pineapple plantation. Until the late 1980s, the public was not welcome. Then David Murdock, chairman and largest shareholder of Dole Food Inc., took control of parent company Castle & Cook. Murdock, a billionaire who often roamed the island in a white suit and Panama hat, decided it was cheaper to grow pineapples overseas, so he yanked out the 17,000 acres of pineapple plants and turned to tourism.

Until 1990, the only place to stay on the island was a rustic 10-room hotel built by Dole in 1923 to house visitors and to provide executives of his pineapple plantations with entertainment. But shortly after Murdock took control of Castle & Cook and renamed it Dole Food, the company spent $400 million to build two world-class hotels. The Lodge at Koele, erected on a hillside in the misty foothills above Lanai City, opened in 1990. The next year, the Manele Bay Hotel opened on a bluff overlooking Hulopoe Bay and the island's best beach. Its 250 rooms, which rent for $250 to $2,000 a day, are nestled in a series of low buildings among the gardens and pools. At the hotel's private beach with its talcum-white sands, guests can swim in a protected marine sanctuary with dolphins and parrot fish. Not long before the Gates wedding, shooting had wrapped at the Manele Bay Hotel for the movie *Exit to Eden,* which starred Dan Ackroyd and Rosie O'Donnell.

Gates and French wanted their wedding ceremony outdoors, on the golf course at the Manele Bay Hotel. The championship 18-hole course designed by Jack Nicklaus was scheduled to open Christmas Day, a week before the nuptials at sunset on January 1, 1994. The actual ceremony would take place on the green grass of the tee box for the par 3 twelfth hole, the so-called signature hole of the course because of its stunning beauty and dramatic location. The tee box is on a spit that juts out adjacent to cliffs that plunge more than 200 feet into the Pacific. Murdock had personally assured Gates that since 99 percent of the island was privately owned, the press could be kept away if they found out. French, who had voiced concerns to friends that if the media found out they would ruin the wedding, was determined not to let that happen. She was all too aware that helicopters hired by paparazzi had flown so low over Madonna and Sean Penn's wedding that the bride and groom could not hear each other. And when Elizabeth Taylor remarried, a reporter for a tabloid paper parachuted into the ceremony. Hoping to prevent details about the wedding from leaking out, French insisted that anyone hired to work on the wedding sign a nondisclosure agreement.

In addition, to mislead the media, misinformation was released. When Gates and French signed up with the Seattle Bon Marché bridal registry, they listed the wedding day as February 14, Valentine's Day. (Among gift requests were upper-middle-class staples such as Waterford crystal—12 highball glasses at $50 a pop; Towle sterling flatware, El Grande pattern, at $232 for a four-piece place setting; and Lenox Westchester china, at $400 for a five-piece setting.)

But accurate word about the wedding did leak out. In late November, *Windows Watcher,* a trade newsletter that keeps close tabs on Microsoft, reported that the wedding was on schedule for sometime in January on the island of Lanai. On December 29, the *Seattle Post-Intelligencer,* the morning paper, confirmed details about the wedding, including the January 1 date. When a reporter phoned Microsoft for comment, Microsoft's public relations czar Marty Taucher called the paper's publisher and requested on behalf of the Gates family that the story not run. In exchange, Taucher offered the paper an exclusive picture of the wedding that was to be taken by a photographer hired for the occasion. Microsoft had planned to release only one photograph of the event to the media, but would give the paper a second photograph, he explained. The paper refused to withdraw, but it did agree to report that the wedding was to take place "somewhere in Hawaii," and not mention

Lanai or the Manele Bay Hotel golf course. The banner headline story ran the next morning, December 30. It had also been sent to the *New York Times* and Associated Press wire services before publication, and by the time the paper hit the streets that morning, other papers, as well as radio and television, had already learned the location of the ceremony.

Gates and French, along with family members, had been on Lanai for a week by the time the media learned the wedding date and location. Months in advance, Gates had booked both families into rooms at the Lodge and at the Manele Bay Hotel. More than 130 people had been invited to the wedding and had taken rooms at the Manele Bay Hotel and the Lodge. For security reasons, Gates also rented most of the rest of the rooms at both hotels even though they were not needed to accommodate his party. As a result, several Hollywood stars who had planned to vacation on Lanai over Christmas were unable to do so.

Gates was footing the entire wedding bill, which was expected to cost well over a million dollars. At the Manele Bay Hotel, family members and Gates and French occupied all but one of the top floor's 13 rooms, which were known as the Butler Suites because a butler saw to the needs of anyone staying on the floor. The rooms cost $1,300 per night. The one suite not used by the wedding party was occupied by hotel owner Murdock.

Wedding guests had been told to travel to Honolulu on their own; from there they would be flown to Lanai on a Boeing 737 chartered by Gates. Several arrived at the Lanai airport in their private jets. The "Friends of Bill" guest list read like a who's who in the *Forbes* annual listing of the richest people in America. In addition to Gates, there were four other billionaires in attendance: best man Steve Ballmer, Microsoft cofounder Paul Allen, cellular phone magnate Craig McCaw, and investor Warren Buffett. Other guests included Ann Winblad and Katharine Graham, owner and former publisher of the

Washington Post, who was a close friend of both Buffett and Gates and his family.

Mary Gates had made the trip, too, despite her illness. After encouraging her son for years to marry, she was not going to miss his wedding.

"Mary was absolutely remarkable," said a family friend at the wedding. "She was very, very sick before the wedding, but I think it's one of those clear examples of a woman rallying, just by her own force of character. To see her at that wedding . . . if you didn't know that she was sick, I don't think you would have picked it up. She was right there. She was full of spark, just like the Mary Gates of old."

On Tuesday, December 28, Gates and French had walked into a small office in Lanai City and paid $16 for a marriage license. Marian Honda, the state marriage license agent, had closed the office at the couple's request while they filled out the forms. Honda had been contacted two months earlier by a Microsoft representative and told about the wedding. She also was asked not to say anything to anyone.

With New Year's Day falling on a Saturday, most of the wedding guests had arrived midweek. Gates had spared no expense to fill their time on the island with fun, parties, and small gifts.

"Throughout the course of our stay on the island," one guest said, "there was a constant stream of little gifts and packages that appeared in each of our rooms. So, when we went back to our hotel room, maybe there was a beautiful basket of fruit; and then another time, there was a little gift or memento of the wedding."

The morning of the day before the wedding, some of the guests played in a golf tournament at the Koele Lodge on an 18-hole course designed by Greg Norman. Gates and his father played together. Afterward, all the men had a luncheon for the groom at the Lodge, while the women had their own luncheon for the bride at the Manele Bay Hotel. A raucous luau complete with a fireworks show was held that night, New Year's Eve, on the private beach below the hotel, where Gates surprised the love of his life with a performance by Willie Nelson, her favorite singer. Nelson had been flown in that day from Honolulu and had been kept out of sight in the hotel until it was time to make his entrance, which came when Gates got up during the luau and announced to his guests, "You know, I want to do something special for Melinda and I thought about singing for her, but you all know I can't sing a note. So I've asked a friend of ours to come and sing."

On cue, Nelson walked out from under some nearby trees. This was one secret that had not gotten out. French was overwhelmed as Nelson began singing with a backup band, and everyone, including Gates and French, danced in the sand.

"He just kept going and going," said one guest about Nelson, who, like French, hails from Texas. "People just kept calling out songs for him to sing. The biggest laugh of the whole evening came when Willie sang the song with the line, 'I've got the money, honey, if you got the time.' That was the humorous high point of the night."

Hundreds of people who live in Lanai City had driven down to the beach that night for the 10:00 P.M. fireworks show, but they were kept more than 100 yards away by Microsoft and hotel security. News of the wedding had spread around the island several weeks earlier. Frustrated reporters and photographers who had begun arriving on the island Thursday had all but disappeared under threat of arrest. Reporters caught anywhere near the hotel had received trespass warnings that stated: "You are hereby notified that your presence and/or patronage is no longer desired on property owned and operated by Lanai Company, including . . . all lands owned by Castle & Cook. This serves as a notice that you are not to return." Media representatives were told they would be arrested if found on private property again. Since about 99 percent of the island is privately owned, there was little point in staying.

A few reporters never made it inland; they were met by security at the Lanai airport and sent packing on the same plane on which they arrived. Only one reporter was actually arrested. He was incarcerated in the Lanai City jail, and released only after he agreed to leave the island. He subsequently sued Gates and Murdock for false arrest, and won. One enterprising freelance photographer managed to reach the golf course by walking through a low-lying scrub forest, where he hid for awhile in one of the large white tents that had been set up for the wedding. He was eventually discovered by security, who escorted him down to the Manele Bay harbor, where he boarded a boat off the island. Nevertheless, some pictures he shot of the wedding site, along with his personal account of his adventures in trying to cover the event, were published by the computer industry trade magazine *PC Week*.

New Year's Day dawned with a magnificent sunrise. Later in the morning, guests were treated to a tour and champagne brunch aboard Paul Allen's 154-foot custom yacht, the *Charade*, which had sailed over for the wedding and was anchored in the Manele Bay harbor, not far from one of the island's landmarks, "Sweetheart Rock," a strikingly beautiful rock formation just off shore.

Even as guests were being transported by motorized launch back and forth to the yacht, workers were putting the finishing touches to the wedding site. Potted plants and palm trees decorated the tee box, where 130 white folding chairs had been arranged facing the ocean, in rows separated by an aisle. By early afternoon, security around the hotel and golf course intensified as the time for the ceremony neared. The golf course was closed, and security officers patrolled the fairways and positioned themselves on hills behind the course. At 4:00 P.M., a red security helicopter took off from the golf course and swooped repeatedly over the hotel beach about a mile away. It then swept low over the golf course and the hills beyond, on the lookout for any intruders.

The first of the wedding guests arrived at the tee box at 5:00 P.M. in a procession of golf carts driven by blue-shirted hotel staff. After they were dropped off, the carts returned to the hotel to pick up other guests. French was the last to be driven out in one of the vehicles, her wedding dress blowing behind her in the wind. Her simple gown, made from Italian silk decorated with pearls and designed by a bridal shop in Seattle, had cost about $10,000, far less than what many society brides spend on their wedding dresses.

The ceremony began with Gates and French speaking to each other "from the heart" in front of Father Sullivan, who wore a white alb and stole.

"It was a particularly beautiful moment," recalled a close friend of the couple. "When we were planning the wedding, Bill and Melinda expressed the desire that before they pronounced their formal marriage vows, they take just a moment, each of them in turn, to express to the other person how very, very much the other meant to them and how getting to know them and falling in love had really changed their whole lives. So, they each took just a couple of minutes, and in very personal words, and talking directly to each other, expressed their love and appreciation and gratitude. That was a little aspect of the wedding that is not a conventional thing, but that was really done very, very beautifully."

There were several scripture readings, including one by French's aunt. When the ceremony ended and Gates and his bride kissed, the guests broke into loud applause.

As promised, Microsoft released one official photograph of the wedding to the Associated Press in Honolulu the next day. But the picture was of such poor quality that few papers used it. However, unbeknownst to the couple, the wedding had been captured through the telephoto lens of a Seattle *Post-Intelligencer* photographer, who was on a boat in the waters off the golf course below the cliffs. The photo later appeared on a two-page spread in *People* and in papers and magazines around the world.

Microsoft had little to say about the wedding. Its public relations firm released a brief statement for the media: "William (Bill) H. Gates III and Melinda French wed last evening in a private ceremony amongst close friends and family. Bill Gates is chairman and chief executive officer of Microsoft Corporation. The small, private wedding ceremony was traditional in style and was performed by a Catholic priest. The bride wore a traditional white gown; the groom wore a tuxedo." The press release then quoted Gates as saying, "We are both extremely happy and looking forward to a long, wonderful life together."

Many of the wedding guests left for Honolulu the morning after the wedding on the Boeing 737 chartered by Gates. The couple left for their honeymoon aboard a private jet for an even more private destination. They spent the next week at the Wakaya Club, a 2,200-acre resort at one end of a five-square-mile private island about 90 miles from the main island of Fiji, described in travel brochures as boasting "emerald lagoons, soaring cliffs and shell-strewn beaches," as well as a nine-hole golf course, tennis and croquet courts, and speedboats. The resort, owned by businessman David Gilmour, has accommodations for only 16 pampered couples, who pay about $900 per night. Children are not allowed. The only access to the resort is by private jet.

It was to prove both a sad and a happy time for the Gates family, for within days of returning to Seattle from the wedding, Mary Gates entered the hospital. The cancer was raging out of control through her body. She would soon go into seclusion, seeing only close friends and family in the last months of her life. She died in her sleep at home on June 10, 1994, at the age of 64. Her son got the call in the middle of the night and rushed to the family home.

"It was a sad hour," said the family minister, the Reverend Dale Turner. "Bill took his mother's death very, very hard. Bill loved his mother and she loved him. They were so close. That love helped to shape his life during his early years, and it blossomed in many ways later on."

After Gates and Allen had moved Microsoft from Seattle to Bellevue (the site prior to the Redmond campus), across Lake Washington, on January 1, 1979, Mary Gates would often call her son several times a day to check on him. She even wrote him letters. When Gates took business trips out of town, his mother often went along. Even well into his late thirties, Gates would try to visit his mother at least once a week.

Gates and other family members spoke at the memorial service for Mary that was held at the University Congregational Church in Seattle a week after her death. More than a thousand mourners packed the church to say goodbye to the remarkable woman who had forged a brilliant career in business, civic activism, and philanthropy. Mary Gates had served as a regent at the University of Washington for 18 years. She was the first woman to be president of the United Way of King County, and she was a director of many corporate boards. She was also a tireless volunteer for the Seattle Symphony, Washington Gives, the Seattle Foundation, the YWCA, and several other organizations.

At the memorial service, Gates and his two sisters recounted stories of games played around campfires, and of their mother's support in school and in their careers.

"I am the son of Mary Gates, and she was a wonderful woman," Gates said. "Not many adult sons are as proud of their mother as I was."

Gates said his mother never stopped stressing the importance of family. "She was always concerned about my getting married. It came up a lot."

He recalled the well-known story of how his mother's connections with former IBM Chairman John Opel had helped Microsoft make the deal of the century when Big Blue needed an operating system for its first personal computer in 1980 and came calling on Microsoft. At the time, Opel and Mary Gates served together on the national board of United Way.

Gates also told the story of how his mother had been influential in wooing Steve Ballmer, then at Stanford Business School, to Microsoft in 1980.

His voice breaking with emotion, Gates concluded by saying, "She would know better how to show appreciation. It has meant a whole lot, and we thank you."

Following his mother's death, Gates turned to the woman he loved for support to see him through the difficult days ahead as he refocused on work and the many battles still to be fought.

"Although his mother had a major influence on him, Melinda will have much more," said one of Gates's best male friends. "For a young woman, she has a lot of common sense. [S]he's a real, both-feet-on-the-ground sort of young person. I have been very, very impressed by her as I [have] gotten to know her. And I think, clearly, while she's full of life and spirit, she has an extraordinarily large quotient of good solid common sense. She will be able to help Bill even more than he realizes."

5

The Davids vs. Goliath

nly a fool would want to be stranded in a winter snowstorm at the Tompkins County Airport in Ithaca, New York, and Steven Sinofsky is no fool. So Sinofsky, one of Microsoft's brightest people, and technical adviser to the boss, Chairman Bill, did the sensible thing and returned to Cornell University, only about three miles away.

He had flown to his alma mater from Seattle in early February 1994, on a recruiting trip, looking for high-bandwidth people like himself who wanted to work for Microsoft and take the company into the next century by helping to write and develop great new software. But that had been business, and had left no time to relax and look around. Now, with the airport closed, snow coming down, and nothing but time on his hands, Sinofsky could reacquaint himself with the campus he knew so well as a student. What he found confirmed his growing concern that Microsoft was slighting the Internet phenomenon that was sweeping inexorably across the land.

Seven years earlier, when Sinofsky was a student at Cornell, the Internet had been a refuge for just the technically savvy, himself included. Now, ordinary students and faculty were using

UNIX workstation computers and TCP/IP networks with relative ease. They were exploring the World Wide Web, exchanging e-mail, sharing information with friends and colleagues at universities all over the world, and sending Gopher on search missions. Students were even accessing their course lists off the Net. These college kids were hip to the Net, exploring a world to which many of the top computer programmers in the country at Microsoft's campus in Redmond did not have easy access.

Certainly this was something to write home about, and Sinofsky dashed off an e-mail to his recently married friend. The message was titled "Cornell Is Wired!" Later in February, after Sinofsky returned to Microsoft, he gave Gates a Web-surfing demonstration with Mosaic. Finally the Internet had the attention of the man in charge of the biggest and most powerful software company on the planet. But that was just about all. Microsoft still had not started to develop a business and technical strategy for responding to this phenomenon from cyberspace.

It would be more than a year before Gates fully acknowledged the importance of the Internet and decreed that all of Microsoft's considerable brain- and firepower be directed at the most serious challenge the company had ever faced. But Sinofsky's e-mail from Cornell, Gates would later tell writer and futurist George Gilder, was the wake-up call that prompted his "Internet Tidal Wave" memo to his executive staff in May 1995.

Sinofsky soon discovered he was not the only one sending e-mail warning Microsoft executives about the Internet boom. James Allard, the programmer who was working on Internet communication protocols in Nathan Myhrvold's Advanced Technology Group, had been growing increasingly frustrated at the company's indifferent attitude toward the Net's unparalleled growth. Recruited by Myhrvold out of Boston University's computer science program, the Net-savvy Allard arrived on campus in 1991, geared up to help Microsoft seize the In-

Ann Winblad, a respected venture capitalist, dated Gates in the mid-1980s. When they broke up, Gates began dating Melinda French, who would become his wife. But Gates and Winblad remained close friends and Gates still spends one week a year with Winblad at her beach house on the Outer Banks of North Carolina. (Photo courtesy of the *Seattle Post-Intelligencer*)

Two days after they got engaged in 1993, Bill Gates and Melinda French took in a basketball game between the Seattle SuperSonics and the Portland Trail Blazers. At the time, French was a product manager at Microsoft. She left the company after the couple married. (Photo by Kurt Smith, courtesy of the *Seattle Post-Intelligencer*)

Bill Gates and Melinda French exchanged wedding vows at sunset on January 1, 1994, on the Hawaiian island of Lanai. This photo was taken with a long telephoto camera lens by a newspaper photographer on a boat positioned off the golf course where the wedding took place. Reporters and photographers had been kicked off the island under threat of arrest by security officers hired by Gates. (Photo by Grant Haller. Courtesy of the *Seattle Post-Intelligencer*)

Gates and best man Steve Ballmer enjoyed a final solitary walk moments before the wedding ceremony began. This, photo, too, was taken with a long telephoto camera lens. (Photo by Grant Haller. Courtesy of the *Seattle Post-Intelligencer*)

Although she was seriously ill, Mary Gates found the strength to attend her son's wedding. She died a few months later of cancer. Gates was very close to his mother and her death greatly affected him. (Photo courtesy of the *Seattle Post-Intelligencer*)

Steve Ballmer is one of Gates's best friends and his most trusted advisor at Microsoft. He was best man at Gates's wedding. (Photo by Scott Ecklund)

Gates laughs at one of Jay Leno's jokes during the launch of Windows 95 in August 1995 at Microsoft's campus in Redmond. Kidding that Gates really wasn't so smart after all, Leno told how he had gone to Gates's home and found his VCR still flashing "12." (Photo by Scott Ecklund)

Above: Pete Higgins, left, one of Microsoft's vice presidents, and Brad Chase appeared on stage with Gates during the launch of Windows 95. Chase was the marketing brains behind what was the biggest and most hyped launch of a product in the history of the computer industry. (Photo by Scott Ecklund)

Left: Bill Gates talks about Windows 95 on launch day in August 1995. (Photo by Scott Ecklund)

Marc Andreessen, who helped create Mosaic for browsing the World Wide Web, was being called "the next Bill Gates" after Netscape took off like a rocket in 1994. (Photo copyright 1996, Netscape Communications Inc.)

Jim Clark founded Silicon Graphics in 1982 to make 3-D. In early 1994, he quit to team up with Marc Andreessen to form Netscape Communications, which quickly seized the lead over Microsoft in the race to control cyberspace. (Photo copyright 1996, Netscape Communications Inc.)

James Barksdale, chief executive officer and president of Netscape Communications, was the key manager who turned Netscape into a well-run business that was able to take on industry giant Microsoft. (Photo copyright 1996, Netscape Communications Inc.)

Nathan Myhrvold is the Microsoft technology guru whose job it is to see far into the future and position Microsoft in emerging new markets. Neither he nor Bill Gates foresaw how quickly the Internet would explode. (Photo by Paul Brown, courtesy of the *Seattle Post-Intelligencer*)

Gary Reback is the Silicon Valley lawyer who represented a group of Microsoft competitors who contested a consent decree negotiated between Microsoft and the U.S. Justice Department. Later, in 1996, Reback began representing Netscape in an antitrust complaint that it filed with the Justice Department about Microsoft. (Photo courtesy of Gary Reback)

Bill Joy, a co-founder of Sun Microsystems in 1982, was an early believer in the Internet and incorporated Internet communication protocols into Sun's UNIX-based computers. Joy is now head of Sun's research and development lab at a mountain hideaway in Aspen, Colorado, called Smallworks. (Photo courtesy of Sun Microsystems)

Eric Schmidt was one of Bill Joy's buddies at Berkeley in the 1970s when they hacked their way around the Internet. Joy went on to co-found Sun Microsystems, and Schmidt became the company's chief technologist. (Photo courtesy of Sun Microsystems)

Rob Glaser, as a vice president of Microsoft, oversaw its transformation into a multimedia company. He left Microsoft to found his own Internet company called ProgressiveNetworks. The company developed a product called RealAudio, which became a standard feature in Microsoft's Internet Explorer. (Photo courtesy of Progressive-Networks)

Above: Tim Krauskopf, seated, the founder of Spyglass Inc., and Doug Colbeth, the company's chief executive officer. When Microsoft needed a browser in 1994 to compete with Netscape, it licensed Mosaic from Spyglass. (Photo courtesy of Spyglass, Inc.)

Left: Senior programmer Ben Slivka was one of the few at Microsoft who early on saw the potential of the Internet. (Photo courtesy of the *Seattle Post-Intelligencer*)

ternet as a great new business opportunity, and to extend the company's reach far beyond desktop operating systems and application programs. He was the first programmer at Microsoft to have the word "Internet" on his business card, which read in full, "Program Manager, Internet Technologies." Working on Myhrvold's nonsanctioned project to develop TCP/IP for Microsoft, Allard had been making a lot of noise about the Internet, so much, in fact, that he had been heard way out in the East Tech building where Jeff Lill and his Marvel team were racing to develop the company's proprietary on-line system. "Allard basically thought that we were nuts not to be doing something for the Internet," said Lill. "He thought we were off base."

On January 25, 1994, shortly before Sinofsky had flown off on his head-hunting trip to Cornell, Allard wrote a long memo to Myhrvold and other senior managers. "I finally just couldn't take it anymore," Allard later told *Business Week*, explaining why he wrote his memo. "I felt the company just didn't get it." Titled "Windows: The Next Killer Application for the Internet," the memo suggested that Microsoft get busy creating its own Mosaic-like browser and include Internet communication protocols in Chicago, which was destined to become Windows 95. Microsoft, he said, had to "embrace and extend." Those two words would eventually become the centerpiece of Microsoft's Internet strategy.

Why didn't Microsoft "get it" sooner? After all, it had some of the smartest people in the industry, including Myhrvold, the technology guru whose job it was to see into the future and help position Microsoft on the road ahead. "Nathan tends to spend a lot of time thinking about the future, but as measured by centuries and millennia, and sometimes he'll disdain to look at decades," said Rob Glaser, who had passed along to Sinofsky his recommendations for making Marvel an Internet-based service. "One of the challenges, when you have real future-oriented people who are great at seeing the world of the possible, is how to marry them with people who know how to see the relationship of the possible and the world of the actual. And while I'm superimpressed with Bill's personal ability to do that, there's no way for any one person to do that across an organization that has 20,000 people, that is in so many different businesses and industries. That's just a structural challenge within any company.... There were other people at Microsoft who certainly thought about the future; but in terms of really mapping corporate strategy for a lot of these fundamental sea changes, I think that it's just inherently an ad hoc process.... Having said all that, though, I want to extend my most effusive praise for how quickly the company pivoted, once the company, and Bill personally, understood the magnitude of the impact and the power of the sea change."

In fairness to Microsoft, Glaser noted, the Internet phenomenon happened very fast, and the difference between being late and being early was a matter of months, not years, and during those months most of the company's talent was focused on Chicago, which was supposed to ship before the end of the year. "Should they have been smarter about understanding these other overall trends? Well, yeah, they probably should have been," said Glaser. "However, it's really easy to get tunnel vision on something you're focusing on."

But Microsoft's hegemony also got in the way: it was used to calling the shots, as it did with DOS and Windows. Microsoft had the band, and the industry marched to its tune. In contrast, the wild and woolly Internet did not look like an environment in which Microsoft was going to be able to call the shots. So Microsoft chose to ignore it, partly out of ignorance, partly out of arrogance.

The company also was worried that the Internet posed a grave security risk across its corporate network of some 30,000 PCs. In early 1994, most employees could not get an Internet connection except on a computer that was not connected to the Microsoft corporate network. There were only two such machines at Microsoft's library, and the company monitored their use with sign-up sheets.

"Microsoft wouldn't embrace the Internet internally because of all these concerns with security, and so none of us knew much about it," said one of the Marvel managers who had been present in December 1993 for Glaser's class on Internet 101. "Most college kids knew much more than we did because they were exposed to it. If I had wanted to connect to the Internet, it would have been easier for me to get into my car and drive over to the University of Washington than to try and get on the Internet at Microsoft."

The company's Information Systems Department wrote a custom version of FTP (file transfer protocol), but to download files from the Internet, a Microsoft employee had to have the approval of a manager, then the approval of a vice president to send the file over the Internet to someone else.

"A couple years before," said Glaser, explaining Microsoft's rationale for its seemingly irrational security concerns, "someone had taken some of the code for Apple's Macintosh computer and put it out over the Internet. There was a big panic. Their proprietary assets had been compromised. And I think that induced in the bowels of Microsoft a sense of, 'My God, this Internet thing is dangerous.' And so, literally, most people at Microsoft were institutionally cut off from the emerging revolution of the Internet."

For much of January and February, while Allard and Sinofsky were trying to excite others at Microsoft about the Internet, Gates was preoccupied with a trial that was being played out before a federal court jury in Los Angeles. In a classic David versus Goliath scenario, Stac Electronics was taking on mighty Microsoft for patent infringement. It claimed Microsoft had illegally used Stac's data-compression technology in the latest version of Microsoft's operating system, DOS 6.0.

In 1993, Stac had earned only as much money as Microsoft had in any given four-hour period. Microsoft had not lost a significant legal fight since the late 1970s when Microsoft, then a tiny company with a handful of employees, had stood up to Pertec Computer Corporation and its hotshot lawyers. Now Stac, a pipsqueak company based in Carlsbad, California, was facing down Microsoft, and it was about to throw a knockout punch against the biggest in the computer industry.

Stac was essentially a one-product company. In 1990, it had developed Stacker, which compressed the data on a computer's hard drive to free up valuable space. With Stacker, a 20-megabyte hard drive, for example, could store about 40 megabytes of information. Stacker was available for both the PC and the Mac, and its sales amounted to about 85 percent of the company's business. In 1992, Microsoft began negotiating with Stac to license Stacker, which was dominating the market. Microsoft wanted to incorporate Stac's technology into the next version of its operating system. The talks dragged on for several months, then broke off. Stac spokespeople said no deal was reached because Microsoft had refused to negotiate any royalty payment to Stac. In pretrial papers, Microsoft claimed that it had offered Stac a licensing fee of $1 million a month, but that Stac CEO Gary Clow had demanded $4 million, and that's why no agreement had been reached. Meanwhile, Stac obtained a patent for its Stacker technology, and Microsoft began working on its own data-compression software, called DoubleSpace, for which it subsequently obtained a patent.

In May 1992, Stac had gone public at $12 a share. But after Microsoft announced it would ship DOS 6.0 with Double-Space, the price of Stac's stock dropped to $3 a share and a shareholder class action suit was filed against it. The company had to lay off about 20 percent of its workforce. By the fourth quarter of 1993, Stac's revenue had dropped 50 percent, to $6 million, versus sales of $33 million in 1992. In court papers, Microsoft claimed Stac had dragged out the negotiations to make its initial public offering more successful, and that it did not state in its prospectus that Microsoft was planning to include its own data-compression product into DOS.

Despite clandestine overtures from both sides, the two companies could not agree on an out-of-court settlement, so the case went on trial on January 18, 1994. The day before, a massive earthquake had rocked southern California, causing widespread destruction and killing a dozen people in an apartment building in Northridge. It was regarded as an ominous start to a trail that was being closely watched by the entire computer industry to see whether a small competitor could stand up to Microsoft's formidable market power and legal muscle and walk away a winner.

It was also seen as an important legal case because of the issue of patents. More software companies, including Microsoft, were obtaining patents to protect their products, and many in the industry were concerned that the patents were so broad that they inhibited innovation and competition, thus doing more harm than good. Case in point: the year before the Stac case went to trial, the U.S. Patent Office had issued a broad patent to Compton's NewMedia for a search technology used in CD-ROM disks manufactured by many companies. If Compton's patent were upheld, it would force companies to pay expensive licensing fees to Compton, a subsidiary of the Tribune Company.

Although patents are more difficult, time-consuming, and expensive to obtain than copyrights, copyrights had proved to be of little use in protecting certain aspects of software. Apple's lawsuit against Microsoft over Windows, for example, had involved copyright issues, not patent protection. Apple claimed that Microsoft had copied the look and feel of the graphical user interface used in the Mac. It sued Microsoft for more than

$5 billion. But in 1992, before a crowded San Francisco court-room, federal Judge Vaughn Walker ruled that some of the similarities between Microsoft's Windows and Apple's Macintosh were technologies that were already licensed to Microsoft and therefore not an infringement and that the rest were beyond the scope of copyright protection. A ruling in favor of Apple's claims, the judge said, would have "afforded too much protection and yielded too little competition." This not only vindicated Microsoft, it also was significant for the industry, clearing away doubts about the rights of software programmers to adapt aspects of other systems.

The Stac case raised even more troubling issues of intellectual property law. Microsoft had been sued before for patent infringement, but this was the first time a case had gone to trial. The jury would hear not only Stac's suit against Microsoft, but Microsoft's countersuit against Stac. The suits had been consolidated before trial. Microsoft claimed that Stac had infringed on its patents, was guilty of breach of contract, and had conspired to commit fraud.

Early in the trail, on January 28, Gates was called to testify, and was grilled by Stac's lawyers in the packed courtroom. Gates denied that Microsoft had done anything wrong. He said the company's programmers worked day and night to develop the company's own data-compression technology and had not relied on Stac's code. "We wanted to do absolutely everything to make sure we weren't taking a risk (of patent infringement)," Gates testified. "There was a consensus that we had a product that we could sell." He also testified that he was not personally involved in the failed negotiations with Stac.

It was not the first time Gates had testified at a civil trial to defend Microsoft's business practices. In 1986, the year Microsoft went public, Gates testified in a $60 million suit brought by bankrupt Seattle Computer Products, which had sold DOS to Microsoft in 1981 for $50,000. After a three-week trial, Microsoft settled the suit for $1 million while the jury was still deliberating.

Nearly a decade earlier, when Gates had taken the stand for the first time in an Albuquerque courtroom, it could have meant the end of his upstart company had his testimony not carried the day. The claimant in that case was Ed Roberts, who had invented the Altair, the world's first personal computer, for which Gates and Paul Allen had developed the BASIC operating language. In 1977, Roberts had sold his company, MITS, to Pertec, a company specializing in disk and tape drives for minicomputers and mainframe computers. But Pertec wanted BASIC—at the time, Microsoft's cash cow—as part of the deal. Gates knew that if Pertec obtained the rights to BASIC, Microsoft would not survive.

When the chief counsel for Pertec arrived in Albuquerque to assess the situation and talk with Gates, he took one look at the long-haired, scraggly, 21-year-old techie and assumed it was going to be no contest, even though Roberts had warned Pertec that it would have its corporate hands full with Gates. "Pertec kept telling me I was being unreasonable, and that they could deal with this guy," recalled Roberts, now a country doctor in Georgia. "It was a little like Roosevelt telling Churchill that he could deal with Stalin."

The Pertec case was held before a judge, not a jury, and went on for three weeks, from 8:00 A.M. until about 5:00 P.M. "It looked like giant Pertec was picking on these poor 19- and 20-year-old guys and trying to steal their life's work," said Roberts. "That's how they played it, and it played pretty well. . . . I told Pertec they needed to deal with Gates hard. But they didn't. It was a fatal mistake. He won everything."

But Gates would not win the Stac case. Time and again during the trial, lawyers for Stac emphasized to the jury how important the data-compression feature was to DOS 6.0. At one point, they showed the jury a videotape of Gates at the launch of DOS 6.0. He was wearing a T-shirt that said, "We came, we saw, we doubled."

When testimony finally ended, the seven-member jury deliberated for six days before returning its verdict on February 23. It awarded Stac $120 million in damages, the largest judgment ever assessed against Microsoft, amounting to almost four times Stac's 1993 revenues. It was a stunning and unprecedented legal setback for Microsoft. With more than $2 billion in cash reserves, it could easily afford to pay the judgment, but its image of invincibility had been punctured. And the verdict came at a time when there was growing speculation that the Justice Department was preparing to bring an antitrust action against Microsoft.

Jurors said later that they calculated the damages based on about $5.50 per unit of the 20 to 25 million copies of DOS 6.0 that had been shipped with DoubleSpace since March 1993. Stac's lawyers had argued that Microsoft willfully infringed on Stac's patent, which would have resulted in trebled damages. But the jury did not agree.

The jury did, however, find for Microsoft on one of its counterclaims: that Stac illegally used access to Microsoft's trade secrets to make Stacker compatible with DOS 6.0. The jury awarded Microsoft $13.6 million in damages. After the trial, Stac CEO Clow admitted that his company used what is known as reverse engineering to make Stacker run smoothly with DOS 6.0. Reverse engineering was a common industry practice, and most software executives did not consider it to be illegal. Nevertheless, Microsoft was clearly the loser.

Stac's victory was widely hailed in the industry as a triumph for small companies trying to compete against Microsoft. Said Clow: "What I think we've shown is a prototype for how small, innovative companies can effectively compete with Microsoft. We've been vindicated. . . ."

Microsoft agreed to remove the infringing features in DoubleSpace immediately. But it also vowed to appeal the judgment. A day after the jury ruled against Microsoft, Gates spoke at a computer conference in San Francisco that was sponsored, in part, by Microsoft. In an attempt to be upbeat about the costly verdict, Gates wise-cracked: "I had a pretty bad day yesterday," he told the audience. "My lawyers told me we might have to pay $120 million—which is a serious amount of money." He also said that software patent disputes were too complicated for juries to understand and that juries usually sided with the underdog rather than "Goliaths" like Microsoft.

Gates apparently was having another bad day a couple of weeks later when he abruptly walked out of an interview with well-known TV anchorwoman Connie Chung after she dared to ask about the Stac case. The interview was part of a segment on Gates for her *Eye to Eye* series. A CBS camera crew already had spent time with Gates on the road and had filmed him carrying his luggage through Seattle's Tacoma-International Airport and stopping at a Wendy's for a cheeseburger and Diet Dr. Pepper—just a regular guy, this 6-billion-dollar man!

On the afternoon of March 16, Chung sat down with Gates in his office, with the camera rolling. Gates was not in the best of moods. He was preparing for an important trip to China, where he planned to meet with Jiang Zemin, Communist Party chief and the country's president, to lobby for better access to China's emerging software market. Gates had just returned from a trip to Europe, and earlier that morning he had tangled with a television crew from the BBC. Nevertheless, Gates reluctantly obliged when Chung asked him to demonstrate, on camera, his trademark knack for jumping over a chair from a standing start. Gates even answered irritating questions from Chung such as "Do you think you're successful?" When Chung asked Gates whether he considered himself to be a nerd, he replied, "If nerd means you can enjoy understanding the insides of a computer and sit in front of it for hours and play with it and enjoy it."

But the interview quickly turned tense when Chung ventured into a sensitive area: Gates's reputation as a bully in the computer industry. Before sitting down with Gates, Chung had interviewed Gary Clow, president and CEO of Stac, who had told her, "A lot of people make the analogy that competing with Bill Gates is like playing hardball. I'd say it's more like a knife fight." Chung repeated Clow's remark to Gates. "I've never heard any of these things," Gates told her, his voice rising and his words etched with anger and irritation. At that point, Gates turned to an off-camera assistant and said, "I'm done."

"Can I ask you one more question?" said Chung.

"No, I don't think so," Gates replied. He then stood up and yanked off his microphone.

With the television camera still rolling, Gates jabbed his finger at Chung, scolding her for repeating the Clow remark. Then he walked out of his office and into an anteroom. He closed the door and would not come back out until Chung and the CBS crew had left. The interview was broadcast on *Eye to Eye* two months later, on May 19, 1994.

Ironically, by then, adversaries Gates and Clow were on their way to becoming business partners. Rather than appeal the Stac verdict, as it had threatened to do, Microsoft decided to negotiate an $83 million settlement. It agreed to pay Stac royalties of $1 million a month for a period of 43 months, as well as purchase $39.9 million of convertible preferred stock in Stac, or about 15 percent of the company. The new partnership gave Microsoft the right to license, for a royalty, any of Stac's existing or future technology unrelated to data compression. In addition, Stac received a license to some of Microsoft's technology in DOS 6.0. The settlement replaced the court award.

Said Clow of his new partner: "This agreement immediately ends our conflict with Microsoft and ushers in a new era of cooperation between the two companies. Having Microsoft as our ally will help us with new business opportunities and be a far better situation for our company. It puts an end to our burdensome legal fees, creates a royalty stream, puts money in the bank and, most important, aligns Microsoft's interests with the interests of Stac."

The "grandfather from hell," Raymond J. Noorda was approaching 70; his memory was failing, and his days as the president and chief executive of Novell were numbered. He looked around the room at the more than two dozen corporate officers, lawyers, and investment bankers gathered in a cabin in Utah's snow-covered Wasatch mountain range outside of Provo. The leaders of Novell and WordPerfect, they had come to this mountain hideaway for secret talks about merging the two companies, a blockbuster deal that they thought would shake up the computer industry and create a software powerhouse, a new Zion that would rise out of the Utah desert able to go toe-to-toe with Microsoft. Only by combining forces to increase their firepower, Noorda believed, did they have a chance to slow Microsoft's growing industry dominance.

It was the afternoon of March 16, 1994. Seven hundred miles away, in Redmond, Bill Gates was walking out of the interview with Connie Chung after she asked if competing with him was like being in a knife fight. In Utah, at the mountain cabin owned by Alan Ashton, one of the founders of WordPerfect, Noorda and the others who were planning their conquest of Microsoft knew all too well about the dangers of competing with "that little squirt," as Noorda had recently taken to calling Gates. Both companies were hurting, losing market share to Microsoft. Listening to the merger discussions among those gathered in what was known as the Great Room of Ashton's palatial wilderness retreat, Noorda reflected on his years at Novell and his battles with Gates, past and present.

Novell Data Systems of Provo had begun as a manufacturer of personal computers, an offshoot of the failed Beehive Computer. Noorda had arrived in 1982, at age 58, almost by accident.

Having wandered into a Las Vegas hotel room that Novell had rented for its programmers to demonstrate prototype software they had developed, he was soon hired to turn the company around. Noorda, a tight-fisted manager who ate at budget restaurants and required company executives to share hotel rooms when they traveled, took Novell out of the hardware business and into networking, where it became established as the industry leader, leaving Microsoft in its wake. (Losing the networking market to Novell topped a written list that Gates kept to remind himself from time to time of the most critical mistakes Microsoft had made.)

Noorda's dislike of Gates went back to 1988, when Gates, concerned about the competition, blocked a pending buyout by Novell of database software maker Ashton-Tate. In front of reporters, Gates delivered an ultimatum to the chairman of Ashton-Tate: if the deal with Novell went through, Microsoft would destroy Ashton-Tate. The deal collapsed, and Borland International later purchased Ashton-Tate. It was the beginning of the end for Borland when Microsoft, in retaliation, purchased Fox, which made a rival database product.

The failed $10 billion merger with Microsoft in late 1991 had left Noorda even more bitter toward Gates. He believed that Gates had led Novell on. "They are snakes," he said of Microsoft to a reporter from *Business Week*. Noorda was determined to get even, but his obsession was costing the company dearly. Novell was mired in debts caused by Noorda's unwise anti-Microsoft shopping spree. Noorda had wanted Novell to have an operating system that would compete with Microsoft's, but the acquisition of Digital Research had turned into a financial disaster. So had Novell's $350 million purchase of UNIX.

"Microsoft has developed a personal conviction that they are anointed to run this industry," Noorda, a Mormon, told writer Richard Rapaport for an article in *Forbes ASAP* in late

1992. In the article, Rapaport described Noorda's hatred of Gates and Microsoft as a Latter Day Saints–style "Blood Atonement."

By late 1993, Noorda was convinced that Novell's lead over Microsoft in networking was threatened because of Windows NT, which had networking features that might eliminate the need for Novell's Netware. About 85 percent of Novell's business was its networking software. The latest version of Netware, however, was not doing well. Neither was Noorda. Two years earlier he had undergone heart bypass surgery and now wore a pacemaker. He had recently acknowledged to reporters what friends already knew, that he was suffering from recurring memory losses that affected his ability to make operational decisions. Noorda had said publicly he would step down as Novell's president by his 70th birthday on June 19, 1994. The merger with WordPerfect would be Noorda's last chance to try to stop Microsoft and avenge himself on his old enemy. And he had seized the moment with missionary zeal.

Like Novell, WordPerfect was suffering at the hands of Microsoft and had recently announced that it would lay off 17 percent of its workforce, more than 1,000 workers, because of slowing sales. Profits were flat. The company's two founders wanted to cash out.

WordPerfect was a private company. All the stock was in the hands of Alan Ashton and Bruce Bastian, who had founded the company in 1977. Ashton had been a computer science professor at Brigham Young University in the early 1970s, and Bastian had been director of the marching band. When Bastian was fired from the band because he did not have his doctorate, he finished his master's in computer science. In 1977, he and Ashton founded Satellite Software International and created a word processing application they called WP. The company was located in the foothills above Orem, about 10 miles from Novell's headquarters in Provo. In 1980, Pete Peterson, a former BYU psychology graduate and Bastian's brother-in-law, was hired to run the company, which later was renamed WordPerfect.

For years, WordPerfect dominated the word processing market, though it gradually lost market share to Microsoft Word. Then WordPerfect made a costly mistake. It failed to develop a version of Wordperfect for Windows 3.0, which was released to great excitement and record sales in 1990. Word-Perfect management was complacent, believing it held an insurmountable lead over Microsoft. Gates pleaded with Peterson to develop WordPerfect for Windows. Peterson refused; he considered Windows nothing more than a passing fad. After Windows 3.0 came out, WordPerfect's lead over Microsoft quickly declined until Microsoft had more customers than WordPerfect. It would never regain its position. Peterson was replaced in March 1992, in part because he had not been aggressive enough toward Microsoft.

WordPerfect's profits were further eroded in the early 1990s by the software price wars, which were part of Microsoft's strategy to keep prices low in order to establish market share. Microsoft could afford the razor-thin profit margins that resulted because it had a steady revenue stream from DOS and Windows. Other companies, like Borland and WordPerfect, did not.

In 1992, Microsoft released its Microsoft Office suite, in which different applications were bundled together and sold at a bargain price not much higher than that of a single application. Microsoft's suite strategy caught the industry off guard, although Lotus Development Corporation managed to counter with SmartSuite, which included its famous 1-2-3 spreadsheet, Notes, and the word processing program Ami Pro.

WordPerfect had no choice but to ally itself in a licensing deal with Borland, which produced the best-selling Quattro Pro spreadsheet as well as the Paradox database. Their suite offering was called Borland Office. But because the applications came from different companies, they did not work well together, and sales of Borland Office lagged far behind those of Microsoft's and Lotus's suites.

Microsoft Office was so successful that other companies were forced to slash prices of their applications in order to compete. Borland, for example, cut the price of Quattro Pro from $495 to $49. Microsoft Office brought in more than $500 million in 1993, compared to $175 million for SmartSuite and less than $50 million for Borland Office. The trend was clear: Microsoft was leaving little room for others in the applications market to go it alone. Only by increasing their firepower through mergers could Microsoft's rivals have a chance to compete effectively.

WordPerfect was clearly at a crossroads and needed help. Before it initiated merger talks with Novell, it had put out feelers to Lotus. On January 10, 1994, new WordPerfect CEO Adrian Rietveld had met with Lotus CEO Jim Manzi at his office in Cambridge, Massachusetts. Rietveld, 40, who was known to his friends as Ad and spoke with a thick Dutch accent, had become WordPerfect's chief strategist while he was senior vice president of sales and marketing. He took the company's reins as CEO on January 1, after Ashton stepped down and joined Bastian as co-chair of the company.

Rietveld was on a press tour in Boston and had just finished talking with the editors of *PC Week* when he paid a call on Manzi. A possible buyout of WordPerfect held a lot of interest for Lotus because Lotus's word processing program, Ami Pro, was the weak link in SmartSuite. Manzi believed that a suite that offered Lotus 1-2-3 and WordPerfect could be a Microsoft-killer; he also thought that Lotus could deal a blow to Microsoft in groupware by merging its popular Notes with WordPerfect.

A year earlier, in the fall of 1993, Alan Ashton had approached Noorda about a possible merger, and at the time Noorda said he was not interested. But by mid-January 1994, when Noorda had recently learned from Philippe Kahn about the talks between WordPerfect and Lotus, his attitude had changed. The last thing Noorda wanted was for Lotus to acquire WordPerfect. Lotus and Novell were battling for second place behind Microsoft in desktop software, and if Lotus bought WordPerfect, Novell would drop to third place. For Noorda, that was unacceptable. There also was bad blood between Noorda and Manzi from a failed merger in 1990, which had collapsed at the last minute because of disagreements over who would run the new company, which would have been twice the size of Novell or Lotus.

If Novell acquired WordPerfect, Noorda believed, Novell could build a business model similar to Microsoft's by offering a suite of applications together with its powerful corporate networking software. But Novell would need a Windows spreadsheet to complete the applications package. It needed Borland's Quattro Pro. Unless Novell could acquire Quattro Pro, the merger with WordPerfect didn't make sense.

In December 1993, Philippe Kahn was attending a conference in Tokyo, listening to a speech by Microsoft's Steve Ballmer. The conference was organized to promote better understanding between Japanese and American businesses. "It was typical Ballmer," recalled Kahn. "He talked for three minutes on Japanese and American relations; the rest was an advertisement for Microsoft."

About halfway through Ballmer's talk, Kahn turned to Duff Thompson, general counsel for WordPerfect, who was sitting next to him. Both Kahn and Thompson were scheduled to speak at the conference, too. "You know Duff," said Kahn, "maybe it's time to come to grips with the fact that it's going to be damn difficult to outprice Microsoft on word processors and spreadsheets and suites."

Kahn then told Duff he was contemplating returning Borland to its roots—building software tools and languages—and reinvesting some of the Suites money Borland was pouring down the drain back into the company. "We've been splitting royalties and talking about a whole bunch of complicated things, like getting our products to work better together," Kahn told Thompson. "Why don't you just acquire the business [Quattro Pro] from us?"

Kahn was aware that his cash-strapped company could not survive unless it got out of the applications business, where it had to compete with Microsoft. Wall Street agreed. Borland's stock had plummeted from a high of $83 per share in early 1992 to about $15 by the end of 1993. Kahn had even come up with a code name for his back-to-roots strategy: Project Boomerang. Only a handful of people inside the company knew about it. The first phase of Boomerang was to sell Quattro Pro, then Paradox and dBase.

WordPerfect had been interested for some time in a merger of the two companies, according to Kahn. "Frankly, we felt the cultures of the companies were pretty far apart," said Kahn. "When we went to a meeting, there were two of us and eight of them. They were a little like IBM. We just didn't feel that we could work together at the time. We had to learn more about each other."

The two companies learned plenty in mid-1993, when they worked out the licensing deal for Borland Office. But the product failed to gain market share against Microsoft Office. "Gates wanted this business so badly that he was willing to give it [Microsoft Office] away for a while," said Kahn. "Because of his position in operating systems, he had no problems doing that because Microsoft was making so much money. Bill was buying share and kicking everybody else from the market."

Borland Office was not making money for either Borland or WordPerfect. A few weeks before the conference in Japan, Thompson and Rietveld had flown to Kahn's home in Scotts Valley, California, to again discuss a possible merger. But Kahn remained cool to the idea. He was, however, interested in selling

Quattro Pro, and that's what he told Thompson when they met in Tokyo.

Not long after the conference in Japan, Kahn and Rietveld talked by phone, and the just-named WordPerfect CEO said he was about to fly to Boston and New York on a press tour. Rietveld didn't say that he planned to meet with Jim Manzi of Lotus while he was in Boston.

Kahn's relationship with Manzi was even more strained than his relationship with Gates. At least Kahn respected Gates; he didn't like the way Gates did business, but he respected him. Kahn had no such respect for Manzi. In 1990, Lotus had filed a copyright infringement suit in federal court against Borland over a feature in Quattro Pro that had the same command system as that in Lotus 1-2-3. At the time, Borland was rapidly gaining market share against Lotus. When a federal judge ruled in favor of Lotus, Borland had to take Quattro Pro off the market quickly to remove the offending feature. (In early 1994, the case was appealed to the U.S. Supreme Court, where Borland would win.) The lawsuit proved to be a crippling financial blow to Borland, and Kahn had never forgiven Manzi, who had pressed the case in the face of widespread industry opposition.

In mid-January, not long after Rietveld told Kahn about his pending trip to the East Coast, Kahn was flying home from his own trip to Boston, where he had met with some Borland customers. On the plane seated next to Kahn was a Lotus vice president whom Kahn knew. During the flight, the Lotus executive had several drinks, according to Kahn, and started talking about WordPerfect. Kahn, who does not drink, just listened, the hairs on the back of his neck standing up as the VP from Lotus hinted that Lotus and WordPerfect were talking.

"In that six-hour flight, he must have told me twenty times how great it would be if Lotus could have WordPerfect," Kahn said. "So I started thinking what I would do if I were Lotus. I would try and break the Borland-WordPerfect alliance, because the combination of Lotus and WordPerfect would certainly guarantee SmartSuite market share. . . . And if such a thing happened, it would be a real bad day for Borland."

Back at Borland, Kahn reflected on what he had heard. "I wondered if it could be true," said Kahn. "I really didn't think the WordPerfect guys would do that to us." Nevertheless, Kahn decided to phone Ray Noorda. "I knew Ray hated those guys at Lotus," said Kahn. "So I told him, 'There's something fishy going on here. We talk to the WordPerfect guys all the time, and they're our friends, or they seem to be. Yet I got the impression from this guy from Lotus that there might be some discussions with WordPerfect. I know you are close to Alan Ashton, so why don't you check it out?' I knew Ray would be worried, because if WordPerfect merged with Lotus, while it would be bad news for Borland, it would also be bad for Novell, because it would eventually bring Novell into the Lotus fold."

When Kahn called, Noorda was not aware that Lotus and WordPerfect had talked. Once Noorda had confirmed Kahn's fears, he was more eager to make a deal with WordPerfect.

Meanwhile, Thompson and Rietveld had arranged a dinner meeting with Kahn at the Sundance Resort restaurant in the mountains outside of Provo on January 26. Kahn came with Bill Jordan, Borland's director of business development. "It's kind of a cultural oasis in Utah," Kahn said of the restaurant, where stills from Robert Redford movies like *Butch Cassidy and the Sundance Kid* decorate the walls. "We could have been having dinner at Spago's in west Hollywood."

Over dinner, Thompson and Rietveld asked Kahn what price he had in mind for Quattro Pro. Kahn told them $400 million. "I said it with a straight face," Kahn said, "and they dropped their spoons in their soup and got splashed. Bill Jordan was having a hard time containing himself."

Kahn then explained why $400 million was a bargain, that acquiring Quattro Pro would allow WordPerfect to become a prime player in suites. "They just looked at me," recalled Kahn.

"These are two very smart people, but they did not seem to have much business experience. They didn't understand that the $400 million was my asking price. They didn't understand I was expecting a bid from them. Instead, they just freaked out. Frankly, Bill and I were expecting people who had a little more business savvy."

After dinner, Kahn and Jordan spent the night in a cabin owned by Ashton, a smaller version of the one where Novell and WordPerfect executives would gather on March 16. Television security cameras canvassed the outside of the cabin. When Kahn picked up the phone and dialed the operator, he was connected with WordPerfect security. Rather than talk business in the cabin, he and Jordan decided to go for a night stroll in the woods. "Bill and I were very concerned that these gentlemen from WordPerfect did not have the business experience to know that we might have to negotiate," said Kahn. During their walk in the woods, Kahn and Jordan decided that Borland's financial adviser, Michael Price, of the investment bank Lazard Frères, should get involved as soon as possible. The meeting with Price took place in New York City on February 17. Borland and WordPerfect agreed to begin due diligence and in-depth negotiations.

On Friday, March 11, a team of executives and lawyers from Novell and WordPerfect arrived at Borland's headquarters in Scotts Valley to begin the first of several weekends of marathon negotiations. Noorda had called Kahn to arrange the meeting. He claimed that Novell was helping WordPerfect financially, but he did not mention that Novell and WordPerfect were talking merger—which would have given Kahn a much better bargaining position. Nor did he tell Kahn that Lotus was making a play for WordPerfect. Kahn assumed that what he had heard on the airplane wasn't true.

Noorda would later tell writer Wendy Goldman Rohm for an article in *Upside* magazine that Kahn was desperate for Novell to buy Borland. Noorda told her that a couple of years earlier, Kahn had even shown up uninvited at a Novell staff meeting to try to talk to Noorda about a merger. The article quoted Noorda as saying that he had physically escorted Kahn to the parking lot and told him he would punch him out unless he left. To which Kahn had replied: "Why don't you like me? You're like my father."

Kahn insists it never happened that way. He admits that he and Noorda indeed talked about a merger once. He also says that Noorda invited him to a Novell staff meeting and that when Kahn later told Noorda that he was not impressed with what he saw, Noorda started screaming at him. "I said, 'Ray, don't scream and shout. You're making me think of my father.'"

There was no shouting between Kahn and Noorda at the March 11 meeting, but the discussions were heated. When the meeting adjourned, on the table was a proposal by Borland to sell Quattro Pro to WordPerfect for $135 million, which included a license for WordPerfect to manufacture a million copies of Borland's Paradox database. In addition, Novell and WordPerfect would assume the first $60 million in potential liability if Borland should be unsuccessful in its appeal of the Lotus lawsuit.

The meeting continued the next day, March 12, in the offices of a Palo Alto law firm that was representing WordPerfect. Additional talks were held on Sunday, March 13. By the end of the weekend, however, the parties remained far apart. Two days later, on March 15, Jim Manzi and a delegation from Lotus flew to Salt Lake City to make a presentation on why WordPerfect and Lotus would make a good team. After the meeting, which was held in the Joseph Smith Conference Center, Manzi was told that WordPerfect would not make any decision until after the next day's meeting with Novell.

All aspects of the proposed merger between WordPerfect and Novell were discussed at the March 16 meeting at Ashton's cabin. Novell was offering $1.4 billion. Late in the afternoon, after the Novell team left, the executives from WordPerfect, including Bastian, Rietveld, and Thompson, took a secret vote on the Novell merger. It was unanimous: the company would be sold to Novell, not to Lotus. WordPerfect and Novell shared Mormon culture; more important, however, was the fact that Novell had the networking infrastructure that WordPerfect wanted. Lotus did not. Also, Novell had always made it clear that it did not know much about the applications business, and the WordPerfect executives were convinced they would be left alone to go about their business.

Novell and WordPerfect wanted to make the announcement of the merger after the stock market closed on Monday, March 21. Before then, the deal with Borland for Quattro Pro would have to be completed. By now, Kahn knew about the merger with Novell. He also knew that Lotus had been negotiating to buy WordPerfect. Until the last minutes, Kahn was worried that WordPerfect would go with Lotus. The terms of the deal with Borland were not finalized until Sunday, the day before the merger was to be revealed publicly. Borland agreed to sell Quattro Pro to Novell for $145 million, including the license for Paradox. Further, Novell would not be held liable should Borland lose its appeal of the Lotus lawsuit.

Novell ended up paying much more for Quattro Pro than it was really worth. Internally, the company had put a $70 million value on its spreadsheet business.

After the merger became official, Borland's legal counsel, Peter Astiz of Baker & McKenzie in Palo Alto, sent a confidential e-mail to Kahn, Jordan, and several other top officers of the company, admonishing them not to gloat publicly over the deal: "I want to congratulate you all on negotiating the company through this period. In the scheme of things, the ability to survive the potential catastrophic cash crunch and get as good a deal as I think was negotiated on QP [Quattro Pro] was a major accomplishment. . . . However, for the time being, I think it best to keep any congratulations to ourselves. Any attempt to categorize the QPro deal other than as good for both sides would pose significant threats to our relationship with Novell. . . ."

The merger made Novell the undisputed number two company in the software industry. But even with WordPerfect's revenues figured in, Novell still trailed Microsoft by about 2 to 1: $2 billion to $4 billion. Lotus was a distant third, with annual revenues of about $1 billion. Borland had all but disappeared.

In the days after the merger was publicly announced on March 21, Novell's stock fell 16 percent. Wall Street questioned the wisdom of deal, as well as the amount. Most computer industry experts said that Novell had made a serious blunder and should have remained focused on its core networking products. An exception was David Coursey, editor of *PC Letter*, who wrote of the merger: "It's Microsoft's worst nightmare. Novell awakes from its slumber, realizes its concept of cooperative competition only goes so far, then gets angry and does something. Well, wake up, Bill, it's happened."

In fact, the merger would turn into Novell's worst nightmare. Months later, it unloaded WordPerfect and Quattro Pro for a small fraction of what it paid.

The most astute and prophetic assessment of the merger at the time came from Microsoft's Pete Higgins, senior vice president for desktop applications: "Novell has a real challenge," he told the *New York Times.* "Mergers are difficult in any industry, but more so in software because you have to combine different code bases, as well as different cultures."

His boss, Bill Gates, took much the same view. Not only was Gates not worried about this new threat, he believed that Novell had made a huge business mistake, that it had been led down a dead-end road by Raymond Noorda, a road paved by his blind obsession with beating Microsoft at any cost.

Bill Gates was on the other side of the world, in China, the day the merger between Novell and WordPerfect was announced in the United States. He was speaking his mind to reporters at a press conference in Beijing, scolding the Chinese government for preventing the marketplace from dictating software standards. He was being his usual pushy and confrontational self. During his short visit to China, Gates would offend just about everyone, including Communist Party leader Jiang Zemin. He had yet to learn that diplomacy usually works better than confrontation.

Microsoft had opened an office in Beijing in 1992. Although personal computers were as rare in China as American automobiles, Microsoft realized the enormous potential of a software market in a country with more than a billion people. In fact, Gates regarded all of the Far East as a potential gold mine for Microsoft. In the first quarter of 1994, Microsoft's revenues from its Far East markets were up 65 percent over the previous quarter, compared with a 4 percent increase in revenues from Europe and a 34 percent increase in revenues from the United States.

By the time Gates visited China at the end of March 1994, about 500,000 personal computers had been sold there, and the number was expected to double by the end of the year. But software piracy was a growing problem. Chinese factories were churning out millions of copies of counterfeit software, costing U.S. companies like Microsoft millions in lost revenue. Borland International had withdrawn from the Chinese market because of rampant software piracy. The Clinton administration was pressuring Beijing to stop the piracy and strengthen its protection of intellectual property rights. Shortly before Gates arrived in Beijing, U.S. trade representative Mickey Kantor had announced that China was being put on a priority watchlist and that trade sanctions could follow if the government did not crack down on the counterfeiting.

While in China, Gates planned to discuss the piracy issue with Communist Party boss Jiang. He also wanted to talk about Windows and free markets. But he was getting a very chilly reception from Chinese leaders. Microsoft had made many mistakes, both cultural and political.

Its first mistake was not asking for advice from the Chinese government before it opened its office in Beijing. Consequently, its China management team was top-heavy with executives from Taiwan, which China considered a renegade province and not an independent country. But Microsoft's most serious blunder was in developing P-Win, the Chinese version of Windows 3.0. The software was developed in Taiwan, not in China. Worse, the Chinese version of Windows contained traditional Chinese characters used in Hong Kong and Taiwan, but not in the People's Republic of China. The characters had been phased out in the 1950s in favor of simplified pictographs to foster national literacy.

Naturally, the Chinese government insisted that P-Win should have been developed with help from the mainland. The country's powerful Ministry of Electronics Industry, the main body that oversees China's computer industry, had refused to endorse Windows. It announced that it was in the process of drafting standards that would determine which PC operating system was best for China.

The ministry was concerned that if it officially endorsed Windows, Microsoft would quickly get a stranglehold on the software market in China, as it had done in the United States. By the end of February, a month before Gates's visit, only 3,000 copies of P-Win had been sold in China. But more than 10,000 copies had been sold of a rival operating system called Chinese Star, which was developed in China and allowed computer users to convert Chinese characters into English.

It was not just the Chinese government that was worried about Microsoft. Some of the comments from Chinese software vendors sounded as if they could have been made by

Microsoft's rivals in the United States. "I think we have good reasons to fear that Microsoft will monopolize the market," one Chinese software vendor told *Newsweek*. And the editor of a Chinese computer magazine told Reuter's news service, "It's clear that Microsoft is pursuing a monopoly strategy in China."

At his press conference a day before his scheduled meeting with Jiang Zemin, Gates sounded as if he was lecturing members of the U.S. government's Federal Trade Commission on capitalism. He said the Ministry of Electronics Industry was tampering with the free market by trying to set the standards rather than letting the market dictate those standards. If the government left things alone, Gates said, the market would surely embrace Windows. Continued interference from the Chinese government, said Gates, would only hinder the development of that country's emerging software industry. "There is no government ministry that has to get involved in every new software that comes into the marketplace," said Gates, who predicted that P-Win would prevail even without an official endorsement from the Chinese government.

Gates did, however, acknowledge to reporters that it had been a mistake to develop P-Win in Taiwan. "We took the approach that brought it to market most rapidly, for the benefit of computer users," Gates said. That explanation might have played well in Seattle or Chicago or New York or Los Angeles, but it did not play well in Beijing. Gates continued on his collision course with the Chinese the next day during his meeting with Jiang Zemin, then one of China's most influential leaders and now, after Deng Xiaoping's death, the most powerful. Zemin told Gates that he needed to spend more time in China. "Learn something from 5,000 years of Chinese history," the Communist Party chief told the king of software. (The message was not lost on Gates, who would return to China 18 months later with his wife, his father, and Warren Buffett for an extended visit that included a train trip across the country.)

In the aftermath of Gates's disastrous March trip, the Ministry of Electronics Industry threatened to ban Windows. *China Daily*, the government's English-language newspaper, even reported that Windows had been banned. Although the story was inaccurate, it highlighted the seriousness of the problem Microsoft faced.

Gates immediately went to work on damage control. He promised that China would be involved in the development of the next Chinese version of Windows. Then Charles Stevens, Microsoft's Far East vice president, sacked much of the company's China management team, and began courting Chinese software companies. Finally, Microsoft initiated talks with the Ministry of Electronics Industry. By the time Gates returned to China with his wife and his pal Buffett, Microsoft had all but locked up the Chinese market for Windows. The Chinese version of Windows 95 would become the standard.

While all this was going on, however, the world had begun moving to Internet time, where Microsoft did not set the standard. While Gates was visiting China in late March, his executives in Redmond were preparing for an important off-site retreat that Gates had called to discuss the Internet and how Microsoft should respond. The retreat was scheduled for April 5. On April 4, Jim Clark and Marc Andreessen formed a start-up company in Mountain View, California, which, after some legal battles over its name, would be called Mosaic and finally Netscape Communications. Gates had nothing to fear from the merger of Novell and WordPerfect. The real threat would come from Netscape, a company that Microsoft took little notice of until it was almost too late.

On his last day on the job at Silicon Graphics, the company he had founded in Mountain View, California, James Clark sent an e-mail to a young man who had recently arrived in the Silicon Valley after graduating from the University of Illinois at

Urbana-Champaign. "Any way that we might be able to collaborate would be of interest to me," Clark wrote 22-year-old Marc Andreessen, whom he had found while clicking through a series of Mosaic pages on the Internet. In his e-mail, Clark explained that he was thinking of starting a new company and wanted to kick around some ideas. Could they meet and talk?

At the time, Clark knew next to nothing about the Internet or Mosaic. But he had heard of Andreessen and his work at the National Center for Supercomputing Applications (NCSA). And Andreessen had heard of Clark; in fact, he had been involved in an effort by IBM to take over Clark's turf. In 1990, while a student at the university, Andreessen worked for two semesters for Big Blue in Austin, Texas, on a project to develop 3-D graphics, with the intent of wresting the market from Silicon Graphics. IBM's product, however, turned out to be slower and more expensive than the machines produced by Silicon Graphics, and Andreessen returned to the University of Illinois to complete his undergraduate degree.

At the time Andreessen was completing his studies in December 1993, the Mosaic development team was dismantling. There was dissension within the team; some had begun to resent management when an article about Mosaic by *New York Times* reporter John Markoff on December 8 ran with a photo of only Larry Smarr, the center's director, and Joseph Hardin, who was in charge of the center's software development. None of the team who had worked so hard on Mosaic were in the picture.

Although Hardin had told Andreessen that he could stay on at the center after graduation, he also told him he could not continue working on Mosaic. Hardin thought the big blond kid from New Lisbon, Wisconsin, was claiming too much of the credit for Mosaic. Since Andreessen didn't much care for Hardin or for Champaign, which he would later describe as mostly "corn fields and pigs," when he graduated in December with a bachelor's degree in computer science, he didn't stay around long enough even to pick up his diploma.

He headed for California and the Silicon Valley, where he had been recruited to work as a programmer for a Palo Alto company that was designing security software for Internet transactions. There he rented a cheap apartment, bought a red 1994 Ford Mustang, and went to work at Enterprise Integration Technologies, which is where Clark's e-mail found him.

Clark was a self-made software millionaire who was looking for a second chance in life and hoped interactive television and the information highway were going to give it to him. Clark had grown up poor and fatherless in rural Plainview, Texas, a panhandle town halfway between Amarillo and Lubbock. In school, Clark was something of a troublemaker, and was suspended several times for such antics as taking a bottle of whiskey on a band trip. He dropped out of high school to join the Navy, where he changed his bad-boy ways when he discovered electronics and passed his high school equivalency test.

After his stint in the Navy, Clark went to Salt Lake City, where he completed a doctorate in computer science from the University of Utah, a greenhouse for talented undergrads like Clark who wanted to study computer graphics, a field then in its infancy. The department's renown was due in large part to the arrival in 1966 of David Evans, a computer professor from the University of California at Berkeley. Evans, whose specialty was computer graphics, had attracted some very bright undergrads who would go on to make names for themselves in the computer industry. In addition to Clark, the group included John Warnock, Nolan Bushnell, and Alan Ashton.

At the time, there was no shortage of research money for the work being done by Evans and his students. The Pentagon was very interested in the military applications of these developments and supplied a generous funding stream through the Pentagon's Defense Advanced Research Projects Agency

(DARPA), the outfit that in 1969 would fund a computer network linking universities and military research labs, a network soon to be known worldwide as the Internet.

In 1978, Clark took his talent and his PhD to Stanford University, where he joined the faculty as an assistant professor. Four years later, he left, to form Silicon Graphics. His goal was to create realistic 3-D graphic simulations on powerful workstation computers rather than on supercomputers. His company acquired chipmaker MIPS and began building the powerful computers that Clark had dreamed about. It didn't take long for Hollywood to discover Silicon Graphics when in the late 1980s filmmakers began using the company's technology to create lifelike special effects, from the water creature in *The Abyss* to the dinosaurs of *Jurassic Park*. Suddenly Silicon Graphics was hot; revenues were soaring.

But Clark was restless, and he squabbled with other company executives over the direction of the company. Clark wanted Silicon Graphics to develop low-cost hardware for the information highway. But he had met with strong objections when he promoted the deal with Time Warner for its interactive television project in Orlando, Florida. "I got tired of pushing against an immovable object," Clark told *Fortune*. "I felt like I wasn't having any influence." In frustration, Clark resigned in early February 1994, and in the process walked away from $10 million in stock options. But the money didn't matter. He still had a 1 percent stake in Silicon Graphics that was worth about $37 million.

When Clark sent his e-mail to Marc Andreessen, he envisioned a company that would produce software for the television set-top box, which Clark believed was the true consumer computer of the future. "There are $100 billion worth of companies out there wondering how they are going to use this data superhighway," Clark told reporter Lee Gomes of the *San Jose Mercury News* when he announced he was leaving Silicon Graphics. "And if you develop relationships and help them connect to this network, there's no reason why they shouldn't want to give you money."

Clark knew that he would face competition from well-established companies, particularly Microsoft, which was making deals left and right to position itself on that data highway. Clark disliked Bill Gates intensely, and so was looking forward to the competition. "Everyone I've spoken to looks askance at Microsoft," Clark told Gomes. "Why should I let them control this market, considering how they have used their power in the market they are in?"

After his initial e-mail, Clark invited Andreessen to his Atherton home, and to go sailing on Clark's yacht. For the next month thereafter, they exchanged e-mail daily about the kind of company they should start. One possibility they discussed was an on-line network for the game company Nintendo. Andreessen even wrote a white paper outlining the project. He also suggested a company built around Mosaic, though even he wasn't sure about the future of the browser. "The Internet was a toy then," he would later tell *Fortune*. "That was when the whole interactive TV thing was peaking; one of those frenzies the industry indulges in when it loses sight of what's happening in the real world. So I wasn't sure about the browser."

Clark's vision of developing interactive software began to fade. He was now willing to take the gamble that the Internet would be the ticket. Initially, he and Andreessen called their start-up Electric Media, but when they learned there was another company with the same name, it was rechristened Mosaic Communications. Clark named Andreessen vice president for technology. They set up shop in an office in downtown Mountain View. Clark invested about $4 million of his own money, supplemented by several times that amount from venture capitalists with Kleiner Perkins Caufield & Byers.

Clark quickly went to work hiring the talent that they needed to turn their vision into a reality. He brought in several friends from Silicon Graphics, but the core of company was made up of several programmers from the Mosaic development team at the NCSA, whom Andreessen had alerted about the planned start-up.

Dave Thompson, a full-time employee of the center, recalled talking to Aleksander Totic shortly before Totic was hired by Clark. Totic had developed the versions of Mosaic for the PC and the Mac. "Aleks was telling me that Marc had plans for starting a company and that he was just waiting to be called. He didn't know when that would be," said Thompson. "A couple weeks later, Aleks was gone."

Their most important hire was Eric Bina, the gifted programmer and full-time NCSA employee who had done much of the coding for Mosaic. Clark invited Bina to meet with him on his yacht. When Bina declined, Clark and Andreessen flew to Champaign to talk with him and several other members of the Mosaic development team. They all met at the University Inn. The full-court press worked. Clark hired five of them, including Bina and Totic.

On Tuesday, April 5, the day after Clark and Andreessen formed Mosaic Communications Corporation, two events occurred on opposite sides of the country that showed that Microsoft was still wavering as to what course they would chart along the information highway. In Kirkland, Washington, not far from Microsoft's headquarters in Redmond, Bill Gates and his top managers met at a 1909 mansion for an Internet briefing by Steven Sinofsky, whose e-mail to Gates two months earlier prompted the meeting. Cross-country in New York City, the Penguin Group announced that it had purchased the rights to a book by Gates about the information highway for an advance in excess of $2.5 million—a book that would not yet embrace the Internet.

Gates was writing his still untitled book with Nathan Myhrvold and Peter Rinearson, a former reporter for the *Seattle*

Times who had done some other writing for Microsoft. Gates had been shopping the book with New York publishing houses since early in March. He had no literary agent and had not met any publishers himself; instead, the negotiations were conducted by a team from Microsoft that included Jonathan Lazarus, Microsoft's vice president of strategic relations. Typically, the Microsoft team played hardball. In a letter to about a dozen publishers who had expressed interest in the book, Gates had set down his terms. He demanded an advance of at least $2.5 million with a guaranteed first printing of 500,000 copies. He also expected the publisher to set aside $125,000 for marketing. In his letter, Gates wrote that he and Myhrvold planned to donate their share of the book royalties to charity.

This was not the way it worked in the book-publishing business: nonwriters or unknown authors didn't set the terms; publishers did. Nevertheless, Bill Gates's demands were met, although Peter Mayer, Penguin's chief executive officer, said that only Gates's "minimal requirements" had been met. The book was scheduled for publication later in the year.

Like Windows 95, the book would be late. By the time it was published in November 1995, the information highway envisioned by Gates and Myhrvold had changed significantly since they had set Microsoft on an ambitious course they believed would position it as the information highway leader. In a state-of-the-company memo, Gates had told employees that Microsoft was placing a "major bet" that the information highway would become a significant growth factor for Microsoft.

Although the proposed venture with TCI and Time Warner did not work out, Microsoft was continuing to make deals intended to take the company away from the desktop and into new markets. In March, Microsoft announced two projects with TCI. One was an interactive cable system capable of delivering a wide range of services, including movies and home shopping. It was to be tested on a few hundred TCI and

Microsoft employees in Seattle later in the year. The other joint project was a cable TV channel for computer users.

Despite such announcements, interactive TV was still more hype than fact. Time-Warner had recently stated that it had postponed its high-profile Full Service Network in Orlando, Florida, because the technology for the set-top boxes from Silicon Graphics wasn't ready, proving that Gates was right when he predicted in 1993 that the industry was moving ahead too quickly, anticipating technology that was not yet in place. Microsoft's own entry into the interactive arena, the project code-named Tiger, was still under development.

Microsoft, nevertheless, continued to scout new alliances that might give it an edge on the information highway. Gates had been talking with Robert Allen, chairman of American Telephone and Telegraph Company, about a possible joint venture, including interactive television. The two had been brought together by Craig McCaw, who was in the process of selling his Seattle-based cellular phone empire to AT&T for $12.6 billion. Gates and McCaw were good friends, and had been working secretly for several years on a project that was, literally, out of this world: a celestial information highway that would bring video, voice, and data transmission to millions of people in the most remote parts of the world—at a cost of about $9 billion and 840 satellites in low Earth orbits. In late March, Gates and McCaw, two of the country's most accomplished entrepreneurs, announced that they had formed a third company, called Teledesic, to build the satellite network communications. McCaw Cellular owned 30 percent of the new company; Microsoft had invested $30 million for an 8.5 percent stake, and Gates and Paul Allen each put up another $10 million of their own money.

Teledesic was scheduled to be up and running by the year 2001. But the many technical and financial hurdles that had to be leaped made it all sound like pie in the sky. Besides, there was already a cheap and easy way to link the world and satisfy its craving for information: the Internet. Which was exactly what Steven Sinofsky was determined to make Gates and others understand at the company's April 5 executive retreat.

It was an ironic coincidence that Microsoft's first off-site conference on the Internet was held one day after the official incorporation of Mosaic Communications. No official announcement accompanied the formation of that company; in fact, it would be May before the first stories appeared in print that Clark and Andreessen were in business together, and that they had drafted some of the Mosaic development team from the NCSA for their own.

The off-site Internet conference had been organized shortly after Sinofsky returned from Cornell. Gates believed that his top staff focused best on a critical issue when they got away from the Microsoft campus for a day or two. This retreat, as it was called, was held at the Shumway Mansion, a four-story, 10,000-square-foot estate in nearby Kirkland.

All of Microsoft's top executives attended the Internet conference, along with James Allard and Russell Siegelman. Sinofsky presented a 300-page report on the Internet and what Microsoft should be doing to respond. One executive who attended said, "It was a very good first step, and it got everyone thinking about the Internet. But frankly, I did not see how Microsoft was going to get much of a return on any investment it made with regard to the Internet. Where would the revenue streams come from? Bill asked the same question: How was the company going to make money?"

The executive staff did come up with a list of Internet-related projects that would at least get the company moving in the right direction. High on the list was Microsoft's on-line service. Siegelman agreed that Internet communications protocols should be built into the service to enable users to access the Net. But he argued against making the service Web-based, which is what Allard wanted, because it would have meant a total redesign. Also on the list was a project to give users of

Word, Microsoft's best-selling word processing application, the ability to create documents for the World Wide Web.

Later in April, during his semiannual "think week" at his secluded second home on Hood Canal on the Olympic Peninsula, Gates spent much of his time thinking about the Internet and writing a memo titled "Internet Strategy and Technical Goals." He sent the memo to Microsoft's managers on April 16. "We want to and will invest resources to be a leader in Internet support," Gates wrote. But he was not yet convinced that Microsoft should make an all-out push.

David Marquardt, a longtime member of Microsoft's board and a general partner at Technology Venture Investors in Menlo Park, California, later told *Business Week* he did not understand why Microsoft was not making a bigger commitment to the Internet. He had asked Gates as much during an April board meeting. "His view was that the Internet was free," Marquardt said. "There was no money to be made."

The cash that fed the Microsoft monster came from its bread-and-butter programs like DOS and Windows, and from its applications like Word. The only danger to that revenue stream was if the Justice Department broke up the company, something Gates had vowed he would never let happen.

Trustbuster Ann Bingaman had not forgotten about billionaire Bill. Since the Justice Department had taken over the investigation from the FTC in August 1993, there had been a constant flow of newspaper and magazine articles speculating on the kind of action Bingaman might take against Microsoft, and when that action might come. But Bingaman had kept quiet, refusing to comment.

But as her staff painstakingly went about its investigation of Microsoft, there was growing concern among some in the Clinton administration that the probe might do damage to the country's brightest high-tech star. Some very powerful people within the administration, according to sources, wanted the matter settled out of court. "There was a lot of concern about what was going on at Justice in the Microsoft case," said a high-ranking official in the White House office of the U.S. Trade Representative. Some of those concerns, the official said, were being communicated quietly to Bingaman and her boss, Attorney General Janet Reno.

Gates would later boast to friends that he told Vice President Al Gore during a meeting in May that if the government tried to break up Microsoft, he would move the company and all its employees overseas, out of reach of U.S. control. Although the vice president's office denied that any such ultimatum was delivered, a White House source confirmed that Gates made his threat to move the company at that private meeting. The source further said that the vice president had been told much the same thing earlier in the year by Microsoft's number two guy, Steve Ballmer, a personal friend of the vice president.

Such threats, real or rumor, in the end really didn't matter. Bingaman's legal team on the Microsoft investigation had decided by late spring that the best attack against Microsoft was one that focused specifically on the way Microsoft licensed its operating system—charging a processor a fee on every computer sold, regardless of whether it came installed with Microsoft's operating system.

Breaking up Microsoft into two companies—one for operating systems and one for applications—was out of the question. Novell, ironically, had made the government's antitrust case against Microsoft more difficult to press by acquiring WordPerfect and Borland's Quattro Pro. Like Microsoft, Novell now owned both an operating system (its networking software) and applications. Also, the Justice Department had learned its lesson when it failed to break up IBM after spending years in litigation and millions of taxpayer dollars. Bingaman's team believed that the department would suffer the same fate if it attempted to split Microsoft. But the government lawyers were convinced they had more than enough evidence to file suit against Microsoft on the licensing issue. Thus, everything else was taken off the table.

The case had become increasingly frustrating for Gates. In June, he had complained to a *Wall Street Journal* reporter that Justice was still requesting documents about Microsoft's business. "We've sent them something like a million pieces of paper," said Gates, "and they need a million more." But later in June, Bingaman called Bill Neukom, Microsoft's chief legal counsel, and suggested that they meet in her office to talk about the case. Several recent stories by industry writers had reported that the government was broadening its investigation of Microsoft. Neukom was told just the opposite by Bingaman, who said that her department was preparing a fairly narrow legal case that would focus on just a few areas of concern, such as Microsoft per-processor licensing fee. She suggested settling the case without a trial, but if Microsoft did not agree, she was prepared to file suit.

Bingaman told Neukom that he could meet with Attorney General Janet Reno if he wanted, which he did, for more than an hour. Reno, who had given the okay to Bingaman to file suit if an agreement could not be reached, also urged Neukom to settle the case.

According to a Microsoft executive, even though Neukom was the lead attorney in the case for Microsoft, he did nothing without the approval of Gates. "When Neukom told Bill that Justice wanted to settle, and that Microsoft might escape without too much damage, Bill gave the go-ahead to start talking," the executive said. "But Bill made it clear that he would have the final say on any settlement. He was determined to get the best deal possible. Anything else and Bill said he would fight a suit in court for as long as it took."

Sam Miller, a San Francisco trial lawyer hired by Bingaman in December 1993 to begin preparing the government's case against Microsoft, said the case was strong. "Microsoft clearly went way over the line in its per-processor licensing arrangement," he recalled. "We had legitimate grounds to bring a suit. Novell's operating system was being excluded. There was a serious potential for damages. That's why Microsoft caved in."

Following the meeting, the first round of serious talks between Neukom and Bingaman took place in Brussels, at the headquarters of the European Commission that was also investigating Microsoft in response to the complaint from Novell. Neukom had insisted that the commission be involved in the negotiations between Microsoft and the Justice Department. The week of July 4, when Bingaman had planned to be on vacation with her husband in New Mexico, she and a small group of lawyers from her department met in Brussels with lawyers from the commission and from Microsoft, including Neukom. The talks lasted a week, but broke off without an agreement.

Meanwhile, Bingaman had given Microsoft a deadline: settle the case by Thursday, July 14, or the antitrust suit would be filed. A few days before the deadline, the talks reconvened in the United States. And despite intense, nonstop talks among the parties, the Thursday deadline passed with no deal.

"These guys don't react to stiff warnings," Bingaman would later tell the *New York Times* in describing the last-minute negotiations. At 3 A.M. Friday, some three hours after the deadline had passed, Bingaman phoned Gates personally to try to end the stalemate. Gates was in Idaho, attending a private conference for some of the nation's top business executives. He was awake in his room when Bingaman called. She told him that he had to agree to the consent decree now, or the next morning the suit would be filed. Gates asked for more time. "We're through," said Bingaman. She hung up the phone and went home to sleep.

The next day, Friday, July 15, Bingaman and lawyers from Justice, Microsoft, and the European Commission continued meeting in her office to reach a settlement. About 3 P.M., Bingaman placed another call to Gates. They talked by speaker phone for more than an hour. "He's the ultimate decision maker," she would tell the *Washington Post*. "I just wanted to get this settled with him."

The negotiations went back and forth. Lawyers representing the parties sometimes left Bingaman's office to huddle privately and then return. Finally, Gates said the words Bingaman had been waiting to hear: "I can live with that." Gates then told Bingaman that Neukom had his authority to sign the consent decree. Nearly five years after it began, the government's antitrust investigation against Microsoft had come to an end. The signed consent decree was filed later that evening in U.S. District Court in Washington, D.C. Lawyers for the European Commission flew home with a nearly identical agreement.

"I just went home," Bingaman told the *Post*. "It was a weird feeling. . . . I wasn't certain it was going to happen." The next morning, Saturday, Bingaman met with reporters to announce the terms of the settlement, which both Bingaman and Reno praised. They boasted that the government had stood up to Microsoft and won an important victory. "Microsoft is an American success story, but there is no excuse for any company to try to cement its success through unlawful means, as Microsoft has done with its contracting practices," Bingaman said.

Reno added that the settlement had "leveled the playing field" for Microsoft's competitors. "While the company fairly and lawfully climbed to the top of the industry's ladder, it used unfair and illegal practices to maintain its dominant position."

Bingaman later talked about the settlement in more detail. "We brought the case that we could, based on the law and on the facts as they exist. I am proud of this case. I am proud of the result." She noted that Microsoft would remain under supervision for six and a half years to verify that it was complying with the terms of the consent decree.

"We got 100 percent of what we would have gotten at trial and on appeal; and we got it now, not three or four years from now," said Bingaman.

To the end, Microsoft refused to acknowledge publicly that it had done anything wrong. "The agreement is not that the allegation is true. Our agreement with the government is that we are willing to accommodate them in these reasonable ways," said Neukom.

In a conference call with reporters, Gates said that the case had become a major distraction and that was why he agreed to settle. He added that the settlement was vindication for Microsoft's practice of not requiring the so-called Chinese Wall between its operating and application divisions.

Reporters wrote that Microsoft had gotten off with what amounted to a slap on the wrist. Computer makers would now be able to offer customers a choice of rival operating systems, such as Novell's DR-DOS and IBM's OS/2, but that would hardly make a dent in Microsoft's business, since most computers sold would still be sold pre-installed with DOS and Windows. Because that's what the public wanted.

Wall Street saw the settlement the same way: as a success for Microsoft and a black eye for the Justice Department. In the days following the settlement, Microsoft's stock rose several points.

Gates would later tell friends that he wished his mother could have lived to see the case settled. Mary Gates had died a month before the settlement. She knew the emotional toll the case had taken on her son over the years.

But it's not over till it's over, and the consent decree was still subject to approval by a federal judge. The Microsoft detractors would get their day in court, presided over by a blunt-speaking federal judge known as Attila the Hun.

The industry was still buzzing over what was generally regarded as Microsoft's "skate" from the Justice Department when Gates teed up with Bill Clinton for a round of golf in August on Martha's Vineyard in Massachusetts. Clinton was on his annual vacation with his family, while Gates and his wife were visiting Katharine Graham, the *Washington Post* publisher, who had a summer home on Martha's Vineyard. Also playing in the group was Gates's wife Melinda, Warren Buffet—a longtime friend of both Gates and Graham—and financier George Stevens.

Although they had played golf together before, Gates and Clinton had little in common. Gates liked the president, but found he could not talk to him about anything technical, which was generally a prerequisite for forming a relationship with Gates.

After golf, they all had dinner at Graham's house. Gates had become closer to Graham since the death of his mother. "I think Bill saw her as taking the place of the mother he had lost," said a friend of the Gates family. "Bill was having a hard time dealing with the death of his mother. Melinda was there for him, of course, but Katharine Graham reminded him of his mother."

Although it did not come up during golf or at dinner, Gates was doing better in the polls than the president. A recent survey by Opinion Research Corporation had found that Gates was number two on a list of the executives whom Americans most admired; Clinton was number five. Heading the list was Lee Iacocca, the retired chairman of Chrysler. Ross Perot, the onetime presidential candidate, was third, followed by Donald Trump. Earlier in the year, Gates's company had tied with Coca-Cola as America's third most admired company in a survey of more than 10,000 business executives by *Fortune* magazine. Rubbermaid came out on top, followed by Home Depot. Obviously, Microsoft's rivals had a much more negative opinion of Gates and Microsoft than the rest of the country did.

On October 6, Gates sent his second e-mail memo to Microsoft's executive staff about the Internet. Titled "Sea Change Brings Opportunity," the memo called upon all of Microsoft's product managers to think about adding features to existing products to take advantage of the capabilities of the Internet. And he reminded his staff that Microsoft's continued growth depended not only on opening new markets, but on getting Microsoft's customers to buy product upgrades. "It takes even more guts to bet on the 'Sea Change' when you are the market leader, but it is the only way to position yourself for massive upgrades."

But Gates himself was still not ready to bet the company on the Internet. A week after his sea change memo, and still fresh from the settlement with the Justice Department that did little to curb Microsoft's appetite, Gates dropped a bombshell on his competitors. Microsoft, he announced, planned to buy Intuit, the maker of the best-selling Quicken financial software program. It was the one area in which Microsoft had tried to compete and failed. Its own financial product, Money, had captured only about 22 percent of the market. Quicken controlled about 70 percent. Once Gates decided, in May, that Microsoft would be unable to catch up, he initiated secret negotiations. Microsoft agreed to pay $1.5 billion, which from Microsoft's point of view was a bargain. It would not only gain Intuit's 7 million customers, but it would establish itself as the major player in on-line banking.

The Justice Department wasted no time in letting Microsoft and the industry know that it planned to take a careful look at the proposed merger. Bingaman was about to get a second crack at Gates and Microsoft. The proposed merger was announced on October 13. Some 24 hours later, a new threat to Microsoft's dominance appeared on the Internet, one that would prove to be far more serious than the one previously posed by Quicken.

6

The Sleeping Giant Awakens

Netscape's epic battle against Microsoft began with the sounds of cannon fire, breaking glass, and croaking frogs. On October 14, 1994, six months after Jim Clark and Marc Andreessen formed Mosaic Communications and hired five members of the Mosaic development team away from the National Center for Supercomputing Applications (NCSA), a test version of the company's first browser was posted on its Internet Web site. Called Mosaic Navigator, it was free to anyone who wanted to download it off the Internet for a journey of exploration around the World Wide Web. After working around-the-clock shifts, members of the exhausted browser development team watched as the first downloads were logged on to a PC screen, each accompanied by playful programmed noises such as cannon fire. It would not be long before the noise resonated all the way up the West Coast to the Silicon Forest of Redmond, where industry giant Microsoft was finally starting to awaken to the Internet spring, like a bear coming out of hibernation.

Borrowing a page from the NCSA marketing book, Andreessen and Clark had decided to give the company's browser away for free in order to get it onto as many computers as possible. (Those users who wanted customer support could buy the software for $99.) Their business strategy was simple: create demand; use the Web to reach customers directly; set the standard in cyberspace; turn the tables on Microsoft.

Conway Rulon-Miller, who had joined Mosaic Communications as vice president of sales in early October, learned at his first sales meeting about the giveaway plan for Mosaic Communications. "I had fierce fights with Andreessen," he would later tell *Business Week.* "I said, 'Excuse me, I might have trouble doing a revenue plan for you.' " But Clark and Andreessen understood that the revenue stream would come not from a browser, but from lucrative Web server software that would be used by companies doing business on the Internet. Mosaic Communications planned to sell its server software for $1,495, or $5,000 for a secured version needed by companies dealing with confidential information such as credit card numbers on the Internet.

A couple of days before Mosaic Communications released its browser, Andreessen told reporter Jared Sandberg of the *Wall Street Journal* that Mosaic Netscape was ten times faster than the version of Mosaic he had helped develop at the NCSA at the University of Illinois. Andreessen also said that Mosaic Netscape had been completely rewritten from scratch and did not contain a line of the original software code.

A curious thing happened when Dave Thompson at the NCSA began playing around with one of those rewritten-from-scratch copies of Mosaic Netscape that he had downloaded off the Net. It was so similar to NCSA Mosaic that it caused a conflict with his computer's operating system. He found he could not run Mosaic Netscape and NCSA Mosaic at the same time. "The operating system would complain that I was trying to run two copies of the same program," said Thompson. "It really looked bad in terms of copying code. The outside may have looked different, but the inside didn't."

Thompson knew a little something about NCSA Mosaic. His former colleague, Marc Andreessen, was getting credit for developing the browser technology that made it so much easier to navigate around the World Wide Web. Fame and fortune were just around the corner for Andreessen, who would be described by some in the media as the next Bill Gates. The idea behind Mosaic, however, had started not with Andreessen but with Thompson's curiosity over some junk mail.

"The whole story about how Marc Andreessen invented Mosaic and all that is a complete fallacy," said Mike Tyrrell, an executive at Spyglass, which licensed the Mosaic browser from the NCSA in 1994 and subsequently licensed it to Microsoft. The real Mosaic story began in November 1992. At the time, Thompson was working for Joseph Hardin, who headed the center's software group of about a dozen programmers. Their task was to develop software tools that scientists could use to look at the streams of data that came from supercomputers.

One day Thompson received a mailing from O'Reilly Associates, a publisher of technical reference books, about a hypertext interface for the Internet called the World Wide Web. Thompson wanted to know more, so he did a search using Archie, a database identifying the location of Net contents. He found what he was looking for at the CERN research lab in Switzerland, where Tim Berners-Lee had created the World Wide Web based on a universal hypertext language. Thompson found two browsers available for free from CERN, and he downloaded both. One was a text-based browser developed by CERN; the other was an X/Windows interface called Viola, developed by a former Berkeley student, Pei Wei. Thompson played around with the browsers and downloaded some documents off the Web.

"To see the hypertext interface applied to the Internet was a pretty cool thing," Thompson said. "I thought, 'Wow!' " He also thought it might be what the center needed—another big hit, because it had been several years since Tim Krauskopf, who had gone on to found Spyglass, had developed NCSA Telnet for connecting PCs to supercomputers and put the center on the map. Hardin's software team had been looking for something new, and now Thompson believed he had found it in his junk mail.

He showed the Web browsers to Hardin and talked with Andreessen, then one of the students at the center. As part of a class project, Andreessen was working on something called Epoch, a limited hypertext editor that allowed the user to flip through directories.

"I thought if Marc could apply this World Wide Web stuff to what he was working on, it would be a really cool addition . . . it would give the editor the ability to browse the Internet," said Thompson. "I showed this to Marc because I wanted him to see how he could expand the technology, from just looking at directories to being able to grab documents throughout the entire Internet."

After discussing the project with Andreessen, Thompson left for an out-of-town conference. By the time he returned a week later, Andreessen had already hacked out a crude prototype of a Web browser with Eric Bina, who, like Thompson, was employed full-time at the center and was generally regarded as one of its most brilliant programmers.

"Marc had gotten pretty excited about this Web stuff," said Thompson. So the two met with Hardin and talked mostly about what kind of browser technology was already available. A week later, Hardin, Bina, Andreessen, and Thompson gathered in a circular meeting room known as the Fishbowl to discuss whether the center should develop a Web browser that would display pictures as well as text, and would be easier to use. "We decided it would be a good idea, that this could be another big hit for the university," said Thompson. "We figured we could do a better job of building something [that was better] than anything that was already out there."

Andreessen would later tell *Newsweek* the apocryphal story wherein the idea for Mosaic came to him when he was eating a pastry with Bina at the Espresso Royale Cafe in Champaign-Urbana. "The culture of hanging out at the Espresso Royale did not develop until several months later," said Thompson, who was 25 years old in late 1992. Andreessen was four years younger. "The start of the browser project came during that second meeting."

Hardin agreed with Thompson. "Marc is no fun to work with. He tries very hard to make sure that anything he touches he gets credit for," Hardin told writer Alan Deutschman for a January 1997 article in *GQ* about Andreessen. The hard-hitting piece, titled "Imposter Boy," was the first to investigate what really happened behind the scenes during the development of Mosaic, and painted Andreessen as a semiliterate programmer who all but stole Thompson's idea.

But Thompson said the *GQ* article went too far. "I have never claimed I came up with the idea of working on a browser," he said. "The idea came out of the meeting with Hardin." Thompson also felt that the *GQ* article, while otherwise fairly accurate, was too negative toward Andreessen and his skills as a programmer. "Marc was always very focused on what he was working on," recalled Thompson. "He was one of those guys who always spent all his time in front of the computer at work. He was either at class, or in front of the computer, or asleep. He had absolutely no social life outside of going out to eat. So he produced a lot of code. He was a perfectionist. He had very little tolerance for bugs in his code. His coding style was better than your average sophomore college programmer. Nothing outstanding, but better than the average sophomore."

After the second meeting in the Fishbowl, Hardin freed up Andreessen and Bina to begin working on the browser with

Thompson. But Thompson soon found himself out of the loop. "I did feel a little left out," he said, "but it was pretty much my own doing. They went off and started coding, and I take some of the blame for not inserting myself more than I did."

The first version of Mosaic by Andreessen and Bina was for UNIX-based machines, not the PC or Mac. Much of the coding was done by Bina, though he also borrowed from the software written by Tim Berners-Lee, which was available free on the Internet. But once Andreessen and Bina had come up with the initial UNIX-based Mosaic browser, Hardin assigned others to the project and they produced versions for the PC and Mac, a move Hardin claimed Andreessen was opposed to because he was concerned that the machines were not powerful enough to display graphics with the same clarity as the more powerful UNIX computers. But Bina disputes Hardin's recollection of the events and says that Andreessen came up with the idea to develop Mosaic for the PC and Mac.

Whatever the truth, one point is undisputed: there was dissension in the ranks of the Mosaic development team. "There was always a problem managing the group," said Thompson. "Marc was sort of the leader without a title. Joseph Hardin was manager of all software development, which included several other groups. So there was a big gap there. The browser group needed some management, which wasn't there. It caused a lot of friction." By the time Andreessen left, near the end of 1993, morale was very low and there was a lot of tension among members of the browser team. "They had split into factions," said Thompson. "People were no longer talking to other people. It was pretty sad." Four months into 1994, those programmers who supported Andreessen would join him and Jim Clark in California at their newly founded company, Mosaic Communications.

The soft-spoken, mild-mannered Thompson ended up at Spyglass. "It's great those guys got the rewards," Thompson said of Bina and Andreessen. "They really worked hard. For me, it was a missed opportunity."

Mosaic Communications had rushed its browser to market in order to stay ahead of its principal competitor, Spyglass. "We don't think Mosaic Communications will be able to set a standard," Bob Rybicki, a marketing vice president at Spyglass, was quoted as saying a few days after Mosaic Netscape was posted on the Internet in October 1994.

But behind the scenes at Spyglass, the company's executives were deeply worried about Mosaic Communications. They were also mad as hell. Two months earlier, in August, Spyglass had obtained exclusive rights from the University of Illinois and the NCSA to license Mosaic. Now, another browser by the same name, developed by some of the same people, was being given away for free by a company that had never obtained a license from either Spyglass or the NCSA. Spyglass and the university were soon talking with lawyers about possible legal action to stop Mosaic Communications from distributing its browser.

"We were trying to build as much value as possible in the Mosaic name," said Tim Krauskopf, founder of Spyglass. "But the name was being diluted by a company that was pursuing a different path and that certainly was not in any agreement to pay royalties to the university."

The university was as upset as Spyglass. It felt that those former NCSA students and employees who now worked at Mosaic Communications had made use of university trade secrets in developing their version of the Mosaic browser. Said Mike Tyrrell, vice president of business development at Spyglass: "We had an agreement that if anyone infringed upon the university's intellectual property, and the university did not pursue such infringement, then we had the right to pursue such infringement. We were basically building a business around Mosaic, and we felt that if any other company started infringing upon the university's technology, we wanted to make sure that the university's technology was protected."

Hoping to resolve the dispute without litigation, Jim Clark telephoned Spyglass CEO Doug Colbeth, and they agreed to meet at Chicago's O'Hare Airport, where Clark told Colbeth that Mosaic Communications had done nothing wrong. It was a short meeting.

Eventually, the university, Spyglass, and Mosaic Communications had more productive talks, although usually through their lawyers and over the phone. Drafts of the proposed settlement were exchanged by fax daily, or, more accurately, nightly. "We were turning around drafts every day for more than a month," said Marcia Rotunda, the associate in-house counsel for the university who participated in the settlement negotiations. "Once the business minds took over, progress was made in terms of getting this thing settled," she said. "Originally, a lot of egos were involved. It was about who's right and who's wrong. Later on, we got the sense that they [Mosaic Communications] decided this was business and they needed to pay the least they could and get on with their business. . . . And we were not all that anxious to have this hanging on either, especially since a former student was involved."

Clark was especially interested in getting the legal dispute settled so he could get the company moving. He had recruited a top gun, James Barksdale, to be CEO. Barksdale had been president and chief operating officer of McCaw Cellular Communications, a Seattle-based cellular phone business. Although Barksdale quietly joined the board of Mosaic Communications, he told Clark he would not agree to take over as CEO until the legal dispute with Spyglass and the university was settled. "Jim did not want to join the company with this potential legal infringement hanging over it," said an executive familiar with the situation. "So for Netscape, getting this thing settled with the university and with Spyglass became paramount."

Early in the talks, Clark agreed to change the name of his company to Netscape Communications Corporation. The name change occurred in late November 1994, although the final settlement was not reached for another month. At the insistence of Clark, terms were to be kept confidential. The parties agreed to say only that Netscape could continue to distribute its browser and did not have to obtain a license from either Spyglass or the university.

The settlement had not come cheap. Although it was not disclosed as part of the confidentiality clause, Netscape agreed to pay the university $2.2 million in damages, plus an additional payment of up to $1.4 million depending on certain licensing deals it might make with other companies for its browser. Netscape ended up paying the university a total of $2.7 million. (The final installment was made in December 1996, two years after the settlement.)

The university split the settlement money with Spyglass, though that deal was never publicly disclosed. "Jim Clark knows this and it really burns his ass," said one Spyglass executive. "We were his main competitor and he actually helped to fund us."

When Netscape announced in December that it had reached a settlement with the university and with Spyglass, Marc Andreessen told reporter David Bank of the *San Jose Mercury News* that the legal fight had left him with bitter feelings toward the university. "You go to school, you do research, you leave, and they try and cripple your business," Andreessen said, "Is this the way you want to be treated? Had I known this would happen, I would have gone to Stanford."

If Stanford would have had him. Rotunda, the University of Illinois lawyer, did not know Andreessen personally while he was at the NCSA, but she had heard about him, and knew his reputation. "We just knew the people here didn't like him, that he had trouble getting along with people," she said.

In early December 1994, *Time* named the 23-year-old Andreessen one of the country's 50 most important young leaders. Wrote *Time:*

> Big, blond, and thoroughly unpretentious, Marc Andreessen had barely come of age when he co-wrote the program that is helping tame the Internet—the vast chaotic web of interconnected computers that is the closest thing today to an information superhighway. In the democratic spirit of cyberspace, Andreessen made the program—NCSA Mosaic—freely available on the Net.

Another of the young leaders named by *Time* was a fellow 16 years Andreessen's senior—Bill Gates. *Time* wrote:

> The people who are closest to Bill Gates (those who feel comfortable enough to pull his smudged glasses off his face and polish them for him) thought his marriage early this year might finally slow him down. If so, there is no outward sign of it . . . he seems intent on extending Microsoft's hegemony into every new medium, from CD-ROMs to digital banking to online services to interactive television. No aspect of life in the information age, it seems, will escape his influence. He's even buying digital reproduction rights to the world's greatest works of art.

It was not just the electronic rights to the world's artworks that Gates was buying to be displayed on giant TV screens on the walls of his mansion that was under construction on the shores of Lake Washington. Shortly before the *Time* top-50 article appeared, Gates bought the Codex Hammer, an original 72-page manuscript of Leonardo da Vinci's diagrams and notes. Through a representative who bid by telephone during an auction at famed Christie's in New York City, Gates paid $30.8 million for his first significant artwork purchase, a record for any manuscript ever sold at auction. (The previous record was $11.8 million.) Before the auction, the manuscript had been expected to fetch about $10 million.

Leonardo da Vinci was one of Gates's personal heroes. Gates greatly admired his scientific genius and vision. Although Gates took only one course in art history before dropping out of Harvard to found Microsoft, he had known the history of the Codex (Latin for book or bound manuscript) for some time, and had told friends that if it ever became available, he planned to buy it. "Going into the auction at Christie's, Bill was determined that he was not going to be outbid," said an acquaintance. "He ended up paying more than he thought he would have to pay, but he had been prepared to go much higher. It really wasn't a question of money for Bill. This was something he wanted. And when Bill decides he wants something, look out." In October, a month before the auction, *Forbes* had named Gates the country's richest person, with a fortune of $9.3 billion.

The Codex Hammer was one of 20 extant da Vinci manuscripts, and the only one still in the United States. The others were in museums in Paris, London, and Milan. Made of just 18 sheets of cream-white linen paper, folded in half to produce 72 pages, the Codex Hammer contains Leonardo's scientific thoughts and predictions, and includes more than 300 illustrations. The major theme of the manuscript is the behavior of water, but it also includes Leonardo's thoughts on many other topics, including astronomy, geology, and meteorology. It offers advice on flood control, dams, and canals. The manuscript predicts the invention of the steam engine and the submarine, and explains the presence of marine shells and fossils on mountains and plains far from the sea. It also explains why waves curl and the sky is blue.

"Experience shows us that air must have darkness beyond it and hence it appears blue," Leonardo wrote. He also wrote that the light of the moon is reflected sunlight—not a significant observation today, but Leonardo made it a century before Galileo proved that the moon does not produce its own light.

Leonardo wrote the text of the manuscript backwards, apparently to disguise his theories, and thus it is legible only when read in a mirror. The notes were composed between 1508 and 1510, when he was approaching 60 years of age.

Leonardo bequeathed the manuscript to a friend, but it did not surface publicly until the death of its second owner, a Milanese sculptor, in 1690. It was later purchased by an Englishman, Thomas Cook, the first earl of Leicester, on a visit to Italy in 1717. For the next 263 years, the manuscript was known as the Codex Leicester. In 1980, American industrialist Armand Hammer, chairman of Occidental Petroleum, bought the manuscript at a Christie's sale in London for $5.6 million, and renamed it after himself. It was the last da Vinci manuscript in private hands; when Hammer died in 1990, it was left to the Armand Hammer Museum of Art and Cultural Center at the University of California at Los Angeles, which subsequently put it up for auction in late 1994 to raise money to fight a lawsuit brought by an heir to the Hammer fortune.

Long before the auction in November 1994, representatives of Christie's contacted Gates's friends and business associates as well as members of the Seattle Art Museum in an effort to pique the interest of the world's richest person. The manuscript was aggressively marketed by Christie's before the sale. By the time it went on the auction block, the manuscript had been shown in cities around the world, including Milan, Zurich, Seoul, and Tokyo.

The bidding war started at $5.5 million and rose quickly. The main competition came from the Cariplo Foundation, Italy's largest bank, which wanted to return the Codex Hammer to Italy as part of its cultural heritage. A representative of the Cariplo Foundation was in a front-row seat at the auction, but had to pull out of the bidding when the price hit $27 million. A Gates representative was bidding by phone, as were several others.

Christopher Burge, chairman of Christie's in New York, described the sale as "an extraordinary moment in auction history." Christie's did not immediately name the buyer, saying only that the person was a private art collector who wanted to remain anonymous. It did not take long for word to leak out that the new owner of the Codex Hammer was Bill Gates, theretofore known in the art world only for buying digital rights to great art treasures, not the real thing.

Gates soon announced that he would not name the Codex after himself, as Hammer had done. Instead, Gates said, it would be rechristened the Codex Leicester, its name for more than 200 years of its history. In a written statement, Gates explained:

> While it has been known by a number of different names, in the nearly five centuries since it left Leonardo da Vinci's studio, it first came to widespread public attention as the Codex Leicester. Much of the important scholarly literature refers to it by this name as well, and I feel strongly that for the sake of continuity and tradition, the name of Codex Leicester should be restored to this remarkable work of art and science.

Gates also promised to share the Codex with the world before permanently installing it at his mansion, by exhibiting it at museums in New York City, Paris, and finally Seattle. When the manuscript finally arrives at Gates's high-tech mansion, it will be kept in a special case in his huge, custom-designed library. A laser light will keep track of how much exposure the da Vinci masterpiece receives. But even after its installation at Gates's home, the prized notebook will still be available to the public—but only virtually. Corbis, the private company owned by Gates that was acquiring the electronic rights to photos and art collections from around the world, made plans to produce a CD-ROM of the Codex Leicester for sale to the public and for on-line viewing.

In 1450, two years before the birth of Leonardo da Vinci, Johannes Gutenberg printed a copy of the Bible on a crude press. Five hundred years later, another revolutionary technology would turn da Vinci's words and illustrations into tiny bits of digital information for viewing in cyberspace.

By the fall of 1994, when thousands of computer users began downloading Netscape's new browser, the number of people using the Internet was exploding by about 10 percent a month. Many of these new users were interested in just one area of the Internet—the World Wide Web. From some 50 commercial sites in January 1993, by October the Web had about 10,000. The number was doubling every few months, and the volume of traffic was doubling every four months. More than 600,000 copies of NCSA Mosaic had been downloaded for free, and upward of 80,000 copies a month were still being grabbed off the Internet.

The Web represented a hotbed of innovation and a golden opportunity for the big three commercial on-line services, which combined had about 6 million subscribers. Compu-Serve, Prodigy, and America Online were all scrambling to find partners with browser technology that would provide their customers with quick and easy access to the Internet. Although Microsoft would not officially announce that it was developing an on-line service until the Comdex trade show in November, it had been negotiating with two companies, Book-link Technologies and Spyglass, about licensing their browsers. Spyglass was marketing the Mosaic browser that had been developed by Marc Andreessen and his team at the National Center for Supercomputing Applications (NCSA). Spyglass had licensed Mosaic to about 20 companies, which in turn planned to peddle about 12 million copies. Booklink, on the other hand, was a tiny company with about a dozen employees; nevertheless, its browser technology was also attracting interest.

Gates and his technical assistant Steven Sinofsky had discovered Booklink's browser when they visited the company's booth at the spring Comdex in Atlanta in late May, about a month and a half after Microsoft's Internet retreat on April 5 at the Shumway Mansion. Gates spent 30 minutes talking about the browser with David Wetherell, who had founded Booklink in February. "We had a good talk at Comdex, and after that we started talking with Microsoft about a lot more things," said Wetherell.

One product idea the two companies talked about was a so-called Internet assistant that would enable users of Microsoft Word to create pages for the World Wide Web, an idea also raised during the April retreat.

Following Comdex, Sinofsky showed the Booklink browser to Brad Silverberg, vice president of Microsoft's operating systems, including Windows 95. Russell Siegelman, who was directing the development of the Microsoft Network, also got involved.

What really jump-started Microsoft's decision to build a browser was a memo that senior programmer Ben Slivka sent to his superiors Silverberg and John Ludwig on August 15, strongly urging that Microsoft assemble a browser development team. But browser technology was not yet a priority at Microsoft. To date, only five programmers had been assigned to help Slivka with the project, and it would be early 1995 before Microsoft began to throw more resources into its own effort to build a browser.

The 33-year-old Slivka was a veteran at Microsoft, having worked on DOS 6.0 and Windows 95. By mid-1994, his responsibilities for Windows 95 were winding down. Much of the code had been written, and debugging was in progress.

Slivka's post-Windows mission was to help figure out a strategy for merging Windows with Windows NT and to come up with recommendations for new features that could be incorporated into the next version of Windows. In examining technology trends, Slivka had begun playing around on the Internet. It soon became apparent to him that the Internet could eventually take the place of Windows as the dominant personal computer platform. The key to tapping the potential of the Internet was a browser, and Microsoft wasn't even working on one. "I wanted to build one, just because it was a fun thing to do more than anything else," said Slivka. "The way it works at Microsoft is if you have an idea and can convince people it's a good thing to do, you can get to do it."

With so few people on the project, it was impossible for Microsoft to build a browser from scratch and have it ready for Windows 95. Booklink's browser technology suddenly became much more attractive. In September, about a month after Slivka wrote his memo, Microsoft began serious talks with Booklink's Wetherell. Siegelman, a crack negotiator, was Microsoft's point man in the talks.

"Our browser was the best in the world at the time," said Wetherell. "Microsoft said they wanted to license it for Windows 95 and for the Microsoft Network. We got very close to making a deal, but they did not sign it."

Early in the negotiations, Wetherell learned what other companies that had done business with Microsoft already knew: Gates does not do royalties. Only rarely has Gates agreed to a licensing contract stipulating that Microsoft pay royalties for a product—although Gates has no problem with contracts stating that the other party pay royalties to Microsoft. Siegelman offered Wetherell a one-time, flat fee of $2 million for the source code to Booklink's browser. Wetherell thought—rightly, it turned out—that the figure was much too low. CompuServe would later pay $100 million for a competing browser. "Microsoft said they would not pay more because there was no money to be made in browsers," Wetherell said. "They thought of it as a commodity. Well, if that's true, isn't e-mail a commodity? So shouldn't Exchange be free? Isn't the operating system a commodity? Obviously, there was a lot of money to be made in browsers. And Netscape proved it. At the time, I thought Microsoft was making a big mistake in their thinking. There was a lot of money to be made, as Microsoft found out later, by giving away things for free."

Although Microsoft would not budge on the $2 million figure, Siegelman did throw in an incentive with potentially a great deal of value for Booklink. Microsoft would give Booklink the electronic rights to a portion of the Microsoft Bookstore, whose content it could market on the Microsoft Network. This sounded attractive to Wetherell, though he was worried about Blackbird, the project that was under way to develop proprietary tools for putting content on Microsoft's Network. Microsoft was hoping that Blackbird would become the industry standard. But Wetherell wondered: What if Blackbird doesn't take off? To which Siegelman replied that that was a risk Booklink would just have to take. "They weren't giving us money to convert their content or to do the conversion ourselves and then market it at the risk that Blackbird would not take off as a standard," Wetherell said. "And as it turned out, Blackbird didn't take off."

By early November, Microsoft and Booklink were just days away from signing a licensing deal when another suitor came calling for Booklink's browser—American Online (AOL), which at the time already had more than 1.25 million subscribers and was expanding its on-line content daily. Although it still trailed Prodigy and CompuServe, AOL was the fastest growing of the three services and was clearly aiming to be number one. It had established strategic alliances with dozens of companies, including Time Warner, ABC, NBC, Knight-Ridder, IBM, and

Apple. More important, AOL had devised an Internet strategy and was aggressively making the acquisitions necessary to implement that plan.

"AOL came in and made us a very good offer," Wetherell said. "We did not go back and forth with Microsoft. It was just simply that AOL made us a terrific offer, and that offer materialized very very quickly. And we accepted." Under the terms of the contract, Booklink's parent company CMG received 710,000 shares of AOL's common stock, valued at the time at $30 million, for all outstanding Booklink stock. It turned out to be a great deal, financially, for CMG. During the negotiations with both AOL and Microsoft, Wetherell had been convinced that AOL's stock was undervalued, which was one reason he spurned the offer from Microsoft. Even though AOL's stock had been in a free fall caused by investors who were worried about the competitive impact of Microsoft's on-line service, Wetherell figured that it would go back up. He was right. That $30 million grew to $73 million within 10 months as the price of AOL's stock skyrocketed. Not a bad profit on a $1.5 million investment made by Booklink to develop its browser.

America Online had promised that it would provide Internet access to its subscribers by the first quarter of 1995, and the swiftness of AOL's move to snatch away Booklink's browser caught Microsoft by surprise. "That woke us up. We had to be a lot more aggressive, a lot more lively," Brad Silverberg would later say.

But, according to Wetherell, Microsoft could have sealed the deal long before AOL came calling. "Once AOL entered the picture, Microsoft was scrambling to try and get the contracts ready. But they sat on the contracts for a long time. Had they moved like they usually move, which is very swiftly—they are the most agile company I've ever done business with—the deal would probably have been done. But AOL was incredibly agile, too."

Wetherell suspected that AOL was less interested in Booklink's browser than it was in keeping the technology away from

Microsoft. AOL's president, Steve Case, was increasingly worried that the Microsoft Network, bundled with Windows 95, would present a formidable challenge to his company. About the same time that AOL won Booklink, it also completed an acquisition of NaviSoft, a developer of software products to help content companies. By using NaviSoft's tools, content companies would be able to launch Internet services such as catalogs, classified ads, or journals without writing a single line of code. America Online also spent another $35 million for Advanced Network & Services, developer and operator of a high-performance data network known as ANSnet for business, research, education, and government organizations. These three acquisitions formed the nucleus of AOL's Internet Services Company, which was put under the direction of David Cole, a venture capitalist and former chief executive officer of NaviSoft and president of Ziff Communications and Ashton-Tate.

Before buying Booklink, Case seriously considered licensing Netscape's browser, but Netscape would not commit to the kind of deal Case wanted. "They were eager to license to us, but not on the terms that we thought would be appropriate, or to make the level of commitment in terms of customizing their technology to meet our needs that we felt was essential, so no deal was ever struck," said Case, who had talked with venture capitalists Kleiner Perkins Caufield & Byers about investing in Jim Clark's company shortly before it was founded in April. Nothing was ever finalized, and Kleiner Perkins found other investors.

America Online wanted to embed a browser within its application, rather than have the browser separate. Netscape's technology, however, was not as modular as Booklink's and therefore would have been more difficult to embed. After a careful technical review, Case decided it made more sense to acquire Booklink than to license Netscape's browser. "We thought that launching a browser and launching a separate application from within AOL would nullify the interactive experience we were trying to create," said Case. "And obviously Netscape had a lot of things on their plate, including entering the corporate market. We didn't feel that they were going to be able to make us the priority that we felt would have been necessary."

Case said that AOL had multiple objectives in going after Booklink, and keeping the technology away from Microsoft was certainly one. "We recognized the growing centrality of the Web and examined a variety of different Web technologies," he said. "We talked to a dozen different companies, and Booklink stood head and shoulders above the pack, in terms of both their product and their technical team. Initially, we were having discussions with them about licensing the technology, but the more we walked down the path, the more we felt it would be better to own it. And, absolutely, part of that motivation was a sense that Microsoft was likely to do a deal with them. Microsoft was considering an acquisition, and we had a lot of concerns that Microsoft could accelerate their entry into our market by piggybacking on Booklink's technology. So the acquisition really gave us some Web technology overnight, gave us some additional insights into the evolving Web market, and preempted Microsoft from acquiring it."

Just days after the deal, at the November Comdex show, AOL's newly acquired Booklink browser received a public relations boost when it was named Rookie of the Year by *Byte* magazine, an award given each year at the trade show to recognize the hottest new company in the computer industry.

Although Microsoft lost out on the browser, it did sign a license agreement for Booklink's Internet technology to be used with Microsoft Word. Booklink developed for Microsoft a product called Internet Assistant for Word, which automatically generates hypertext markup language, or HTML, the standard Internet file format, freeing Word users from having to learn the HTML format and manually input the HTML pages needed to create Internet documents.

On November 18, Prodigy became the first of the top three commercial on-line services to provide access to the World Wide Web. Ten days later, CompuServe linked up with a Seattle company, Spry, which was selling a version of the popular Mosaic browser. CompuServe, owned by H&R Block, paid a staggering $100 million in cash and stock for Spry. The Internet market had become red-hot. In late November, MCI Communications Corporation announced that it was teaming with Netscape to offer Internet access and software by January 1995. It was the first major success for Netscape. Microsoft, meanwhile, was in serious talks with Spyglass about its browser. Ironically, months earlier, a Spyglass executive had been rebuffed by Microsoft when he called to ask if Microsoft might be interested in licensing Mosaic. Microsoft had told him that it would build its own browser. Now it was Microsoft that wanted to make a deal with Spyglass. And it turned out to be the most critical deal Microsoft would make as it rushed to catch up with Netscape and the rest of the industry that was now running on Internet time.

The phone call that Michael Tyrrell had been hoping for came early in the afternoon of Friday, November 11, 1994. Tyrrell, executive vice president of business development for Spyglass, was in his office in Cambridge, Massachusetts. For the past several months, he and Microsoft had been going back and forth on whether Microsoft would license the Spyglass browser for Windows 95. But after American Online reached an agreement with Booklink for its browser, the talks had begun to heat up. Suddenly, Microsoft was showing much more interest. On the phone that morning was Thomas Reardon, program manager for Microsoft's browser development group and the company's principal representative in the talks with Spyglass. Reardon worked with Ben Slivka, who had written the August memo urging Microsoft to have a browser ready to go with Windows 95.

"We are ready to talk," Reardon said. "We'd like you and Tim [Krauskopf, founder and vice president of Spyglass] to be out here first thing Monday morning. We want to get this deal done by next week." Tyrrell responded that he did not want to fly all the way out to Seattle for a meeting unless Microsoft was serious. "We are very serious," Reardon told him. "We want to move, and move fast. We want to get this done."

After Reardon hung up, Tyrrell phoned Spyglass headquarters in Naperville, Illinois. He wanted to give the good news to Krauskopf. "Get your bags packed," Tyrrell told him, "we have to be at Microsoft first thing Monday morning. They are ready to make a deal!"

Both Tyrrell and Krauskopf realized just how important an agreement with Microsoft would be for the future of Spyglass. A few months earlier, in August, Spyglass had signed a contract with the National Center for Supercomputing Applications that gave Spyglass the master license to sell the Mosaic browser that had been developed at the center, meaning that any company that wanted to license the browser now had to come to Spyglass. Microsoft had wanted to deal only with the center, not with Spyglass, but now, if it wanted Mosaic, it would have to negotiate with Tyrrell and Krauskopf.

"This was such an important contract to Spyglass," said Tyrrell. "Netscape had already released its browser, and it had more features and they were getting more notoriety than we were, by leaps and bounds. This deal with Microsoft was everything to Spyglass. It was everything."

For Krauskopf, it was the realization of an entrepreneurial dream that had started when he was a student at the National Center for Supercomputing Applications, one of five big centers around the country that had been funded by the government to help research scientists using supercomputers, in much the same way that Tim Berners-Lee had been given a charter to help high-energy physicists at CERN, the research lab in Geneva. Berners-Lee had invented the World Wide Web as a way for scientists to exchange information. In the mid-1980s, as part of the center's brain trust under director Larry Smarr, Krauskopf and another student developed NCSA Telnet, which became the standard communication protocol for logging in to a supercomputer with a PC or Macintosh. NCSA Telnet was the first experiment in "freeware" that brought the Internet to every PC and Mac. Today, it is used by every university in the country. Mosaic was the next free software developed by the university, and it brought the Internet to the masses.

Telnet made it possible for scientists to transfer millions of numbers from supercomputers to personal computers for the study of astronomy, hydrodynamics, and other fields. But they could not do anything with all those numbers without the software to display them as images. Krauskopf wrote a series of scientific visualization programs, and in 1990, with some prompting from friends and a loan from Apple Computer, he founded Spyglass to commercialize that visualization software. The company was initially headquartered in Champaign, Illinois, home of the supercomputing center at the University of Illinois. "At the time, scientific visualization was very hot and we were going to grow that product line to become profitable and establish the company," said Krauskopf. "We wanted to go out and capture a certain portion of the market for people who needed to do imaging and analysis of scientific numbers. and we achieved that. At that point, we had not as a company embraced the Internet at all. My ties to the Internet were very solid, but that's not what the company was doing. The Internet was very useful for universities, but it had not yet branched out into commercial applications. Most scientists could not see how to do their jobs without it. But it was still very much for research only."

The first version of Mosaic for UNIX machines was released by the university in early 1993. In September and October, Mosaic became available for the PC and Macintosh, respectively. By this time, about 100,000 copies a year of Telnet were being downloaded for free to universities on high-volume servers. By early 1994, those same servers were downloading 50,000 copies a month of Mosaic, prompting Spyglass to reinvent itself and focus on Mosaic and the Internet.

While Krauskopf handled the technical duties, CEO Doug Colbeth visited with companies with a potential interest in licensing Mosaic. "We concluded that this thing was going to explode so fast that we could not create the company that we needed to service it. So we decided to leverage other companies that were out there, like Digital, FTP Software, NetManage, Sun, Novell. . . . We would license the product to them and they would distribute it through their channels. That way, we did not have to hire people for end-user support."

In April 1994, Spyglass became the ninth company to receive the rights to distribute Mosaic when it signed a licensing contract with the university. The other eight companies had signed what amounted to small-scale licensing deals, of $10,000 to $100,000; they had committed to selling a small number of copies of Mosaic to their customers. Spyglass, on the other hand, committed to selling millions of copies. "That first commitment we made to the university was the largest by far, by probably a factor of 10, of any commitment that they'd gotten before," said Krauskopf. "It showed how serious we were as a partner."

Other companies that had already licensed Mosaic included Spry and Santa Cruz Operations. "All those other companies had licensed Mosaic from the university with end-user business models in mind," said Tyrrell, who was the sixth employee at Spyglass. "We believed that Mosaic would become so pervasive, and would end up inside operating systems and applications, that we decided the best long-term business model was, in effect, to take NCSA's place in the licensing chain and to become an OEM [original equipment manufacturer] supplier of technology."

After acquiring the April license from the university, Spyglass soon negotiated deals with Digital Equipment Corporation and FTP Software for the browser. More agreements followed. Spyglass was more than meeting the commitment it had made to the university. Consequently, in August, the university agreed to give Spyglass the master license for Mosaic.

Spyglass next prepared a list of the biggest potential OEMs that might want to license Mosaic. Number one on the list was Microsoft. "We put an asterisk by their name," said Tyrrell, "because any deal you do with Microsoft, you have to be very careful that Microsoft doesn't become your biggest competitor."

In late August or early September 1994, Tyrrell approached Microsoft about a licensing deal for Mosaic. He was the one whom Microsoft told that it wasn't interested. "It came from several levels at Microsoft," Tyrrell said. "I was told that they were not interested; or that they would build their own browser."

Then in early October Netscape's browser hit cyberspace. It was free, and it could be downloaded off the Internet. The rush was on. Within days, Microsoft was indicating to Spyglass that it might want to license Mosaic after all. Tyrrell flew out to Redmond to propose to James Allard how the two companies could structure a deal.

In subsequent negotiations, Reardon took over as Microsoft's point man. Generally, Sinofsky, Allard, and Slivka are credited for pushing Microsoft toward the Internet, but Reardon was instrumental, too. "He was as influential as anyone," said Tyrrell. "He was the person beating the drum for browsers in the Internet at large. He and Allard are cut from the same cloth."

Tyrrell believed that Microsoft changed its mind about licensing Mosaic not so much because of the threat of Netscape, but because IBM had decided to put a browser in OS/2. Big

Blue's souped-up operating system, with the Star-Trekky name of Warp, was released a few days before Netscape's browser. Among the many new features in Warp not available in Microsoft's Windows was a browser that made it easy for anyone using the operating system to connect to the World Wide Web. IBM also began a $50 million ad blitz to convince people to transport from Windows to Warp. Although when Warp was launched, Windows had more than 50 million customers and OS/2 only about 4 million, Gates was clearly worried about Warp, browser or no browser.

Mitchell Kertzman, who sold Powersoft Corporation, the Boston-based software company he founded, to Sybase in 1994, recalled a conversation he had with Gates during that time regarding OS/2. "Bill Gates was still thinking about OS/2," Kertzman said. "You would think, 'Does Bill Gates think about OS/2? Hell no. That war has been won.' But he was still thinking about it. When Microsoft displaces an OS/2 customer in a corporation, Bill knows about it. That's amazing. This is the least complacent company you have ever seen. I urged people at Powersoft to emulate them. We took every little competitor seriously. We learned that from Microsoft. Microsoft always wants to win."

Once Microsoft had decided it wanted to license a browser, as a negotiating tactic, it quickly let Spyglass know that it had some competition. Tyrrell was told that Microsoft had a couple of internal groups working on a browser, and that it was also talking to other companies about their browser technology. What Microsoft didn't say was that it had been trying to do an end run around Spyglass and was talking to the NCSA about licensing Mosaic directly from the university. "Spyglass had the master license and every commercial organization had to go through them," said one NCSA official. "Microsoft did not want any part of that. They wanted a direct relationship with the university. It was the hotbed of the Internet. Microsoft also probably figured they could get a better deal if they came to us rather than Spyglass."

But Krauskopf downplayed Microsoft's attempt to license Mosaic from the university rather than from Spyglass. "It was not uncommon for our customers to contact the university and be referred to us as the commercial channel for Mosaic. Microsoft was not alone. You would expect them to explore their options, and one of the things that went on in the fall of 1994 was us educating Microsoft about what our arrangement with the university really was."

Meanwhile, Spyglass was learning about Microsoft. CEO Colbeth, a software executive who had been recruited in 1991 by Krauskopf to raise venture capital for the fledgling company, talked with people and companies that had done business with Microsoft. That background information proved invaluable in the formulation of the business strategy that Spyglass would use in the upcoming negotiations with Microsoft. Specifically, the strategy was to set a market value for Mosaic and not play games, in an effort to stay abreast of Microsoft, which is known for cutting to the chase and having an instant response to anything the other side comes up with.

"Smoke and mirrors are going to be blown away," said Krauskopf. "There are so many people who I think have gotten where they are by using negotiating tricks that they are not prepared to deal with a company like Microsoft that simply attacks whatever trick you put in front of them."

After AOL had bought Booklink and the talks between Microsoft and Spyglass about licensing Mosaic heated up, Reardon made it clear that Microsoft was interested in a browser only for Windows 95 and that there would be no royalty payment. Further, he said, Microsoft would pay a one-time fee only. Tyrrell said no. Microsoft's offer directly contradicted the marketing strategy Spyglass had developed for licensing Mosaic, which was to charge a fee of about $1 for each copy of

Mosaic that was sold by a customer. If Spyglass agreed to Reardon's terms, Microsoft could turn around and license Mosaic to Spyglass customers, and could potentially charge those customers less than Spyglass did.

"We saw the classical Microsoft in those negotiations," said Tyrrell. "They essentially wanted all the rights in the world for very little money; and we promptly stated that we would not do that type of deal and could never do that type of deal, and if Microsoft were in our shoes, it would not do that type of deal, either."

The negotiations continued, with Spyglass trying to sell Microsoft not only on the value of Mosaic, but also on the "time-to-market" value—the amount of time it would take Microsoft to release a browser if it used the Mosaic code as a base, versus the time it would require to build its own browser from scratch. It was a factor Microsoft had already calculated. Microsoft executives had concluded that it would take six months to a year to build a browser, whereas if it had the Mosaic code, it could have a browser out of development and ready for testing within a couple of months. But Reardon did not reveal this to Spyglass. His position took two poses: one, that Microsoft would build its own browser; and two, that the Mosaic name was not worth that much.

Said Krauskopf: "We kept coming back with, 'Here's the time to market. The code is good. There are other companies using it. Mosaic is one of the most widely known noncommercialized names; and by the way, look how much attention Netscape is grabbing in the headlines.' Netscape was a major source of irritation for Microsoft at the time."

As the negotiations dragged on through October and into November, Tyrrell found himself doing business at what seemed to him some very strange hours, often after 11 P.M. eastern standard time. E-mail was exchanged at all hours of the day and night. "I had numerous conversations with them very late at night, from hotel rooms across the country and from my home," said Tyrrell. "The phone would ring late at night and my wife would say, 'Don't tell me that's Microsoft again.' It was just the Microsoft way of doing business. I don't believe they ever really sleep."

Eventually, in November, the broad parameters of a licensing arrangement took shape, though nothing was finalized and Tyrrell was still not certain Microsoft was going to agree to a deal. Finally, Reardon called to set up a meeting in Redmond for the morning of Monday, November 17. Tyrrell and Krauskopf flew out on Sunday. The next morning, about 8:30, Reardon escorted them into one of the buildings on the Microsoft campus. They were walking down a hallway toward a conference room when Krauskopf spotted Ben Slivka. "Hello, Ben," said Krauskopf. "Long time no see." The two had gone to school together at Northwestern and had known each other well.

Krauskopf asked Slivka what he did at Microsoft, and Slivka said he was in charge of the Internet engineering crew. "That was very pleasant surprise for me, to go walking into our big meeting with Microsoft and see Ben," said Krauskopf. "It was a very nice feeling." But what occurred next was not so pleasant. First, Krauskopf and Tyrrell signed a nondisclosure agreement, followed by an intense, six-hour technical grilling by Allard, Slivka, and Reardon. By this time, they were familiar with Mosaic, having downloaded copies from NCSA, but they wanted to know all about the version of Mosaic that Spyglass was selling. Had it been improved from the version available from NCSA over the Internet? Tyrrell and Krauskopf made the case for the code, the Mosaic name, the university relationship, and the time-to-market value.

"Our code had a lot of mileage on it, which was good," said Tyrrell. "We had already licensed it to 10 or 12 other major OEMs, which had also beaten up the code. So, it was a good starting point for them to go build a browser on top of." Numerous times during the six-hour interrogation, the Microsoft team would leave the room to confer, only to return with another series of rapid-fire questions.

Finally, they brought John Ludwig into the room. It was time to get down to the business of how much Microsoft was willing to pay to license Mosaic, which was Ludwig's job as general manager for the Windows 95 group. Ludwig started by putting a figure on the table. It was significantly lower than what Tyrrell and Reardon had discussed a week earlier on the phone. "That's totally unacceptable," Tyrrell told him. "We would not have made the trip all the way here if we had known that's what you had in mind. And I'm speaking for Spyglass and the university."

Ludwig, Allard, Reardon, and Slivka left the room. When they returned, Ludwig asked Tyrrell what the figure had to be. "Well," Tyrrell told Ludwig, "it better start with a two and have a whole bunch of zeros after it."

Tyrrell had determined a value for Mosaic long before he and Krauskopf had sat down that morning to negotiate a licensing deal. Tyrrell had figured it would cost Microsoft about a million dollars to develop its own browser, not counting what it would cost to commit a team of programmers to work around the clock for six months to a year to get a browser out the door. There was also the added value of the Mosaic name.

"For the money they paid us, Microsoft got a bargain," said Krauskopf. "It would have taken them six months to a year to develop their own browser, and if they had accelerated that time to market, it would have ended up costing them a lot more than they paid us. . . . We were convinced it was the right play for them. And it was right for us. It was critical to the kind of success we wanted to build on. It legitimized our strategy of doing leverage deals, because we knew that this was going to get distributed, and distributed by an engine that could make it successful."

The $2 million that Microsoft agreed to pay Spyglass was the same amount that Microsoft had offered Booklink for its browser a few weeks before. The essence of the deal was that Microsoft would get a single snapshot of the Mosaic code and very limited distribution rights. It could use the code to build a browser for Windows 95 and Windows NT, but not for Windows 3.1, the Macintosh, or UNIX-based machines. After some fine-tuning, it was up to the lawyers to ready a final copy of the agreement to be singed by Gates and Spyglass CEO Doug Colbeth.

That same Monday, while Reardon, Allard, and Slivka were in Redmond putting together a tentative agreement to license the Mosaic browser, long lines and a packed house welcomed Bill Gates as he opened the Comdex trade show in Las Vegas with a keynote speech on the future of the information superhighway, where, he predicted, virtual money from wallet computers would replace cash, and wall-size screens would bring interactive television into the home.

Although his oratorical skills will never rival those of a fiery southern preacher, Gates can always hold the attention of an audience of the faithful, and so, accompanied by a Microsoft interactive video, he had the techie crowd of 5,000 entertained with his vision of the future. The content of his speech, though, was old news. The information highway, movies on demand, and those 500 television channels had been the hot talk of Comdex the year before. And many of the interactive TV trials that were supposed to have gotten under way in 1994, including some in which Microsoft was involved, had been delayed or canceled. Thus, Gates, that day, had to acknowledge that it would take 10 years for the information highway to really be paved. But, Gates assured the crowd, Microsoft would be a part of that future by creating standards for the distribution of information along that highway.

Coincidentally, Microsoft's more immediate future was being decided even as Gates spoke, by the three true-blue Internet believers who were holed up in a conference room of Building 3 on Microsoft's campus. They believed that people wanted to cruise the Web, not point some remote control device at a TV set-top box. And for that, they needed a browser. Due in large measure to the vision and the tireless efforts of Allard, Slivka, and Reardon, Microsoft now had one.

Following his keynote address at Comdex, Gates held a news conference to announce the industry's worst-kept secret: Microsoft would launch its own on-line service, to be called the Microsoft Network, MSN for short. Although Microsoft had discussed its plans with industry executives and had been negotiating to line up content for the service, the company had never before publicly acknowledged its plans. Now it was officially out; MSN, to be bundled with Windows 95, was scheduled for launch in April (the date would soon be pushed back to August). MSN, Gates promised, would be available in 35 countries that had telephone access to the network. With the simple click of the mouse button, any computer user running Windows 95 would be able to log on to the Microsoft Network.

That ease of registration had the competition crying foul, building on the criticism that had been mounting since Microsoft announced in October its plans to buy Intuit. If Microsoft obtained Intuit's popular Quicken program and made it available through the Microsoft Network, critics claimed, it would give Microsoft a dominating platform for an on-line banking service.

It wasn't only the usual suspects who were complaining this time. A few days before Comdex, during a discussion on the future of electronic commerce at BusinessNet, held at New York City's Waldorf-Astoria Hotel, executives of Prodigy, CompuServe, and America Online asserted that they could be at a significant disadvantage if Microsoft tied MSN to Windows 95, and that Microsoft would be able to use its dominance in operating systems to leverage itself into a similar position among the on-line services. "The Windows operating system is what the dial tone is to the phone industry," explained AOL's Steve Case, meaning that in the same way that consumers who pick up a receiver automatically get a phone company's dial tone, anyone who signed on to a computer would be on Microsoft's line.

Case contended that Microsoft should offer MSN as a stand-alone service, not connected to Windows, so it would have to compete fairly with the other three services. And he strongly suggested that perhaps it was time for the government to step in and regulate Microsoft, just as it had regulated the phone companies to allow competition. "There needs to be a level playing field on which companies can compete," said Case.

At his Comdex news conference, Gates said that competitors' fears about MSN were misplaced. "We don't think this is anticompetitive at all," Gates told reporters. "If this is about splitting up the market, it's a poor market for all of us." While Gates defended MSN, Russell Siegelman gave reporters a demonstration of the service, which was set up to run on a bank of computers at Microsoft's campus in Redmond. Siegelman promised that MSN would be priced to meet or beat the competition. Initially, it would have a selected number of content providers, but it would eventually be open to everyone, even industry rivals.

Industry analysts predicted that the Microsoft Network could have 20 million subscribers by the end of 1995, in sharp contrast to the other three, none of which had more than 3 million subscribers. Given Microsoft's formidable wealth and power, Microsoft seemed poised to bury its competition in the on-line world. A city once shaken by underground atom bomb tests now felt the antitrust rumblings, which resounded all the way to Washington, D.C., and the United States Department of Justice, where some of Gates's old pals were well under way in their investigation of Microsoft's proposed purchase of Intuit.

Jeff Lill, the number two guy on the MSN development team, had skipped Comdex and was resting at a summer home with his wife in Phoenix. Getting the service up and running for a live demo at Comdex had left him exhausted. He had fought many battles over the last few months, technical as well as political, to get ready for the fall show.

"I was planning to go to Comdex, but I was tired and I needed a break," said Lill. "It had been a marathon effort to get it from just barely working for a demo for Bill in October to actually working at Comdex [a month later]. It took a really tremendous effort. The whole development group was pretty exhausted by that point."

Lill's most difficult challenge had been to convince Siegelman and others, including Gates, that Microsoft Exchange, the mail program; would not work with the Microsoft Network. A significant number of programmers in the Advanced Technology Group had been working on Exchange for several years. Despite several delays, it was supposed to be ready to be shipped to customers in 1995. It was a critical project that was intended to make Microsoft competitive with Notes, the best-selling mail system from bitter enemy Lotus Development Corporation. The revolutionary Notes software, often referred to as groupware, made it possible for groups of people connected to different PCs to work together. They could store their material in central files where it could be easily viewed, updated, or changed by others in the group. Notes was so popular that it was even being used by the staffs of the White House and the Central Intelligence Agency. In short, Notes was a Microsoft-killer. No wonder the Exchange project had Gates's special attention.

"Notes was the one thing Microsoft really felt bad about," said Lill. "Lotus had put together a strategy and a product and made it happen, and for some reason Microsoft could never get its arms around Notes and compete with it. The Exchange guys were chartered to do it, but they were having a hard time. Maybe they spent too much energy worrying about Notes. Then the Internet came along, and it seemed that was a way to finally leapfrog Notes. It was kind of funny how quickly their worrying about Notes changed to worrying about the Internet."

Although Exchange was still under development in mid-1994, it seemed like the perfect mail service for the Microsoft Network. And that's exactly what Lill had told Gates a few months before Comdex, during a briefing on how things were going with MSN. After that briefing, Lill and the rest of the top managers on the MSN team made the long walk back from Gates's office in Building 8 to the East Tech building on the edge of the 300-acre campus. Lill began talking with one of the other technical guys, to whom, despite what he had just told Gates, he admitted that he was having doubts that Exchange would work. It had not been designed for the large numbers of servers that would be needed to handle the millions of potential customers that would sign up for the Microsoft Network.

"Frankly," recalled Lill, "I wasn't getting the support out of the Exchange group that I needed to make it happen. And frankly, in their defense, they were just trying to ship a product for an office server rather than the mega-servers we needed for the Microsoft Network. My design goal was to have 40,000 to 50,000 mailboxes per server. Their design for Exchange was to have maybe 200 to 300, certainly no more than 500 mailboxes per server. So it just didn't fit. But politically, it was a very difficult battle to say, 'Oh, we're not going to use it; we're going to write our own,' which is what we ended up doing."

The day after the briefing, Lill went to lunch at a Thai restaurant just off campus, a favorite of many at Microsoft, including Gates. While he was eating, Lill decided what to do: he would have a quick prototype of a mail and bulletin board system built for MSN. "I wanted something low-budget, low-risk, and high-performance," said Lill. Later, he told Siegelman that he was going to take five or six programmers and assign them the job of building the prototype. Siegelman gave his okay. Lill sent a general e-mail to the MSN technical team, which numbered about 100 programmers, explaining his plan to build a mail and bulletin board prototype system *not* based on Exchange. He said the project would have the highest priority, and it would probably determine the fate of the on-line service.

"I told the entire team to give these five or six guys anything they needed," said Lill. "If they needed servers, get them servers. If they needed space, get them space. This was a make-or-break project. It was to have the highest priority."

Lill's e-mail went to everyone on the MSNDEV (Microsoft Network developers) mailing list. But other Microsoft employees who were not part of the MSN development team were also on that mailing list, in order to keep with what was happening on the project. Usually, an interested staff member just had to ask, and Lill would put him or her on the list. "I was pretty open about letting people get on the list," he said. "It was the best way to get a feel for what was going on inside the project."

As it turned out, a Microsoft employee in Australia, at what Lill described as "this little outpost," received a copy of the e-mail and immediately forwarded it to Gates with an attached note saying that it was crazy not to incorporate Exchange into the Microsoft Network after so much effort had been put into the development of the sophisticated mail system. Gates, of course, had only recently been told by Lill and Siegelman that Exchange *would* be used, and that everything was going great. When Gates got the e-mail from Australia, he forwarded a copy to Siegelman with a terse note of his own: "Are things *this* insane in the MSN group!?"

"Russ was not happy," said Lill. "But I ignored that and Russ took the heat. I did have a problem, though. Microsoft probably had a hundred labor-years invested in Exchange, and here I was going to take six guys and in a few months build a mailing system. It just didn't seem feasible."

In fact, the prototype took only a few weeks to build, and when Lill ran a side-by-side performance test against Exchange, the prototype was a hundred times faster. Although Siegelman was catching hell from Gates and was now in the camp of those who wanted Exchange, Lill had convinced Nathan Myhrvold that the newly designed mail system would work better than Exchange on the Microsoft Network.

By September, also in preparation for Comdex, now two months away, the Microsoft Network team was preparing for another critical go/no go meetings with Gates—with one major difference: Gates wanted a live demo. How well the Microsoft Network worked in the demo would determine whether it would be included in Windows 95.

Shortly before dawn the day of the demo, the Microsoft Network came alive for the first time, not in the lab but running on servers from a data center in downtown Bellevue. Hours later, Gates and Myhrvold watched the first live demonstration. Gates even took part in an on-line chat with someone in France and in Australia. "We were chatting worldwide," said Lill. "It was a very nice demonstration. It was just amazing, considering the whole thing did not even work the night before. We had a contingency plan to demo this for Bill in the lab. But with Comdex coming up, we knew we had to get it up and running out of the data center, which had a butt-load of servers."

Once he knew that Microsoft's on-line service actually worked, Gates turned his attention to a pressing business matter that he was hoping to wrap up before Comdex. He had to convince his friend John Malone that TCI should invest in the Microsoft Network and not in America Online. Even though TCI and Microsoft were collaborating on interactive TV projects, those experiments were not going to produce results anytime soon, if ever. So Malone was looking to make a major investment in one of the on-line services, which were seeking telecommunication partners whose cable networks could deliver video and graphics much faster than telephone lines could. Although Malone had put out feelers to Prodigy, he actually had his eye on Paul Allen's remaining 9 percent stake in

America Online. Malone had talked to Steve Case about buying Allen's holdings, and Case assured him that not only would there be no objections from the AOL board, but taking Allen out of the picture would be welcomed.

There was bad blood between Allen and AOL. A year earlier, in 1993, AOL had adopted a poison-pill strategy to prevent Allen from taking control of the company. Microsoft's cofounder had started buying stock in AOL soon after the company went public in early 1992. At the time, the stock was selling for about $11 a share. Allen wanted AOL as part of a broad strategy in which he was buying or investing in companies he believed would become key players on the information highway. By 1993, Allen owned two software companies, Starwave and Asymetrix, and had made substantial investments in a dozen other businesses, including $300 million for an 80 percent stake in Ticketmaster. He also had formed Interval Research, a think tank in Palo Alto, California, to which he had pledged $100 million in support over 10 years. Allen was hoping that it would become another PARC (Xerox's famed Palo Alto Research Center). To that end, Allen had hired David Little, one of PARC's best minds, to oversee Interval Research.

Allen also continued buying stock in America Online, and by 1993 owned about 25 percent of the company. Microsoft, too, had designs on AOL. Siegelman had met with Case several times to discuss a possible acquisition, but Allen's interest in AOL was making negotiations difficult for Microsoft. In early May of 1993, Siegelman had sent Gates a memo in which he complained that Allen "has made our life much more difficult." "It was hard to understand what the heck was going on," said Lill. "At the time, I was privately asking myself, 'God, don't Bill and Paul have lunch and sort of coordinate on this stuff?'"

That summer, Case flew to Seattle to talk face to face with Allen about his intentions. Later that day, Case also met with Gates. Microsoft's founders were both interested in the same thing: acquiring America Online. But now they were rivals. "It was a very strange situation, because Allen was on Microsoft's board," said Case. And Allen also owned the second biggest chunk of Microsoft stock after Gates.

"We were really just feeling each other out and getting a sense of the situation," Case said of his meeting with Gates. "Obviously, we had a lot of respect for Bill and Microsoft. But it was our view then, and frankly our view now, that we could best develop this franchise as an independent company not tied to any specific technology or any specific communications company or any specific software company or any specific media company. And that path of independence has paid off. Our market value in 1993 was probably one-tenth of what it is today."

Because of Allen's close ties with Microsoft, Case did not want him to get control of AOL, either. "If we had been willing to consider an acquisition by Paul, I suspect he would have pursued it vigorously," said Case. "And if he had been successful, I presume he would have had to get off Microsoft's board, because clearly what we were doing was going to be increasingly competitive with Microsoft. But things did not develop in that direction, because we tried to cut off the discussions with Allen at the pass."

Fearing a hostile takeover, AOL flooded the market with millions of shares of new stock, thus making it too expensive for Allen to buy a majority stake in the company. By the summer of 1994, a frustrated Allen had dumped more than half of his share of AOL stock—for a cool $75 million profit. Malone was poised to buy Allen's remaining 9 percent stake in AOL in September, when Gates came on aggressively with a full-court press. He convinced Malone that the Microsoft Network, bundled with Windows 95, was a much more attractive investment than America Online. There would be no deal with Allen, who soon sold the rest of his AOL stock for another $30 million profit. "This is positive news," a spokeswoman for America Online told the *Wall Street Journal* upon learning that Allen no longer had a stake in the company. "We believe it closes the chapter on Paul Allen and America Online."

TCI had wanted to invest in the Microsoft Network all along, according to Case, but Gates had been unwilling until Malone began talking with America Online. "As soon as Gates became concerned that TCI might fall into the AOL camp, he quickly expressed a willingness to sell a stake in the Microsoft Network to TCI," said Case. "But prior to that he had been unwilling to entertain such a notion."

Before Comdex, Malone and Gates reached a tentative agreement that TCI would invest $125 million in the Microsoft Network, a 20 percent stake. The partnership papers were not signed, however, until after the trade show. When the deal was finally announced publicly, some members of the MSN development team were stunned. "We were shocked, just absolutely amazed," said one MSN manager. "We had not even launched a project yet and suddenly we had a market value of $625 million!"

Immediately after Comdex, Lill told the development team to relax and to take their two-week vacations. "The group was exhausted," he said. "I told everyone we would get the project started back up in January. Comdex had been a success. We were happy to be alive. We felt that we had the majority of components running. We obviously had a lot of bugs, and we had some implementation work to do, but we felt like we were going to be able to make it. In one sense, Comdex actually got us on the map inside the company. Internally, people started saying, 'Hey, maybe they are really going to make it, and maybe this will really matter.' We started getting some other groups coming in and wanting to participate."

The Internet had finally moved up a notch or two in importance. One of the team's managers, Anthony Bay, was assigned responsibility for making the Microsoft Network work on the Internet. For that, Microsoft needed an Internet service provider to supply the telecommunications lines to connect computer users to the Microsoft Network and the Internet. There were many such service providers, including Ablecom, Netcom, PSINet, and UUNET Technology. Microsoft began talks with UUNET in early December and quickly reached an agreement to purchase a minority stake in the company, which was based in Falls Church, Virginia. Microsoft also got a seat on the UUNET board. "I put in a significant number of my resources to make sure that we could deliver Internet access simultaneously with the launch of MSN," said Lill. "Frankly, considering how aggressive the whole schedule was to begin with, I was taking a big risk . . . but the Internet was starting to be cool."

In early December, only a couple of weeks after Comdex, the Microsoft Network lost the media spotlight to Netscape Communications Corporation, which was the center of attention at the Internet World trade show at the Hilton Hotel in downtown Washington, D.C. It was standing room only around Netscape's booth, while Microsoft attracted hardly any attention. A *Wall Street Journal* reporter covering the show wrote that Netscape was the "new star of cyberspace." The trade show itself was testimony to the booming business of the Internet. Attendance had tripled since the 1993 show; the number of companies displaying Internet-related products had jumped from 40 to 115.

Netscape may have been the star, but its main rival, Spyglass, was also drawing large crowds. "We had a little booth, probably 10 feet by 10 feet, and at one point there were so many people crowding around that you could not even see it," recalled Spyglass flak Randy Pitzer. "I actually got trapped and could not get out of the booth. They were trying to take my last press kit. Someone grabbed it out of my hand. It was a madhouse."

Although Spyglass and Microsoft had managed to keep their negotiations secret, there had been speculation that a deal for Mosaic was in the works. "We all knew that Microsoft

needed a browser, and they did not have enough time to develop something in-house," said Karen Rodriguez, who was
covering Internet World for the trade magazine *InfoWorld.* "So
the question was, where were they going to get the technology?
All that was out there were Spyglass and Netscape."

By this time, Spyglass and Microsoft had pretty much
wrapped up their negotiations. In early December, a few days
before Internet World, Reardon and a lawyer for Microsoft
flew to Boston to meet with Tyrrell and the lawyer for Spyglass.
The four went to a Boston Celtics basketball game and spent
the next day working on the contract at the Boston law firm of
Hale & Dorr, which was representing Spyglass. "Once we
reached general terms with Microsoft, negotiating the actual
agreement with them was very, very, very reasonable and fair,"
said Tyrrell. "I've done lots and lots of big OEM agreements,
and [Microsoft is] very, very reasonable and fair to deal with,
once you have the basic structure of the deal in place. They
don't waste time. I'm a huge Microsoft fan, even though I've
sat across the table from them. I admire the hell out of them.
And it's guys like Reardon and Allard that I really admire. They
are cut from the Bill Gates cloth, in the sense that they are brilliant technically; they understand the big picture; they love
strategy, they love to think strategy, they want to know your
strategy, they want to know everybody's strategy; and they're
tough negotiators. They don't waste time and they get things
done. That's an amazing, amazing, amazing company."

The agreement between Spyglass and Microsoft contained
a provision that Microsoft would credit Spyglass and the
NCSA in an "about box" that users could open when they
clicked on Microsoft's browser. But there was to be no formal
announcement of the deal. During Internet World, however,
reporter Rodriguez had lunch with Spyglass CEO Doug Colbeth, who dropped such significant hints that something was
in the wind with Microsoft that Rodriguez went with a story.
Once the word was out, Bill Gates went nuts. He called Thomas

Reardon into his office and demanded to know where the leak had come from. Reardon said he didn't know. Gates said there had better be no more leaks.

Reardon called Mike Tyrrell in Cambridge. "All hell is breaking loose out here. What's going on?" Tyrrell, who did not know about Colbeth's lunch talk with the *InfoWorld* reporter, insisted that the leak had not come from Spyglass. "When the story broke, we refused to confirm it," said Tyrrell. "The deal had not even been signed yet. There was no way we were going to say anything. That would have been stupid."

A clean copy of the contract between Spyglass and Microsoft was ready to be signed on Friday, December 9. Gates insisted that Colbeth sign first. But before he could do so, he had to talk with the university and get its blessing. By the time he had a letter of approval from the university and contacted Microsoft late that Friday afternoon, he was told he had missed Gates by about 30 minutes and Gates would not be able to sign until the following week.

That next week proved to be hellish for Krauskopf and Tyrrell. As the tension mounted, they worried that Netscape had made a last-minute deal with Microsoft, much as AOL had come in at the eleventh hour and snatched Booklink away from Microsoft. By December 14, the day of the Spyglass Christmas party, which was held in a campus building at the University of Illinois in Urbana-Champaign, the contract still had not been signed by Gates. From the party, Tyrrell was calling his voice mail and Microsoft every half hour throughout the evening. "I did not enjoy the Christmas party at all," said Tyrrell. "I was a complete basket case. It was a salesperson's worst nightmare. I had a huge cell-phone bill. This was such an important contract for Spyglass. And as each minute went by, the likelihood that Father Murphy would tap me on the shoulder and give me the bad news increased dramatically. I was worried about the competition getting in there and getting Microsoft's business."

It was not until Friday, December 16, late in the afternoon on the East Coast, that Reardon phoned Tyrrell and congratulated him. Gates had just signed the contract. "This was a great deal for Spyglass, and I believe a great deal for Microsoft," said Tyrrell. "It's not often that you can walk away from a deal, particularly a deal with a company of Microsoft's size and reputation, and six months later both companies can look each other in the eye and say that was a fair deal. When everything was said and done, this was fair to both. We got a fair price for the technology, and Microsoft saved itself perhaps as much as the year it would have taken them to build a browser and get back in the race against Netscape. And by then, who knows? Netscape might have had an insurmountable lead, and no one would be talking about how quickly Microsoft was able to make that turnaround."

On the afternoon of December 16, Microsoft issued a news release, but not regarding the just-completed deal with Spyglass. It came from Microsoft's public relations department, and it denied a news account published on the Internet that the company had agreed to buy the Catholic Church. Microsoft, a Johnny-come-lately to the Internet, was the victim of a huge cyberprank. As best as it could be determined, around December 1, a very clever cyberprankster had posted a fake dispatch from the Associated Press, the world's largest news organization. Datelined Vatican City, the story reported that Microsoft had agreed to acquire the Roman Catholic Church in exchange for an unspecified number of shares of Microsoft common stock. "If the deal goes through," it read, "it will be the first time a computer software company has acquired a major religion."

Under terms of the alleged deal, Microsoft would get exclusive electronic rights to the Bible and the Vatican's prized art collection, including works by Michelangelo and da Vinci.

Pope John Paul II would become the senior vice president of the combined companies' new religious software division. Two Microsoft senior vice presidents, Steve Ballmer and Mike Maples, would be invested in the College of Cardinals.

Further, the story quoted Gates as saying, "We expect a lot of growth in the religious market in the next 5 to 10 years. The combined resources of Microsoft and the Catholic Church will allow us to make religion easier and more fun for a broader range of people."

Finally, according to the Internet story, the Microsoft Network would make sacraments available on-line for the first time. "You can take Communion, confess your sins, receive absolution—even reduce time in Purgatory—all without leaving your home."

The story concluded by predicting that the Microsoft acquisition could spark a wave of mergers. It quoted Herb Peters of the U.S. Southern Baptist Conference as saying that other churches would now have to scramble to strengthen their position in the increasingly competitive religious market.

Although the story was obviously a hoax, conservative talk show host Rush Limbaugh read it on his national television program. Soon thereafter, Microsoft was fielding calls and e-mail from angry people who believed the story to be true. Microsoft was not amused, and on December 16, the company issued this terse statement: "The story has no truth and was not generated by the company. The company is not aware how the electronic message originated, but maintains strict policies internally concerning the proper use of electronic communications." Subsequently, a legitimate wire service story about the hoax carried by the Associated Press quoted Microsoft spokeswoman Christine Santucci as saying: "Given the seriousness of the issue, it's not something we wanted to be associated with."

Hoax though it was, the story made news around the world, and finally proved to Bill Gates just how big the Internet had become.

7

Nothing but Net

It was no longer fun. Bill Gates had won.

Philippe Kahn, president, chief executive officer, and chairman of the board of Borland International, once the third biggest computer software company in the world and the leading contender for the title of "The Next Microsoft" was fed up. Despite a reputation for having an unlimited appetite for work, fun, food, and mischief, he had been beaten down by this last year. He was tired, damn tired; tired of having to tell good men and women who worked for him that the company faced further restructuring and more cutbacks, tired of Wall Street analysts and institutional investors calling for his head. Most of all, he was sick and tired of being a punching bag for the industry press, which blamed him for everything that had gone wrong at Borland. The recent flurry of negative stories about him had become a major distraction, overshadowing anything positive the company tried to do.

As he sped along Highway 17 in the predawn darkness, the whine of his powerful motorcycle piercing the thick blanket of fog that hung over Scotts Valley, all he wanted was to get to the

San Jose Airport, climb into the cockpit of his plane, and fly off into the December morning, leaving behind all the bullshit.

It had gotten so bad around the office that he had even ducked the big Borland news conference the day before, leaving his staff and public relations people to explain to analysts and the press that the company would suffer another substantial quarterly loss, followed by another major layoff, the second of the year. But that was yesterday, and with a new day about to dawn, Kahn was off on vacation, to the ski slopes of Aspen, Colorado. There, in the mountains, he would sort it all out, decide his future.

In Kahn's wilder days, when he was collecting speeding tickets that built on his reputation as the bad boy of the computer industry, Kahn would hop into his white Porsche and race along Highway 17 from Borland's headquarters in Scotts Valley, on the outskirts of Santa Cruz, to the San Jose Airport in less than 30 minutes. He loved the challenge, the exhilaration, of slamming the sports car hard into the serpentine turns at high speed, zipping up and down the mountain on the edge. But he had long ago gotten rid of the Porsche. Now he tooled around on his Honda CBR900/RR motorcycle. The 120-horsepower engine could propel this fastest commercial motorcycle made at speeds of more than 170 miles per hour.

But as much as Kahn wanted to get to the airport this morning, he had to take his time. An enveloping fog made it too dangerous to speed. When he finally reached the airport about 7:00 A.M., Kahn rode his motorcycle over to the hangar where he kept his plane and began preparing it for the trip. Just being around the plane took his mind off the problems at Borland and filled him with excitement and anticipation for the adventure and long flight ahead. He had owned the plane for about a year. It was an Extra 300, a stunt plane, the same kind flown by three-time U.S. acrobatic champion Patty Wagstaff. With a glass bubble cockpit on a body made of lightweight carbon fiber composite, the German-made Extra was a high-tech hot-rod of the skies, a real aviator's plane—and a handful to fly. Kahn called it Looney Tunes. Some might say the moniker reflected the nature and passions of its saxophone-playing pilot.

The airport was still socked in when Kahn finished his pre-flight preparations, so there was nothing to do but wait. Alone with his plane and surrounded by an eerie quiet produced by the absence of the usual air-splitting roar of jet engines, Kahn watched through the hangar door as the morning fog slowly burned away. It was two days before Christmas, 1994. Only a couple of miles away was Stevens Creek Boulevard, where it had all begun in a cheap motel a dozen years earlier.

He had arrived in San Jose in 1982 by bus from the San Francisco Airport, a 30-year-old Frenchman with a tourist visa, a black belt in karate, and $5,000 borrowed from his dad. He was alone; his wife and two daughters were back home at an artists' colony in the south of France. His eclecticism was homebred. His father was a die-hard socialist. His mother, a singer and filmmaker who had survived Auschwitz, died when Kahn was in his early teens. Although Kahn was a promising student of mathematics with a passion for music, he dropped out of one of the world's great universities in Zurich after reading Henry David Thoreau's *Walden*. The book had such an impact on him that he disappeared into the high reaches of the French Pyrenees, where he tended a few goats, practiced his music, and contemplated his future.

When he finally came down from the mountains almost a year later, Kahn took a job teaching mathematics. He also began to rediscover the rewards of capitalism, and bought an Apple II computer with some of the money he made. By this time, the personal computer revolution was well under way in America, and Kahn had decided he wanted to be part of it. And the headquarters of the revolution was in the Valley of Silicon Dreams.

Upon arrival in America, he was unable to get a job in San Jose with companies like Hewlett-Packard, because he did not have a green card. Undeterred, the crafty Kahn started his own computer consulting business, which he called MIT, for Market In Time. The acronym was no coincidence. By the time the original MIT took notice and started making noise about a lawsuit, Kahn had moved from San Jose across the Santa Clara mountains to Scotts Valley, where he was doing business in a small office above an auto repair shop, using the imposing name Borland International. It was there that the legend began.

But now his days as Borland's leader were numbered. He wanted out. Earlier in the year, Kahn and his live-in girlfriend, Sonia Lee, a respected Silicon Valley graphics designer, had started a new venture called Starfish, which was dedicated to producing small and fast software products called slimware— the fewer lines of code the better. Kahn was flying on this December morning to meet Lee in Aspen. She had left several days earlier, driving in their 18-foot motor home with Samuel Kahn, Philippe's young son from his now ended marriage. After the vacation, Kahn planned to drive back to Scotts Valley with Lee and his son. A friend would fly his plane back from Aspen.

By 10:00 A.M., the fog lifted at the San Jose Airport, and Kahn strapped himself in Looney Tunes and taxied out to runway 29. Cleared for takeoff, he gave the plane full throttle and accelerated down the runway. Kahn gave a wing waggle to the controllers in the tower and headed east, leaving Borland and his troubles far behind.

A week later, on December 30, 1994, two days before the New Year, Kahn phoned a reporter acquaintance. He, Lee, and his son had stopped for the night near Dinosaur National Monument on the Colorado-Utah border, en route back to Scotts Valley. The topic and tone of the discussion that night was set immediately by Kahn. He wanted to talk about the man he viewed as the Satan incarnate of the computer industry: Bill Gates.

"It's just amazing how destructive he is," said Kahn, comparing Gates to John D. Rockefeller, who created the Standard Oil monopoly. He complained that Microsoft's "predatory pricing" of its products had crippled Borland and other software companies. "He's made it unprofitable for the rest of us. There is no balance of power." Gates, he insisted, would eventually control every aspect of the computer industry, from applications and operating systems to home banking and interactive television. "It will be a total dictatorship," Kahn said. "This guy will go down in history as one of the most ruthless and powerful people of all time."

Kahn had heard that the *Wall Street Journal* was soon to release an article about just how ruthless Gates was, and he was worried that Gates would use his enormous influence to have the article killed. Kahn believed he had every reason to be worried. For years, Gates had Kahn in his sights. In the mid-1980s, when Borland's Turbo Pascal was blowing away Microsoft's competing product, Gates held meetings that became known around Microsoft as Borland War Councils, during which his staff plotted how to beat the fun-loving Frenchman. Gates reportedly walked into one such meeting, threw Kahn's picture down on a table, and said, "How can I get rid of this guy?" A product group at Microsoft passed out T-shirts that read "Delete Philippe." Some prankster at Microsoft sent one of the shirts to Kahn.

Kahn recalled that he once had found Gates at an industry conference in the late 1980s sitting alone in a corner, looking at a photograph in his hands. "It was a picture of me," said Kahn. In the early 1990s, an ex-Borland employee who went to work for Microsoft sent Kahn a photo of what allegedly was a room at Microsoft filled with pictures of Kahn. Kahn showed the photograph to the author of this book.

In an interview for an article that appeared in the *New York Times Magazine* in 1991, Kahn described Gates's technical capabilities as all talk. "It's an image he's trying to put out," said Kahn. When Gates was asked to respond to Kahn's remark by Stephen Manes and Paul Andrews, the authors of *Gates,* a book about Microsoft published in 1993 by Doubleday, Gates exploded: "Fuck this guy! I mean I really hate this guy. . . . I'm so much more technical than that guy."

For Kahn, the unkindest cut may have come not from Gates but from his former wife, Martine. When they divorced in the early 1990s, the first man Martine dated was Bill Gates. "It made Philippe a little crazy," said Martine.

In late 1994, during a trip overseas, Kahn had eaten dinner one night with someone he described as a Microsoft executive. "He told me that Gates hates me, that it's even shocking to Microsoft people," recalled Kahn. "He said Gates has sworn to destroy me personally by all means; that he is obsessed; that he is paying people to spin bad news about Borland. I can't think of anything that I've done or said about the guy. It's pretty scary, given the power that he has."

Whether Gates was obsessed with Kahn or Kahn with Gates really didn't matter. The long and the short of it was that Microsoft had won and Borland had lost. On January 11, 1995, shortly after Kahn returned from his vacation in Colorado, Borland announced that Kahn had resigned as president and chief executive officer, though he would remain on the board. The board had shoved Kahn aside because of a disagreement over the direction in which he wanted to take the company— back to its roots. "I wanted to sell off everything but tools, including Paradox and dBase, and get out of the suites business," said Kahn. "But the board didn't want to follow through with 'Project Boomerang.' We got into a match and they fired me."

USA Today's story on Kahn's resignation on page 2 of the business section the next day was directly above a piece about Bill Gates by *USA Today* business columnist Kevin Maney. Headlined "Getting One's Fill of the Ubiquitous Bill," the article began, "I'm so sick of Bill Gates I could barf." Maney went on to complain that Gates was everywhere he turned: on the covers of magazines, in newspapers, on television. Gates recently had begun writing a weekly newspaper column that appeared in papers around the country, Maney said. Gates was also the subject of an entire newsgroup on the Internet, on which people around the planet could post "thousands of messages a day about nothing but what Gates says, how he looks, and whether his house on Lake Washington near Seattle is an architectural disgrace," wrote Maney.

Already ubiquitous or not, Gates was about to be in the news a lot more. The day before Kahn "resigned," his good friend Gary Reback, a Silicon Valley lawyer, filed a long brief on behalf of three unnamed Microsoft competitors, asking federal Judge Stanley Sporkin in Washington, D.C., the judge known as "Attila the Hun," to block the Justice Department's antitrust settlement with Microsoft. Among the supporting documents that Reback used to make his case was an old Microsoft memo that talked about "sticking it to Philippe." It would become a critical piece of evidence in helping to convince Sporkin that Anne Bingaman had treated Gates with kid gloves and that the consent decree was not in the best interest of the public. Kahn would finally get to stick it to Gates.

It was just the luck of the draw—literally—that the most significant antitrust case in the history of the personal computer industry had landed in the lap of one of the most colorful, controversial, and independent judges on the federal bench. In the United States District Court for the District of Columbia, consent decrees are assigned by lottery to federal judges, who determine whether they are in the public interest. The Microsoft case had gone to Stanley Sporkin, three days after it was filed on the night of July 15, 1994. Consent decrees are routinely approved after a 60-day public comment period and a hearing, which is required by the Tunney Act. (The act was passed by Congress in 1974 in response to allegations that the government was making sweetheart deals with companies to settle antitrust cases.) But the 63-year-old Sporkin was no rubber-stamp judge. A recent profile in a Washington, D.C., news magazine had described him as "the most irritating judge in town."

If Microsoft's lawyers had wanted to confirm that description, they could have looked in the *Almanac of the Federal Judiciary*, in which lawyers anonymously give their opinions about judges. The almanac described Sporkin as "quixotic," with a harsh and crusty courtroom style. "It's a real carnival in his courtroom," the almanac read.

Sporkin was the son of a federal judge in Philadelphia. He graduated from Yale Law School, and in 1973 he became the enforcement chief of the Securities and Exchange Commission, the watchdog agency of Wall Street. During his tenure there, the crusading Sporkin was nicknamed "Attila the Hun" in reference to his aggressive efforts to prosecute companies accused of offering bribes to foreign governments. He pioneered the use of consent decrees to force corporations to admit to the bribes.

During the biggest scandal of that decade—Watergate— the White House had pressured Sporkin to delay an investigation of financier Robert Vesco, who had secretly contributed $200,000 to the Nixon campaign. Sporkin refused. On the Watergate tapes, when Richard Nixon was heard complaining to John Dean about those "Jew boys" at the SEC, he had Sporkin, among others, in mind.

Sporkin's boss at the SEC at that time was William Casey, and when Casey was named CIA director, he brought Sporkin along as the agency's general counsel. President Reagan named Sporkin to the federal bench in 1984, but the nomination approval process dragged out for 18 months because of the reputation Sporkin had earned of being tough on business. Conservatives did not like him. Once he was on the bench, though, he became known as a judge who did not mind mixing it up with either prosecutors or defense attorneys, a sometimes loose cannon with an independent and iconoclastic judicial philosophy.

Sporkin presided over the Charles Keating lawsuit to overturn the government takeover of Keating's Lincoln Savings & Loan, during which he told defense lawyers, "You're not going to strong-arm this court." He eventually took control of the case, grilling Keating for five hours, and accusing him of "looting" Lincoln funds.

On a cable TV monopoly case, Sporkin shot down lawyers for the cable companies with this remark: "Find out why we have to pay $5 a month for a remote control when we can buy one for $15. If that isn't a monopoly, then I don't know what one is."

Despite his iconoclastic image, however, Sporkin's judicial record did not show him to be a loose cannon. By 1992, the *Legal Times*, reporting on more than 350 opinions, found that Sporkin had been reversed 21 percent of the time on appeal, a figure only slightly higher than the 17 percent average for judges in the district.

When the consent decree against Microsoft landed in his lap, Sporkin was semi–computer literate—he had learned how to use a personal computer so he could play chess—but he knew next to nothing about Microsoft or the computer industry. On the advice of his son-in-law, who worked for *Money* magazine, Sporkin read a book about Microsoft while he was on vacation that summer. The book was *Hard Drive: Bill Gates and the Making of the Microsoft Empire,* by James Wallace and Jim Erickson, published in 1992 by John Wiley & Sons.

Sporkin held the first hearing on the Microsoft consent decree on September 29. It proved to be vintage Sporkin. "Maybe it wasn't someone's lucky day when I got this assignment, but I think I have a little experience in consent decrees," Sporkin told Anne Bingaman. Although the hearing was open to the public, no reporters showed up, either because they didn't know about it or because they assumed that the consent decree would get the usual quick-and-dirty approval.

But as Sporkin talked, it became clear that this case would be anything but the norm. Peering out over his glasses, the judge said he had boned up about Microsoft by reading *Hard Drive.* He said he wanted answers to troubling questions the book raised about the way Microsoft did business, which Sporkin said had not been addressed in the consent decree. He also noted: "I . . . thought it would be a good idea to know as much about Microsoft as they're going to know about me."

Addressing Bingaman, the judge said: "As I read the book, it doesn't seem to be one that's trying to be unfair. I mean, it seemed somewhat balanced. They [the authors] seemed to think that the company had done a lot of good things. But there are a number of practices . . . things like putting out announcements that are misleading or not true to freeze the competition, and something called vaporware. . . . I don't know what's true or not. But if they are doing that, I think you ought to look into it."

In addition to the issue of vaporware (products that don't exist but are preannounced to forestall competitors), Sporkin said that he was concerned about another issue raised in *Hard Drive:* complaints by Microsoft rivals that the company's applications developers had gotten inside information from the operating system developers, which gave Microsoft an unfair advantage. Sporkin told Bingaman he wanted these issues fully explored during the settlement hearings.

Vaporware would be a key issue for Sporkin in the months ahead. Vaporware was first brought to wide attention by Ann Winblad in 1982, long before she started dating the man whose company would become most closely identified with the practice. Then, Winblad had her own software company, and she had visited Microsoft to find out if it still planned to develop a version of the UNIX operating system, on which software produced by Winblad's company ran. "Basically, it's vaporware," a programmer whispered to Winblad during her visit. She began spreading the word around the industry.

By 1985, Gates's use of vaporware was so well known that he accepted the first Golden Vaporware award at the Alexis Hotel in Las Vegas, to the strains of the song "The Impossible Dream." The mock award was presented for Windows, which had been announced two years earlier and still had not been released.

The practice of preannouncing products was widespread in the industry, though Microsoft seemed to do it more often than others, and when industry giant Microsoft preannounced a product, there was a chilling effect on the competition.

At the second hearing on November 2, Sporkin again focused on the Microsoft business practices that he had read about in *Hard Drive*. "[The authors] cite chapter and verse," the judge told Bingaman. "I want to be satisfied . . . that, in fact, the person was writing fiction," said Sporkin.

Bingaman's staff was aggressively examining Microsoft's proposed purchase of Intuit, in part by soliciting responses to the merger from banks and the computer industry. Among those contacted was Silicon Valley technology lawyer Gary Reback. He was known to Bingaman's staff because of briefs he had filed with the FTC, urging it to take action against Microsoft.

What separated Reback, 45, a native of Knoxville, Tennessee, from other attorneys in the case was his technical background. He had worked his way through Yale as a computer programmer, received his law degree from Stanford, and later joined the Palo Alto firm of Wilson, Sonsini, Goodrich & Rosati, one of the biggest in the Silicon Valley, with more than 300 lawyers. Its founder, Larry Sonsini, was an influential member of Novell's board.

At the time Microsoft announced it was buying Intuit, Reback was defending Borland in the copyright suit that had been brought against the company by Lotus. When Bingaman's staff asked Reback if he wanted to weigh in on the Intuit merger, he agreed, and began by asking some of Microsoft's competitors if they wanted to finance a white paper opposing the merger, which was filed with the Justice Department in November.

There was widespread speculation in the industry press at the time that Sybase helped fund Reback's white paper, though the company denied it. Sybase, which produced database software for tracking corporate information, was starting to lose market share to Microsoft and saw the Intuit merger as a giant nail in its coffin. "Sybase freaked out when Microsoft announced it would buy Intuit, and secretly paid Gary," said a well-known industry executive who had firsthand knowledge of the payment.

As part of the Intuit deal, Microsoft announced that Novell would buy Money, Microsoft's finance software program that trailed in market share far behind Intuit's Quicken. Microsoft knew the merger with Intuit would never pass legal muster if it held on to both products. Gates convinced Novell CEO Bob Frankenberg to take Money off Microsoft's hands. Frankenberg, who had replaced Ray Noorda when he resigned after his 70th birthday, had met secretly with Gates in the summer of 1994 to patch up differences between the two companies. Gates guaranteed Frankenberg that Microsoft would pay Novell millions of dollars if Money bombed. Once the Intuit merger was announced, however, Novell was roundly criticized for taking Money. Frankenberg looked like a patsy.

"What the hell did Novell think it was doing?" asked Philippe Kahn. "It was absolutely amazing. What Novell did was legitimize the Intuit deal, which should never have been legitimized."

In late 1994, Novell's legal counsel visited with Bingaman's staff and quietly urged them not to approve the Intuit merger. But if they did, the lawyer said, Novell wanted Money.

Kahn saw the Intuit deal as another example of Microsoft's hegemony, and of Gates's ambition to control the industry. "At the time, I felt the only thing that was going to stop the guy was his ego," Kahn said of Gates. "He's got a shitload of it. You sit down and you listen to this little prick going on about how he's going to put everybody out of business. . . . It's not right, for the industry, for the customers. . . . In an industry that is growing as fast as ours, why is nobody making money but Microsoft? Something very bizarre is going on at the top."

After writing his white paper opposing the Intuit merger, Reback went to Lake Tahoe with his family for the Christmas holidays. While there, he was contacted by a journalist who asked him about the two hearings Sporkin had held on the consent decree. At the time, Reback did not know what had taken place at the hearings, so the journalist faxed him transcripts. Reback immediately realized that the consent decree was in the hands of a judge who might actually reject it, so he cut short his Tahoe trip and rushed back to his Palo Alto office and faxed copies of the transcripts to several companies, asking if they wanted him to prepare a brief urging Sporkin to reject the settlement. Although three companies signed on, they told Reback that they feared retaliation by Microsoft and did not want to be named.

Fortune reported that the three companies were Apple, Sybase, and Sun Microsystems. But the same industry executive who had reported that Sybase had underwritten Reback's white paper on Intuit said that Novell, not Sun, paid Reback. Executives of Apple, Sybase, and Sun would neither confirm nor deny that they were involved. Novell also denied paying Reback.

Under the Tunney Act, the public could comment on the consent decree for 60 days, in this case, until October 18, 1994. By that date, only five comments had been received, none of them of any significance. But when Sporkin delayed the third hearing, which was scheduled for December, to January 20, Reback won the time to file his brief, which he did on January 10.

In obtaining documentation for his brief, Reback got help from Borland. In 1987, Microsoft had filed suit against Borland when one of its executives went to work for Kahn. Microsoft was worried that the executive would reveal trade secrets and wanted the court to restrict the executive's new duties at Borland. The court papers filed by Microsoft contained the "stick it to Philippe" note along with another one that revealed that Microsoft had preannounced a vaporware product to hold off buyers of Borland's Turbo Pascal. Obviously in 1987, Microsoft had no idea that those papers would come back to haunt it big time.

On Friday, January 20, Sporkin held the third and final hearing on the consent decree. It was exceedingly acrimonious. All of the frustration and anger that Anne Bingaman had felt since the first hearing in September boiled over. She and the judge clashed repeatedly during what turned out to be an eight-hour shouting match in a courtroom packed with lawyers, many representing Microsoft's competitors, who had come to watch the action.

Bingaman started the hearing by asking Sporkin to approve the consent decree, to which Sporkin quipped, "Will the government give me a pen to sign or can I use my own? I've got to have some role here."

She then urged Sporkin not to substitute his judgment for that of the Justice Department, which had spent considerable time investigating allegations against Microsoft. "Unfortunately," said Sporkin, "I took this role very seriously, and I got involved in this case. And that's my problem: I got too involved in this case perhaps. But there are certain things that are gnawing at me." Sporkin demanded to know why the Justice Department had not taken a tougher stand against Microsoft and more thoroughly investigated the numerous allegations.

A lot of finger pointing and table banging ensued. "I don't think this decree is in the public interest," said Sporkin, waving his finger at Bingaman. "I'm the prosecutor, you're the judge," Bingaman responded, pounding the table. "I decide what makes out a winning case, and if I don't want to file it, nobody can make me!" Sporkin accused Bingaman of "stonewalling" the court. "I'm not!" she fired back.

Much of the hearing focused on the vaporware documents that Reback had recently submitted with his brief. Sporkin felt that Microsoft had misled the court by claiming it did not have any documents regarding vaporware.

Sporkin referred to Microsoft's lawyers as LLFLS—lawyers looking for loopholes. "You can stand on your head. I cannot accept your word anymore. You have lost your credibility," Sporkin told Microsoft lawyer Richard Urowsky.

Sporkin also said that the note, which Reback had entered into evidence, about Microsoft trying to block Borland's Turbo product with vaporware was "as close to a smoking gun as you can get." To which Urowsky retorted that the practice of promoting products before they were ready for market was common in the industry. "If these documents are supposed to be a smoking gun, then there is no conceivable case to be made here." Urowsky also argued that the documents did not prove illegal conduct.

Sporkin would not let the point pass. He called the documents "conspiratorial." Replied Urowsky: "Your honor, it's called competition. It's the very heart of a free market economy." "I cannot accept your word," Sporkin shot back. "This is a trusting judge . . . but you've lost your credibility."

Before the hearing adjourned, Bingaman urged Sporkin not to accept any more submissions in the case from other parties. Answered Sporkin: "If somebody throws over the transom . . . some more documents like those that Reback gave me, I'm not going to just say 'Hey, I can't see them,' and throw them away. It would be like a police officer who gets a report of a crime and says 'I'm off duty. Go and see somebody else.' "

More submissions did come in. Andrew Schulman, the programmer and writer who had complained to the FTC about Microsoft's hidden features in Windows that developers for other companies were not told about, faxed a letter to Sporkin's chambers saying he was opposed to the decree and that he had asked his publisher to send the judge a copy of his latest book, *Unauthorized Windows.*

On February 13, Sporkin received a startling three-page letter from Apple's general counsel, Edward Stead, claiming that Gates, that very day, had had a meeting with Apple CEO Michael Spindler during which Gates said that Microsoft might stop developing applications for the Macintosh computer if Apple continued to develop a product called Open-Doc. "Since Microsoft is the largest supplier of software applications for the Macintosh, this threat was a serious one," Stead wrote. The letter also claimed that in 1994 Microsoft had threatened to withhold a beta version of Windows 95 from Apple unless it dropped its copyright suit against Microsoft.

Stead would later tell *Fortune* how helpless he had felt when he read what Gates had to say about the settlement with the Justice Department. "Bill Gates had stated publicly that the settlement wouldn't require Microsoft to change its basic ways of operating," said Stead. "And a few days after that, he was on the evening news, golfing with President Clinton on Martha's Vineyard. What were we supposed to think?"

The day after Sporkin received the Apple letter, he issued a 45-page opinion that the consent decree was not in the public interest. The federal judiciary had not handed down such a ruling since Judge Harold Green in 1982 refused to approve the consent decree breaking up AT&T until it was modified to help the Baby Bells.

"Simply telling a defendant to go forth and sin no more does little or nothing to address the unfair advantage it has already gained," Sporkin wrote. If he had approved the decree, Sporkin said, "the message would be that Microsoft is so powerful that neither the market nor the government is capable of dealing with all its monopolistic practices."

Sporkin again criticized the Justice Department for not conducting a more thorough investigation before it settled the case. "The picture that emerges from these proceedings is that the U.S. government is either incapable or unwilling to deal effectively with a potential threat to this nation's economic well-being," Sporkin wrote.

Further, the judge said, Microsoft needed to grow up. "Microsoft has done extremely well in its business in a relatively short period of time, which is a tribute both to its talented personnel and to this nation's great ethic that affords every citizen the ability to rise to the top. Microsoft, a rather new corporation, may not have matured to the position where it understands how it should act with respect to the public interest and the ethics of the marketplace."

In the aftermath of his Valentine's Day massacre of Microsoft's consent decree, Stanley Sporkin became something of a judicial folk hero to Microsoft competitors, big and small, that over the years had yearned for someone to stand up to Bill Gates and take him down a notch or two. Although most antitrust experts predicted that Microsoft and the government would prevail on appeal because Sporkin had overstepped his authority by trying to get Anne Bingaman to bring additional charges against Microsoft, for the moment, Microsoft had suffered a resounding legal setback that was reverberating through the industry and giving hope to all those who lived in the shadow of the Silicon Forest giant.

Armed with Sporkin's gutsy ruling, competitors continued to fire away at Gates and Microsoft. Novell CEO Bob Frankenberg, speaking at a computer conference in Phoenix, Arizona, said that Novell had not ruled out an antitrust lawsuit against Microsoft. "There are some potential problems with restraint of trade there," said Frankenberg, whose comments came as something of a surprise in light of the fence-mending visit he had made to Microsoft soon after succeeding Ray Noorda.

During that same conference in Phoenix, Steve Hayden, an advertising executive doing work for IBM, concluded his presentation by unbuttoning his shirt to reveal a T-shirt bearing a picture of Sporkin and the words "Our hero." The audience roared.

In early March, the issues raised by Sporkin erupted into a public war of words between Gates and Jim Manzi of Lotus. Manzi fired the first salvo in an article published by the *Wall Street Journal* on its editorial page. Manzi praised Sporkin for having the courage to stand up to Gates. "Microsoft has systematically blocked rate-of-change competition, and has actually slowed the rate of innovation in the marketplace," Manzi wrote. "When winners can parlay their success into permanent industry-slowing advantages, we must acknowledge a new form of anticompetitive behavior."

Gates counterpunched a few days later. His article, in part personal, took up about a quarter of the *Journal*'s editorial page. "It is understandable," Gates wrote, "that Mr. Manzi would prefer to measure performance in terms of competitor criticism; Lotus has not fared well with customers under Mr. Manzi's leadership. It was larger than Microsoft when Mr. Manzi became CEO, and today it is less than one-fifth of Microsoft's size." He went on to describe Manzi's complaints as "shrill," and said that complacency by Lotus, not unfair competition, had resulted in Microsoft moving in to fill the void left by Lotus when its flagship spreadsheet lost market share.

Gates also wrote at some length about the five-year antitrust probe of his company, and the decision by Sporkin to reject the final settlement:

> Microsoft has been subjected to what I believe is one of the most thorough audits of any business in modern times. It was a major distraction and cost the company tens of millions of dollars. It

was virtually unprecedented to have both the Federal Trade Commission and the Justice Department conduct separate investigations. During this time, our competitors hired plenty of lawyers, economists and other experts to "help out," and every complaint they would conjure up was put forward and investigated by the government. At the end of this exhaustive process, the government found cause for concern only with certain aspects of our licensing practices with PC manufacturers. We agreed to make some modest changes to accommodate the government's concerns not because we had done anything wrong but because by agreeing to these changes we could focus 100 percent on building great software. Although Judge Stanley Sporkin's decision to reject the agreement has provided some fireworks at the end of the process, I am confident that the consent decree will be entered.

When a journalist informed Philippe Kahn about the exchange between Gates and Manzi in the *Journal,* Kahn wrote an "open letter" to both men, which the paper also published on its editorial page. In his letter, Kahn was much more critical of Manzi than of Gates; he focused on the Lotus executive's decision to bring the Quattro Pro copyright suit against Borland. A federal appeals court had recently ruled for Borland in the case. Kahn wrote:

> Mr. Manzi, you accuse Mr. Gates of anticompetitive practices. This is very hypocritical. If anyone has used anticompetitive practices in the software industry, it is you, Mr. Manzi. Let me refresh your memory. Over four years ago, you unfairly attacked Borland by alleging copyright infringement. You knew, like all of us, that "systems" and functionality cannot be copyrighted. Nevertheless, you relentlessly tried to put our company out of business.

In contrast, Kahn was downright nice in some of his comments to Gates, though he did ask him not to "stick it" to the industry. "As you know, a lot of issues were raised recently when Judge Sporkin read an internal Microsoft memo where some of your executives expressed an intention to 'stick it to Philippe.' You can understand that it's a bit worrisome for me to be in the sights of one of the most powerful companies in the world (it's also flattering!)."

Kahn went on to praise Gates for all that Microsoft had accomplished.

> Unlike Mr. Manzi, who tried to use the legal system to gain a competitive advantage, you, Mr. Gates, competed in the marketplace—and you did a very good job of it. You deserve credit for that. You've actually done such a great job at it that today Microsoft clearly dominates the software industry. Some say that Microsoft is like a government that has been democratically elected but is now tempted to take advantage of its position of power. Mr. Gates, prove these critics wrong. Use your position of leadership to foster industry practices that will help the software industry grow to its next stage of maturity, assuring our customers that the software industry will remain fair and competitive for decades to come.

In what seemed to be an astonishing turnabout, between the lines of his letter Kahn was making a peace offering of sorts to his old nemesis. Kahn's new company, Starfish, was developing products to run on Windows 95, and some cooperation was in order. Gates had already extended a peace offering when he sent Kahn an e-mail when he resigned as Borland's CEO, saying he hoped Microsoft and Starfish could enjoy a good working relationship.

In early March, both Microsoft and the Justice Department asked the U.S. Court of Appeals in Washington, D.C., to disqualify Sporkin and to reassign the consent decree. In her brief, Bingaman said that Sporkin had overstepped his authority and that his decision was "an invitation to anarchy." She said that Sporkin had acted contrary to the Tunney Act when he questioned the Justice Department's decisions on the kind of case to bring against Microsoft. "The United States concluded that Microsoft was engaging in particular unlawful practices that diminished the prospects for innovation and competition," she wrote. "It negotiated a decree for complete and prompt termination of these practices."

If the appeals court did not step in and remove Sporkin from the case, Bingaman said, the only recourse for the department would be to file suit against Microsoft "with all the irretrievable costs and uncertainty of result that such a course would entail. Without immediate appeal, the parties would return to their adversarial roles."

In its appeal brief, Microsoft argued that Sporkin was "fixated" on the book *Hard Drive* and improperly relied on allegations raised therein to reject the consent decree. The brief was unusually personal. "From the very outset," the brief read, "Judge Sporkin's views about Microsoft were shaped by *Hard Drive*. It is apparent that in Judge Sporkin's mind, a book based largely on conversations with Microsoft competitors and disgruntled former employees had replaced the complaint as the yardstick with which the sufficiency of the consent decree was to be measured."

Microsoft also contended that the involvement of Gary Reback's law firm raised ethical questions. "The law firm . . . has never explained how it can act as regular counsel for Novell Inc. (and have a partner on Novell's board of directors) while at the same time directly attacking Microsoft's planned acquisition of Intuit, in which Novell has a substantial interest as the purchaser of a personal finance software product to be divested by Microsoft. That important ethical question has been simply swept under the rug by the District Court."

In sum, Microsoft urged that Sporkin be removed from any further proceedings on the consent decree. "By engaging in its own fact gathering, the District Court assumed an inquisitional role of a European magistrate, a clear basis for disqualification."

A three-judge federal appeals panel promised to expedite a hearing on the case. Later that spring, the panel took the rare step of removing Sporkin, and reassigned the consent decree. In a stinging rebuke of Sporkin, the appeals panel said it was "deeply troubled" and "distressed" at his handling of the case. The court added that Sporkin did not have the authority to second-guess the Justice Department on the kind of case it chose to bring against Microsoft. And it chastised Sporkin for allowing the three computer companies that had bankrolled Reback's brief to go unnamed. The court said it did not know of any case where someone was allowed to bring action against a defendant anonymously. "Such proceedings would, as Microsoft argues, seriously implicate due process," adding that Sporkin "did not fulfill his duty to consider the impact of anonymity on the public's interest in knowing the identities of the participants, nor did he consider the possible unfairness to Microsoft."

Sporkin also came under criticism for relying on the book *Hard Drive*, an action which the appeals court found had "contaminated" the hearing process. "The book's allegations are, of course, not evidence on which a judge is entitled to rely," the court wrote. It also said that the Tunney Act did not permit a judge to order the Justice Department to conduct a new investigation, and that Sporkin was misguided in accusing the Justice Department of not filing the strongest case possible against Microsoft. "Remedies which appear less than vigorous may well reflect an underlying weakness in the government's case."

In an unsigned section of the opinion, the court noted that Sporkin had made "several comments during the proceedings which evidenced his distrust of Microsoft's lawyers and his generally poor view of Microsoft's practices."

The case was reassigned to U.S. District Judge Thomas Penfield Jackson. On August 21, 1995, Jackson held the first and only hearing on the decree. Jackson began the proceedings by saying, "This hearing will be short and sweet, ladies and gentlemen. I have my own pen." A few moments later he declared, "The decree has been entered." The case that had dragged on for more than five years was over in 17 minutes. Later in the day, on CNN's *Larry King Live*, Gates said about the settlement, "It's great to see it finally come to a close, because there were a lot of years there where we were producing a lot of documents."

Three days later, on August 24, Microsoft launched Windows 95.

During the spring of 1995, all the while the Justice Department was teamed up in court with Microsoft in the ultimately successful effort to have Sporkin removed, it continued to scrutinize the company outside the courtroom. Bingaman and her staff were hard at work investigating complaints from the big three on-line services that claimed that Microsoft would have an unfair advantage in the marketplace if it were allowed to bundle the Microsoft Network with Windows 95. At the same time, Bingaman's staff also was winding up its examination of Microsoft's planned purchase of Intuit, a deal that one industry pundit said would mean "everybody's most favorite software company being bought by everyone's least favorite software company."

The planned merger had drawn immediate fire when it had been announced in 1994 because of industry fears that Microsoft would be able to expand its already extensive reach into the emerging market of electronic commerce and on-line services. As the Justice Department began its investigation, it requested thousands of documents about the acquisition from Intuit and Microsoft. Some of those documents, in which executives of both companies discussed how the merger would eliminate competition, would give the department the ammunition it needed to block the deal.

In one document, Intuit Chairman Scott Cook described Microsoft as "Godzilla," in reference to the legendary Japanese monster that destroyed everything in its path. Cook had used the name in a memo to his board during negotiations with Microsoft in 1994. He wrote that Intuit's "future vision is both vulnerable to and would benefit from Godzilla's strengths." A merger with Microsoft, Cook went on to say, would give banks one clear choice of software product. "Our combination gives [financial institutions] one clear option, eliminating a bloody share war. . . . That, in turn, enriches the terms of the trade we can negotiate" with the institutions. Cook's point was that since Microsoft and Intuit already dominated the market, banks and other financial institutions would have only one place to go after the companies merged, and the software companies could set their own pricing terms.

According to another document obtained by the Justice Department, Microsoft had told Intuit that it would spend as much as $1 billion to aggressively promote Money over Quicken unless Intuit agreed to the merger. The threat was implicit in a memo written by a Microsoft executive to Gates, which explained that he had told Cook to accept the merger or else face the consequences. "I tried to tell him how much we could do with $1 billion. I tried to be nonthreatening, but let him know we would do something aggressive."

These documents and others became part of the public record when, on April 27, the Justice Department filed suit in federal court in San Francisco to stop the merger. Bingaman told reporters that the merger would stifle competition in the personal finance software business. "Allowing Microsoft to buy a dominant position in this highly concentrated market would likely result in higher prices for consumers who want to buy personal finance software, and would cause those buyers to miss out on the huge benefits from innovation," said Bingaman.

She also said that Microsoft's proposed solution of selling off its Money product to Novell would not realistically preserve competition in the marketplace. "This so-called fix just won't work," she said. "Novell simply can't replace Microsoft—

with its leading position in the personal computer software industry—in competing against an entrenched, dominant product like Intuit's Quicken."

Microsoft now had a choice: it could take its case to trial against the Justice Department, or it could walk away from the merger. After first insisting that it would fight the government tooth and nail, Microsoft realized that there were more important battles to fight down the road; and in this case, the chance of victory was doubtful. So, on Saturday, May 20, Gates announced that the merger was off. Microsoft agreed to pay Intuit $46.25 million in compensation for terminating the deal. Asked by reporters how the failed merger would affect Microsoft's future business strategy, Gates replied sarcastically, "The way this might affect our business is that we'll probably wait at least a week or two before doing anything like this again."

Six days later, on May 26, Gates sent a memo to his executive staff that signaled he had finally set his watch to Internet time. Microsoft was about to become a very different company. In the memo, titled "The Internet Tidal Wave," Gates wrote that he believed that the Net was the single most important development in the computer industry since the IBM PC. "I have gone through several stages of increasing my views of [the Internet's] importance," he wrote. "Now I assign it the highest level of importance." It was time for Microsoft to get moving or be left behind.

Bill Gates had become increasingly paranoid about Netscape, a company that by late spring of 1995 had only 200 employees, had posted a loss of $2.7 million in the most recent quarter, and did not expect to show a profit until sometime in 1997. On paper, it appeared to be the kind of harmless but irritating business gnat that Microsoft otherwise might swat away nonchalantly. But in only six months more than 5 million copies of Netscape's Navigator browser had been either sold or down-loaded free off the Internet, giving Netscape an estimated 70 percent chunk of the browser market. That was the kind of market share usually reserved for only one company in the computer industry.

Netscape was hot. It was the most talked-about Internet company on the planet, and a lot of investors wanted a piece of the action. In April, Netscape sold 11 percent of its stock to five media and software companies: Times Mirror, the Hearst Cor-poration, Adobe Systems, Knight-Ridder, and TCI Technology Ventures, a unit of cable giant Tele-Communications Inc. There were rumors on Wall Street that Netscape would soon make a public offering.

Paul Maritz, a member of Microsoft's inner circle who ad-vised Gates, had posted his own Internet memo in February, titled "Netscape as Netware," in which he warned that Netscape could end up dominating the Internet much as No-vell did the networking market. No one had to remind Gates that heading his list of Microsoft's greatest mistakes was losing the networking market to Novell. Novell set the standard, not Microsoft. Now Netscape, not Microsoft, was looking to set an Internet standard. And that was unacceptable to Gates, who resorted to the familiar strategy he had used just recently with Intuit: If you can't beat a company, buy it.

When Netscape came calling on Microsoft to request Win-dows 95 code in advance of the scheduled August launch date so it could include certain features in its browser and server software, it gave Gates the opening he was looking for. He talked to Jim Barksdale, who had joined Netscape in January as its chief operating officer, about a possible buyout. When that didn't work, Gates proposed that Microsoft buy a 20 per-cent stake in the company and a seat on its board of directors. "Clearly, he understood our plans from day one," Barksdale would say later. "But we had read the book on Microsoft, so we said no thanks." Netscape founder Jim Clark added that the offer was nothing more than an attempt by Microsoft to try to control the Internet, as it did the desktop. "It's not in Microsoft's bones to cooperate with other companies," he said.

At Microsoft, attitudes about the Internet were considerably different from those a year earlier when the company held its first Internet retreat at the Shumway Mansion. As programmers came off the Windows development team, they were put to work on Microsoft's browser, Internet Explorer, which was intended to be available as an add-on to Windows 95. Subscribers of the Microsoft Network also would be able to download the browser.

Gates put Maritz in charge of the company's Internet efforts. "We went through all the stages—denial, grief, anger, acceptance. Then we got on the job," Maritz would later tell *Newsweek*.

Gates's Internet Tidal Wave memo was purposefully leaked to the press as an announcement to the industry that Microsoft was not going to be left behind, according to a Microsoft source. "Frankly, I think Bill was getting tired of all the stories about Netscape," said the source. "I don't know who actually leaked the memo, but it was done with Bill's knowledge."

It had taken Gates weeks to draft the multipage, single-spaced memo. It began by confirming his belief that the Internet was going to set the course of the industry for the foreseeable future.

> I want to make clear that our focus on the Internet is critical to every part of our business. The Internet is the most important single development to come along since the IBM PC was introduced in 1981. It is even more important than the arrival of graphical user interface (GUI). The PC analogy is apt for many reasons. The PC wasn't perfect. Aspects of the PC were arbitrary or even poor. However, a phenomena grew up around the IBM PC that made it a key element of everything that would happen for the next 15 years. Companies that tried to fight the PC standard often had good reasons for doing so but they failed because the phenomena overcame any weakness that resisters identified.

Gates instructed his staff to begin using the Internet whenever possible, and to encourage their staffs to use it, too. He suggested possible Web sites to explore, such as Yahoo! "Also of interest are the ways our competitors are using their Web sites to present their products," Gates wrote. "I think Sun and Netscape and Lotus do some things very well. Amazingly, it is easier to find information on the Web than it is to find information on the Microsoft Corporate Network."

In a section of his memo called "Next Steps," Gates wrote: "Over the last year, a number of people have championed embracing TCP/IP, hyperlinking, HTML and building clients, tools and servers that compete on the Internet. However, we still have a lot to do. I want every product plan to try and go overboard on Internet features."

The day after Gates sent his memo, Internet evangelist Ben Slivka sent one of his own, titled "The Web Is the Next Platform." Slivka, who had been working almost around the clock on Microsoft's browser, suggested that the Web could eventually replace Windows. "I don't know if I actually believed that would happen, but I wanted to make a point," he later told *Business Week*. Slivka had been urging that Microsoft begin work on a browser for Windows 3.1. The licensing agreement with Spyglass restricted Internet Explorer to Windows 95 and Windows NT.

On June 1, Microsoft held its second off-site Internet retreat, at the Red Lion Inn in downtown Bellevue, not far from where Microsoft had set up office in January 1979 after moving from Albuquerque, New Mexico. In a short talk, Gates repeated some of the points he had made in his memo. Then Slivka talked for more than an hour. At one point, when he suggested that Microsoft consider giving away its browser on the Web, à la Netscape, Gates exploded and called him a "communist," a word he had applied a couple of years earlier to an FTC commissioner who had suggested that Microsoft share its technology with competitors.

The second retreat also focused on a hot new Internet product from Sun Microsystems called Java, which had been introduced with great hoopla on May 23 during the Sun World conference at the Moscone Center in San Francisco. Among Java's most enthusiastic fans was Netscape's Marc Andreessen, who had joined Sun CEO Scott McNealy on stage to give the product a thumbs-up.

Java was an object-oriented programming language that had been developed by Sun programmers James Gosling and Patrick Naughton for possible use in interactive TV set-top boxes. They had called it Oak. Sun hoped to get the bid to work with Time Warner on its Full Service Network in Orlando, Florida, but the cable company had picked Sun's crosstown rival Silicon Graphics for that experiment, and Oak seemed to have little future. Then Bill Joy, Sun's co-founder, saved the day. He realized that Oak could be adapted for the Internet, and the job was given to Naughton and Gosling. Oak was renamed Java in January 1995.

Java's features made it delightfully easy to jazz up a Web page, to make it come alive with audio and visual effects. But most threatening to Microsoft was that programs written in Java could run on almost any computer, not just machines with Windows. At Sun's Smallworks research lab in Aspen, Colorado, Bill Joy was already working on an operating system built around Java that would end the need for Windows on the PC. More intimidating to Microsoft was that Sun was planning to make the Java source code free over the Net so that programmers could develop Java-based applications. In August, Netscape would become Java's first corporate customer. It planned to use Java in the next version of its Navigator browser, which was due out in late summer or early fall.

Initially, however, Microsoft considered Java a language tool, not a significant application that would be of value to most computer users. When most of the 40 or so company executives got their first peek at Java during the June 1 off-site retreat, there was no rush to jump on the bandwagon. James Allard, who had written the Internet memo in January 1994, told *Business Week:* "Like the early reaction to my memo, the reaction [to Java] was lukewarm."

Although Gates had committed Microsoft to ride the Internet tidal wave, his most immediate concern was getting the much-delayed Windows 95 out the door and onto millions of computers. But his old friends at the Justice Department were making his life miserable once again. They were on another antitrust fishing trip. This time, the department was concerned that Microsoft would have an unfair advantage over the other on-line services by bundling the Microsoft Network with Windows 95.

America Online, Prodigy, and CompuServe had been complaining publicly since mid-1994, but they got a chance to go on record when Justice Department lawyers spoke with executives of the three companies during its probe of the Intuit merger. In early June, the department announced that it had issued a subpoena against Microsoft, ordering it to turn over documents that might be relevant to its investigation of the bundling of MSN with Windows 95. It also sent out a sweeping request for documents from the on-line services and from companies that planned to provide content on the Microsoft network.

But Gates had had enough. Microsoft turned the tables on Bingaman by asking a federal judge in New York to block the subpoena; the company claimed that it was the victim of a "campaign of harassment by the Justice Department." Its 12-page petition described as "ridiculous" the concerns that Microsoft would have an unfair advantage. "When America Online, CompuServe, and Prodigy have millions of subscribers and MSN has zero, it seems a stretch for the DOJ to assert any probability of Microsoft achieving such a monopoly."

The petition further accused the Justice Department of having an "insatiable appetite" for investigating Microsoft's every venture. "If it appears that something may provide Microsoft with an advantage over its competitors—no matter how mundane and obviously legitimate that advantage may be—it is presumptively regarded by the DOJ as a proper subject for investigation."

In late June, the *Wall Street Journal* reported that the Justice Department in its latest records request had asked Microsoft to provide all documents concerning "the future of computers and computer technology." The report prompted Senate majority leader Bob Dole to tell reporters, "If this report is accurate, DOJ is out of control." He accused the department of being overzealous in its investigation of Microsoft. "A company develops a new product, a product consumers want. But now the government steps in and is in effect attempting to dictate the terms on which that product can be marketed and sold," said Dole. "Pinch me, but I thought we were still in America." The senator's comments were included in the Congressional Record.

The Justice Department responded to Microsoft's petition on July 13, asserting that Microsoft's marketing and sales strategy for its on-line service might be in violation of the Sherman Antitrust Act. In a brief filed with the New York court, department lawyers said that Microsoft was taking advantage of its de facto monopoly in one market (operating systems) to gain an edge over competitors in the growing market for electronic information and services, and asked the court to order Microsoft into negotiations to comply with the government's demand for additional documents. Finally, it requested that the court give Microsoft 10 days to turn over the documents unless it immediately began good-faith negotiations.

While the lawyers slugged it out in court, it was damn the subpoenas and full speed ahead in Redmond, where the biggest product launch in the history of the computer industry was planned for August 24.

Shortly after noon on Friday, July 14, a pickup truck pulled up alongside the building on Microsoft's campus where the team of programmers developing Windows had worked for what seemed like an eternity of seven-day weeks and days that began early and often ended after midnight. The truck was filled with 180 bottles of iced Dom Perignon and several cases of whipped cream. This was the day that Windows 95 went "golden." No more changes would be made in the 15 million lines of computer code before it shipped. The product that Microsoft was banking on to help maintain its dominance of the desktop was finished.

"It was a death march, especially at the last," Rick Waddell, who headed a team of programmers that created the Windows 95 networking code, would later tell a reporter. He said he had sat down with his wife before the project began and tried to explain the long days ahead. "It was a chance to shape the way computers will be used, to make an impact on the way people live. If that doesn't give you a rush, you're in the wrong business."

Finally, it was time to celebrate, with a little thank-you gift from Gates himself. Whatever those 180 bottles cost, it was a tiny drop in the bucket for Gates. Earlier in the month, *Forbes* had named him the world's richest person, with $12.9 billion. His fortune had increased nearly $5 billion in the past year, enough to move his friend Warren Buffett to second on the list, with $10.7 billion.

The party began without Gates. "You give 450 geeks champagne and whipped cream and it's an ugly sight," said Waddell. "Before long, we were going through other buildings, pulling people out. It all started around 1:00 P.M. and by 7:00 P.M. we were swimming in the fountains."

Microsoft had more reason to celebrate three weeks later, on August 8, when the Justice Department announced that it would not pursue an antitrust action against the company before the launch of Windows 95. Bingaman had blinked. But she had also made it clear that the investigation had not ended, and that the department might still decide to take action against Microsoft at a later date over the MSN bundling issue.

The department had been heavily lobbied in the days before the announcement by Microsoft allies who wrote to Bingaman that any delay in the launch of Windows 95 would be devastating to the software market, where many companies had made huge investments in developing applications for Windows 95. Firms such as CompUSA, Egghead, Symantech, and Corel urged the department to allow the launch to go forth as planned. "Any interference in the shipment of Windows 95 will not only adversely impact business in the United States, but also will have a worldwide impact," wrote Michael Cowpland, chief executive of Corel, a Canadian computer graphics company. Gordon Eubanks, chief executive of Symantec, warned of "extraordinary market disruption" if the launch was delayed. Microsoft later admitted that it had encouraged the firms to write letters asking the Justice Department not to file suit to stop the launch.

Later in the day after the Justice Department said it would not take action before the Windows 95 launch date, Microsoft sent an e-mail to its employees admonishing them not to gloat about the victory, but to respond, if asked, that they were happy with the decision and had believed all along that Microsoft had done nothing wrong by including its on-line service with Windows 95.

Less than 24 hours later, the attention of the computer industry shifted some 900 miles south to Mountain View, California, where Netscape Communications Corporation had gone public in one of the most stunning debuts in stock market history. In just a few hours of Wall Street hysteria, the year-old company, with $16.6 million in revenue for the first half of 1995, was valued at more than $3 billion, making instant paper millionaires of many of its employees. In contrast, it had taken

General Dynamics Corporation 43 years to become a corporation worth $2.7 billion. Netscape did it in a day, and its main product, Mosaic, was available free of charge.

The public offering had been one of the most anticipated ever. In the weeks before the stock traded on Wall Street for the first time, investors from around the globe had been frantically calling Netscape and its underwriters asking how they could buy shares in the company. Robert Strawbridge, a summer intern at Hambrecht & Quist, one of the underwriters, was in charge of emptying the San Francisco's company voice mail each day. "People were desperate," he told the *Wall Street Journal.* "The calls would come in from people saying, 'I've never opened an account before, but this one I have to own. Can someone please, please, please call me back?' " It was the same kind of chaos over at Netscape, where a finance department receptionist had her hands full fielding calls from would-be stockholders.

Before the trading began, demand for Netscape was so high that the company and its underwriters increased the initial offering from 3.5 million to 5 million shares and doubled the offering price from $14 to $28.

When the stock officially opened, the first trade went for $71 a share, more than one and a half times the initial offering price. The stock climbed quickly to a high of $75 a share before cooling off and closing at $58.25. It had chalked up a 108 percent gain, the third biggest one-day jump in Wall Street history. Jim Clark's 9.7 million shares were worth $565 million. Marc Andreessen's 720,000 shares were worth $58.3 million. Not a bad profit for 16 months of work. Four months after going public, Netscape stock would soar to an astounding $171 a share. Overnight, Clark was a billionaire. Microsoft was 12 years old before Gates reached billionaire status.

At Netscape's offices on the morning of the initial public offering, Clark had ordered an espresso cart and free bagels and pastries, but it was mostly work as usual, because programmers were rushing to complete Navigator 2.0. There was no time to rest on laurels. As Microsoft knew and Netscape was about to learn, it was a lot easier getting to the top than staying there.

Coincidentally, the day of the Windows 95 coming-out party on August 24, 1995, was the anniversary of the eruption of Vesuvius in A.D. 79, and the advertising blitz that had erupted from Microsoft prior to the big event was nearly as choking as the ash from the famous volcano. Microsoft's marketing team had put together a brilliant campaign and carried it out to perfection. The entire world was talking about Windows 95 by launch day, and the hottest ticket was to the invitation-only party at Microsoft's campus in Redmond. Lee Gomes, a writer for the *San Jose Mercury News,* described it as "how the Ten Commandments would have been launched, if only God had had Bill Gates's money."

Along the midway, an encampment of tents was filled with technology companies showing off their latest products—developed for Windows 95, of course. Even Philippe Kahn was there, demonstrating the latest version of SideKick for Windows 95, developed by his new company, Starfish. When his old "pal" Gates came by, they had a lengthy conversation. "It was strange to see the richest man in the world come to talk with a software guy," said Kahn, who had never been impressed with Gates's technical knowledge. "He got tripped up in the conversation and was not making much sense. It's almost like there is something he wants to prove that he can't prove. I almost felt that he was envious because he knew that what I was showing was my personal design, and that everyone was saying it was great software. I think that hurt him more than if he lost his $12 billion."

Toward evening, as Kahn was leaving the campus with his laptop, he ran into Brad Silverberg, Microsoft's vice president in charge of operating systems, including Windows. Silverberg had worked for Kahn before jumping ship to Microsoft, so there was some residual bad feeling. As they talked, a young woman who worked for Microsoft approached them. She had a poster from the Windows 95 launch and asked Kahn if he would autograph it. Kahn declined, saying he was just a software guy and didn't do that kind of thing. "I saw that Brad was surprised," said Kahn, "and I think it kind of got to him. Bill does that kind of rock-star stuff all the time. The young woman kept insisting and I kept saying no, and finally she asked Brad if he would sign it. Brad told her, 'If Philippe won't sign, how can I?' I think it was a philosophical moment for Brad."

Before they parted, Silverberg told Kahn that he hoped the two could be friends again. "He said there are few innovators, and that maybe I was the Tucker of the software business," said Kahn. "I told him I hoped I could at least pay my bills. It's funny. People are surprised when I tell them that I need to work for a living. It doesn't bother me. What I'm now sure of is that the journey is the reward, and what I really like to do is to innovate and build products and technology."

In the course of their conversation, Silverberg had told Kahn that Microsoft had purchased the rights to the Rolling Stones song "Start Me Up." The story behind the deal reveals the extent to which Microsoft was willing to go financially to make Windows 95 the most-talked-about consumer product since New Coke. Initially, Microsoft wanted to acquire the rights not only to "Start Me Up," but also to a song by the rock band R.E.M. called "The End of the World as We Know It," which released in 1987. But the talks never got as far as money. R.E.M. was not interested. The Georgia-based band turns down all requests to sell the rights to any of its songs.

Microsoft especially wanted "Start Me Up" because a key feature in Windows 95 was the Start button. It was the perfect song for an advertisement. But Mick Jagger and Keith Richards, lead singer and guitarist of the Stones, who own the rights to all the band's songs written since 1972, had never before allowed one of their songs to be used for an advertisement. Earlier Stones songs, for which Jagger and Richards do not control the copyrights, have been used in commercials and advertisements.

Microsoft approached the Stones through the company's connection with music mogul David Geffen, who was partners with Steven Spielberg and Jeffrey Katzenberg in their new movie studio, Dreamworks SKG. In March 1995, Microsoft had invested about $10 million in a 50-50 venture with the studio to create a new generation of computer games, interactive movies, and multimedia entertainment. Geffen had plenty of juice in the music industry. Early in his career he was vice president of Creative Management (now ICM), which represented groups such as Peter, Paul & Mary, the Doors, and Crosby, Stills, Nash & Young. Later, he founded Asylum Records and brought to the label Jackson Browne, the Eagles, and many other famous artists. He founded Geffen Records in 1980 and sold it to MCA 10 years later.

Although Microsoft would claim that it paid only a couple of million for "Start Me Up," in fact, it paid six times that much. According to a source with firsthand knowledge, Geffen approached Jagger through his agent and asked what it would take to buy the rights to the song. Jagger told him $12 million. "Jagger was half kidding," the source said. "But Microsoft was in a big hurry, so they took the deal, unlike anything else in the software industry, where they negotiate to death."

Whatever the price, "Start Me Up" became the theme song of the Windows 95 advertising campaign. Microsoft did not, however, use the song's refrain, "You make a grown man cry"—a judicious decision, as the tricky and time-consuming installation required by Windows 95 reduced many eager purchasers to just that state. Help lines that had been set up to assist Windows 95 customers were flooded with calls. Typical of the complaints was one from Philip, the owner of Steel City Bolt & Screw in Birmingham, Alabama. He spent some six hours on the phone over two days talking with Microsoft technicians while trying to get Windows 95 to work on his computer. "I'm ready to throw the whole thing against the wall," he told the *Wall Street Journal*. "My phone bill is going to cost me more than I paid for this."

Microsoft's much ballyhooed on-line service also had its problems. Fears that the Microsoft Network would quickly dominate the market quickly dissipated. While customers purchased Windows 95 at a record clip, few clicked on the MSN icon to subscribe to the service—and those who did found it slow and buggy. By late fall, the service had fewer than 500,000 customers. Leader America Online had more than 3.5 million. It would be another year before Microsoft reinvented MSN for the Web and got it right.

By far the most serious complaint about Windows 95 was that Microsoft programmers had deliberately rigged it so that, once installed, competing Internet browsers would not work; Windows 95 defaulted to Microsoft Explorer 1.0. "Whenever you installed Internet Explorer, it effectively destroyed the other browsers on your system. And this change was made after the beta version had come out," said Eric Schmidt, chief technology officer for Sun Microsystems. In other words, it appeared that Microsoft had added the destructive code to its browser after the final beta version had been tested publicly, but before the finished product shipped. Among the browsers that were disabled or broken by Windows 95 was Netscape Navigator.

"This was pretty serious skulduggery or whatever you want to call it," said Schmidt. "I can't tell you what the intent of these things were. I don't know what decisions Microsoft made. I don't know if they sat around and decided this or not. But, it's indicative of what happens with a de facto monopoly when your competitor [Netscape] has 10 million users. I'm not arguing maliciousness here; I'm arguing power. It's an example of the extraordinary power that Microsoft has."

Microsoft eventually acknowledged that some browsers designed for earlier versions of Windows did not work well with Windows 95, but it angrily denied that it deliberately programmed the software to disable competing browsers. Nevertheless, the Justice Department quietly began another investigation of Microsoft based on the complaints.

It had been a long 12 months for Bill Gates. He had fought the Justice Department and won, then fought it again. Tiny Netscape had come out of nowhere to shove Microsoft into the unfamiliar role of underdog. And the push to get Windows 95, the Microsoft Network, and Microsoft Explorer all out the door had been draining. Gates was exhausted. In September, he left on a two-week vacation to China with his wife and several other couples. It had not been announced publicly, nor would it be, but Melinda was pregnant. The baby was due late the following April.

The China group included Gates's father, Bill Gates Jr.; Warren Buffett and his wife; Seattle Art Museum director Mimi Neill, a Chinese art scholar; and William Gerberding, former president of the University of Washington. Also joining the entourage was an international bridge master. Gates and Buffett loved to play bridge.

On his previous trip to China, Gates had been admonished by Jiang Zemin, China's president and Communist Party boss, to come back and get to know China's history, her culture, and her people. On his second visit, Gates did just that. He and his group were the first private citizens to ride across China on the "Mao Train," named after the late Chinese leader Mao Tse-tung. During much of the train trip across the country, while others in the group took in the spectacular scenery, Gates and Buffett played bridge. The group also explored China by boat along the Yangtze River. Melinda organized various activities, including karaoke singing in the ship's ballroom. During a visit to the Great Wall, Gates tried to fly a kite, but there was not enough wind. The trip also included a visit to a McDonald's restaurant, where Buffett paid for the meal with discount coupons he had brought with him.

It was only the second real vacation Gates had taken since he and Paul Allen had founded Microsoft in 1975. The other had been to Africa in 1993, before he and Melinda were married. He made only one business stop during this trip, a quick visit to Microsoft's office in Beijing. While in the city, Gates also met with Jiang, who greeted him more warmly this time. Gates, Melinda, and Buffett posed for pictures with the leader.

Among the souvenirs Gates brought back was a nine-foot clay replica of a warrior statue that had been unearthed near the city of Xian some 20 years before. Gates planned to put the terra-cotta relic in the yard of his new home, which was still under construction.

The vacation was something of an early birthday present for Gates, who would turn 40 on October 28, a couple of weeks after he returned from China. Before leaving on the trip, Melinda had organized a birthday party for her husband at their still unfinished $50 million home on Lake Washington. Gates had hoped to move in by his 40th birthday, but construction delays had made that impossible. Some of the delays had been caused by Melinda, who wanted significant changes after she and Gates married: she wanted her own bathroom, dressing room, and a study. She also hired a different architect for some of the interior design. The remodeling had pushed back completion until the spring of 1997. (The chief appraiser for King County estimated that once the construction was finished, taxes on the 45,000-square-foot home would run about $500,000 a year.)

So it was a work in progress that Melinda turned into an 18-hole putt-putt golf course. The 80 or so guests came in costume. Bill and Melinda dressed in old-fashioned golf attire. As a surprise, Melinda had four of Bill's women friends outfitted as cheerleaders, with letter sweaters that spelled out B-I-L-L. The four included old flame Ann Winblad and Heidi Roizen of Apple, both of whom had been high school cheerleaders.

In his 16th-floor office in an aging building at 85 Broad Street in lower Manhattan, New York's financial district, the software industry's most respected and influential analyst, Rick Sherlund, was about to do the unthinkable. He was taking Microsoft's stock off Goldman Sachs's Priority Recommend buy list for the first time. The Firm, as Sherlund liked to call Goldman Sachs, had been Microsoft's underwriter when the company went public in 1986. In the years since, Microsoft's stock had never disappointed. Countless investors had grown rich by following the Firm's simple advice: buy Microsoft.

Just days before Gates's 40th birthday, the software giant had once again posted an impressive earnings report. The big boost in Windows 95 sales had propelled Microsoft's profits in the quarter that ended September 30 to $499 million, an increase of 58 percent from a year earlier. Total sales for the quarter surged to $2.02 billion, a 62 percent increase. Microsoft's quarterly profit of 78 cents per share had handily beat Wall Street estimates of about 70 cents. Since Windows 95 hit the market on August 24, an estimated 7 million copies had been sold, far above the predictions of industry analysts. Dataquest, a San Jose research firm, had recently announced that Microsoft had pushed its share of the $3 billion suites market to an astonishing 90 percent, leaving competitors Novell and Lotus with just 5.5 percent and 4.6 percent, respectively. And Microsoft's lead in this area was expected to accelerate, since it was the only software company shipping a suites product that ran on Windows 95.

Microsoft was riding high as usual. But Sherlund was taking the long view, and he was concerned. Even though Gates

had been preaching in memos that Microsoft had gotten religion about the Internet, his company had yet to publicly announce a strategy for competing with Sun, Oracle, Netscape,
and other companies that had embraced the Internet earlier.
Thus, on Thursday morning, November 16, 1995, Sherlund
lowered the Firm's rating on Microsoft stock, which had been
selling for around $90 a share. And when Sherlund talked, Wall
Street listened. He was ranked the number-one analyst by *Institutional Investor* magazine and was the acknowledged expert
in a 15-company group that included all the top software companies. The market responded immediately: the company's
share price plunged 5 percent, which represented a $6 billion
loss in Microsoft's market value.

Less than a month later, on December 7, Bill Gates would
give the most important speech of his life to reporters and
analysts, laying out Microsoft's Internet strategy and putting
Netscape and other rivals on notice that they had awakened "a
sleeping giant." At the time, it appeared that Microsoft had
hastily conceived its Internet strategy in response to the negative publicity following Sherlund's November pronounce-
ment. In fact, long before Sherlund lowered the boom, Microsoft was formulating its strategy, hoping to have it ready in
time for Gates to make the big announcement on December 7.
Even the "sleeping giant" remark was scripted to sound like a
spur-of-the-moment thought.

But several pieces of the Internet puzzle had to fall into
place before Microsoft could make its move. On November 16,
the same day Sherlund sounded the alarm about Microsoft,
Mike Tyrrell, executive vice president of business development
for Spyglass, was meeting with Microsoft's Thomas Reardon
and John Ludwig in Redmond. Reardon was still program
manager for Microsoft's browser development group. Ludwig
had been promoted from general manager of the Windows 95
group to one of the vice president spots. Over the next couple
of days, they hammered out another licensing deal for Mosaic.

The negotiations had started earlier in the summer, after Reardon, James Allard, and others had convinced Gates that Microsoft needed to build a browser for Windows 3.1 and the Mac. "We had been telling Microsoft all year that they needed to develop a multiplatform code base," said Tyrrell. "With Reardon and Allard and others at their level, we were simply preaching to the choir. And they were preaching inside Microsoft that a browser for Windows 3.1 and a browser for the Mac were paramount if Microsoft was going to stop the Netscape avalanche."

The reasons were obvious. Windows 3.1 was the most popular operating system in the world, installed on as many as 100 million computers. The Mac had millions of users, too. Netscape had a browser that worked on both Windows 3.1 and the Mac. Microsoft did not. The licensing agreement that Microsoft had negotiated with Spyglass in 1994 allowed it to use the Mosaic code base only to develop the Microsoft Explorer browser for Windows 95 and for Windows NT, meaning that if Microsoft wanted to modify its browser to work on Windows 3.1 and the Mac, it needed a new licensing agreement with Spyglass.

During the spring and summer of 1995, Microsoft had watched helplessly as Netscape grabbed a bigger and bigger share of the browser market, convincing top executives at Microsoft that the company needed to build a cross-platform browser. "Microsoft is a paranoid company," said Tyrrell. "And they were paranoid about Netscape. Guys like Allard and Reardon were respectful of what Netscape had accomplished. They would fight them tooth and nail, but they respected what Netscape had done. It's just that when Microsoft finally decided they had had enough, Microsoft had a lot more firepower to draw from."

Microsoft had refused to pay Spyglass royalties in its 1994 licensing agreement for Mosaic—it had paid Spyglass only a flat fee of $2 million. Microsoft tried the same tack again. But

Tyrrell stood his ground, aware that his bargaining position was strong. Microsoft had to give in. It agreed to pay Spyglass something less than $1 per copy for every browser Microsoft sold for the Mac and Windows 3.1. But it did succeed in negotiating a royalty cap. Further, Spyglass was prohibited from revealing that it was getting royalty payments from Microsoft.

Once the preliminary details of an agreement were worked out at the November meetings, the two companies exchanged drafts for the next couple of weeks. The final agreement was signed at the Boston law firm representing Spyglass on the afternoon of December 6, the eve of Microsoft's big Internet announcement. Tyrrell then jumped on a plane at Logan International Airport and headed to Seattle with Spyglass founder Tim Krauskopf. They wanted to be part of history.

The Spyglass deal was in the bag, but time was running out for Microsoft to complete a licensing agreement with Sun for its all-world Java product. Publicly, Gates was still bad-mouthing Java, even though he had authorized his staff to license the product from Sun before he stepped to the microphone on December 7. Gates was hedging his bets, just in case Java became an industry standard. He had recently told *Business Week,* when asked about Java, "What's new about Java versus other programming languages? Why is *Business Week* writing about Java? Just having another computer language doesn't change the dynamics of any of these things." As an alternative to Java, Microsoft was pushing its own Web programming language, Visual Basic. In addition, Blackbird, containing the proprietary tools that Microsoft had created for its on-line network, was being reworked for the Web.

Sun had announced in San Francisco in May that it planned to license Java to Netscape. Subsequently, it completed licensing agreements with several other companies, including Oracle. "Of all the strategies that we thought about for Java, one involving Microsoft adopting Java was not even on the list," said Eric Schmidt, Sun's chief technology officer. But there had been some discussion at Sun about trying to convince Microsoft to license Java; at one point, Schmidt and Bill Joy considered flying to Redmond to talk with Gates. But the idea was nixed. "We decided to do that later in the cycle," said Schmidt. "In other words, we would solidify our position with Netscape and other partners like Oracle, which is what we did."

The first contact between Sun and Microsoft about Java came on a cold winter morning in early November at Princeton University. Schmidt was a graduate of Princeton; so was Nathan Myhrvold, Microsoft's technology guru. By coincidence, both were supposed to be at Princeton on Friday, November 10. Myhrvold was speaking at an alumni event, and Schmidt was there to review the computer science program. Schmidt's secretary called Myhrvold's secretary to find out which hotel Myhrvold was staying in. Schmidt then phoned Myhrvold's room on Thursday night and left a message. Myhrvold, who did not arrive until 1:00 A.M., called Schmidt early the next morning. Schmidt said he thought it was time that Microsoft woke up and smelled the Java. The two agreed to meet in a lecture room called McCosh 10 at the university, where Myhrvold was supposed to make his speech. They talked for more than an hour about Java.

"I was in sales mode," said Schmidt. "I told him Microsoft should license Java. Nathan had been impressively briefed. He knew everything there was to know about Java. I didn't need to explain anything to him. Microsoft had clearly done a full evaluation of this situation. They had independently thought through what options they had . . . Nathan was extremely focused on Netscape. He knew a great deal about a technology called Livescript, which Netscape had just acquired." (Livescript would be later renamed JavaScript.)

It was agreed at the Princeton meeting that Myhrvold would brief Gates and Paul Maritz on the content of the discussion. On Monday morning the following week, Schmidt got a call from Roger Heinen, Microsoft's vice president for languages, who worked for Maritz. Heinen and Schmidt knew each other from their days in the Silicon Valley, when Heinen was Apple's vice president in charge of the Mac operating system. "We want to license Java," Heinen told Schmidt. "Send us your contracts."

Sun delayed sending anything to Microsoft for about a week. With sensitive contract information about to be turned over to Sun's number-one enemy, company executives wanted to think everything through thoroughly. Finally, Sun sent a licensing team to Redmond with contracts in hand. At least one member of the team would remain until the deal was done. Several days later, on Monday, December 4, Heinen flew to Sun's headquarters in Mountain View, California. It was the first real meeting about Java between the two companies at the executive level.

"What's your price?" Heinen asked. Sun named a figure, and Microsoft made a counteroffer the next day, Tuesday. Time was running out. Microsoft had to have the contract signed before the December 7 show in Seattle. Like Spyglass, Sun was in a good bargaining position. Microsoft had a serious deadline problem. "They wanted this deal badly," said Schmidt. "We thought we could do a deal that was very favorable to us and to our shareholders, on terms that we could live with, given the timing. And Microsoft seemed happy with that."

On Wednesday, December 6, the two sides had a draft agreement to show to the lawyers. Schmidt phoned his boss, Sun CEO Scott McNealy, who was in New York City at the time, and told him: "Look, Scott, I'm really going to do this deal. You understand the implications, right? It's a huge deal for Sun, a huge deal for Java, a huge deal for the industry, by any measure." McNealy told Schmidt that he understood, and asked him to call him at his hotel room when the deal was done, no matter how late.

Schmidt had to be in Aspen for a talk he was supposed to deliver the next morning, the same day Gates was to make his speech, so that afternoon, he drove to the San Francisco Airport to catch the 4:00 P.M. United flight to Denver, with a connecting flight to Aspen. As he was walking through the airport, his cell phone rang. It was Paul Maritz at Microsoft, wanting to verify that some language Microsoft wanted remained in the contract. "At this point," said Schmidt, "we had given up trying to get any kind of press release ready for Bill's announcement the next morning. We were just trying to get an agreement signed."

Schmidt's plan, once in Aspen, was to go immediately to Bill Joy's house, where he could use a fax machine to get the final draft of the contract from Microsoft. But when Schmidt arrived in Denver, he learned that his connecting flight to Aspen had been delayed. At about 9:00 P.M. Denver time, 8:00 P.M. in Seattle, he frantically phoned Heinen in Redmond to tell him that he didn't have access to a fax machine and had no way to get the final draft of the contract for review. Just when Schmidt had decided to take a van to Aspen—a five-hour trip—the plane was repaired. Schmidt arrived in Aspen about 11:00 P.M. and went directly to Joy's home.

Schmidt and Heinen exchanged a few more drafts of the contract by fax, each side making minor wording changes. The agreement was finally signed at midnight, Aspen time, and Schmidt immediately phoned McNealy from Joy's house. "We did it!" he shouted. "It's signed. They're going to announce it tomorrow morning." "Great," said McNealy. "Now I want to go back to sleep." It was 2:00 A.M. in New York.

The next morning, Schmidt called Jim Barksdale at Netscape to inform him that Sun had licensed Java to Microsoft. Barksdale would tell reporters later that day that he was pleased, since it was an endorsement of Netscape's Internet strategy. Schmidt next called Steve Case, president of America Online. Case had been talking to Sun about licensing

Java, too. "I wanted him to know this did not make Java any less valuable for AOL," said Schmidt.

"It had been a very special week for Sun," said Schmidt. "This was a very big deal for us. . . . We knew what we were getting ourselves into. We understood that we were dealing with Microsoft. We had had some experience with them in the past that had not been very good. But I felt confident we had made the right decision. . . . On the downside, Microsoft was clearly behind, which was an opportunity for other companies to get ahead. By enabling Microsoft to better compete, we had effectively closed that window of opportunity for those other companies. We gave Microsoft some very important keys to the castle. But in our defense, we saw this as good for Java. It was better to work with Microsoft than not. And eventually they would have built a Java clone. We had heard rumors that one was already in the works."

For much of the two weeks before what was being billed as Microsoft's Internet Strategy Workshop on December 7, Bill Gates had been on a book tour for *The Road Ahead,* which had been published in late November, a year behind schedule. On the cover was a picture of Gates, hands in pockets, standing on an unfinished two-lane highway that stretched into the distance behind him. The picture was taken by celebrity photographer Annie Leibovitz on an unfinished section of highway near the remote eastern Washington town of Connell. Gates and Leibovitz were flown to the site by helicopter one day in the summer of 1994. Stripes had been painted down the middle of the highway just for the photo shoot.

One of Gates's first stops on the book tour was New York, where he appeared on *Late Night* with David Letterman. Gates drew huge crowds wherever he spoke on his tour. At Georgetown University, demand was so great that students had to enter a raffle for the 700 or so available seats. The National Press Club, too, was sold out, for the first time since the actress Sharon Stone appeared there.

On Tuesday, December 5, just two days before his talk in Seattle, the book tour took Gates to San Francisco, where he engaged reporters in a lively discussion about the Internet. "It's kind of a neat thing to have the Internet exploding, and to have this gold rush atmosphere," said Gates. But he bristled when someone suggested that Microsoft had been late arriving at the Internet party. "Who knew on this date that the Internet would be as big as it is?" retorted Gates. "If you can find him, crown him."

From San Francisco, Gates returned to Seattle to begin final preparations for his speech. At 8:00 P.M. Wednesday, he and other executives gathered at an auditorium at the Seattle Center in the shadow of Seattle's landmark Space Needle for a dress rehearsal. Gates would later tell a reporter that it was an eight-cheeseburger night.

The next morning, after only a couple of hours of sleep, Gates climbed out of bed, showered, put on his customary slacks and open-neck shirt, got into his Lexus, and headed across the Lake Washington floating bridge to the Seattle Center. There had been no time for breakfast. It was time to answer the critics. No one kicked sand in Gates's face and got away with it. After all, he had the biggest, most powerful, and most feared software company on the planet, and it was now ready to join the fray, powered by unlimited resources and talent.

As he took the stage on that morning of December 7 before hundreds of industry analysts and reporters, Gates wasted no time making sure that everyone in the audience knew the significance of that date in history. He recalled the famous words of Admiral Yamamoto after the Japanese Imperial Navy launched its surprise Sunday morning attack on Pearl Harbor, sinking 21 American ships, destroying 185 planes, and killing more than 200 servicemen: "I'm afraid all we have done is to awaken a sleeping giant." Microsoft and the computer industry, Gates said, had entered a second PC revolution—this one to be fought over the Internet.

Microsoft, he promised, would immediately begin a major push to win a larger share of the browser market. He revealed that the company had completed a new licensing agreement with Spyglass and would develop a browser for Windows 3.1 and the Mac, and that it had also licensed its browser to CompuServe. The audience stirred noticeably when he said that Microsoft's browser would be given away for free. Eventually, he said, it would be incorporated into the Windows operating system. He also said that the Microsoft Network would be redesigned as a Web site, rather than a stand-alone service, something James Allard had recommended a year earlier.

The speech/workshop lasted seven hours, with Gates and other company executives delivering a point-by-point presentation of how they were going to remake the company and set it and its nearly 20,000 workers on a new direction. The outline of the comprehensive overhaul of the most successful software company of all time surprised many in the audience. "I wasn't expecting them to come out so aggressively," said Craig McCallum, vice president of finance and business development for CompuServe. But Chris LeTocq, an analyst for the Dataquest market research firm, spoke for many when he told a reporter, "Somebody has been playing in the pit bull's backyard, and guess what? The pit bull has teeth."

During the lunch break, Microsoft treasurer Greg Maffei, a cell phone up to his ear, had walked up to Paul Maritz and told him, "Netscape's down $30." "Good," replied Maritz, a sly smile spreading across his face. A few seats away, another Microsoft executive who had overheard Maffei murmured, "That's not good enough."

By the end of the day on Wall Street, Netscape's stock had dropped $28.75, to close at $132.50. Microsoft's stock had dropped 12.5 cents, closing at $90.50.

On the stage with Gates while he was making his opening address were Mike Tyrrell and Tim Krauskopf of Spyglass, sitting between Brad Silverberg and John Ludwig. Spyglass had gone public earlier in the year. The announcement that Microsoft had completed another licensing agreement with Spyglass was a significant event for Spyglass. Then Gates dropped his bombshell that Microsoft would give away its browser. "Oh my God!" Tyrrell said to himself. He leaned forward in his chair and exchanged shocked looks with Krauskopf.

"I'm sitting there and I literally take the contract with Microsoft out of my briefcase and I'm reading sections of it between my legs and Bill is talking," said Tyrrell. "I instantly had this fear of what it all meant. We had never thought about Microsoft giving [the browser] away for free. What did that mean for Spyglass? It really didn't mean anything, but it was a very, very, very complicated contract with all sorts of definitions for different types of distribution, and I needed to make sure that, given all the money we had paid our lawyers, . . . we had a contract that would protect our interest no matter what Microsoft did."

No wonder Tyrrell didn't know anything about it: Gates and Maritz had decided only that morning to go along with a recommendation from the browser development group to give away Microsoft Explorer for free, said a source. It had been discussed for days, but the final decision had not been made until that morning. Sitting there on the stage, it suddenly made much more sense to Tyrrell why Microsoft, during the waning days of negotiations with Spyglass, had insisted on a royalty cap.

The next morning, as he drove to the Seattle-Tacoma International Airport for his flight back to Boston, Tyrrell was pumped over what he had heard the day before. "We had been fully immersed in the Internet for the last two years—living, breathing, sleeping, eating the Internet, and the Web, 24 hours a day, 10 days a week," he said. "After hearing Gates lay out their strategy and showing this incredible corporate commitment to the Internet, I was a true believer. This was a war Microsoft was going to win." Tyrrell picked up his cell phone, called his broker, and placed a sizable order for Microsoft stock.

EPILOGUE

It was all very hush-hush. No one was supposed to know that the very pregnant woman who quietly checked into Bellevue's Overlake Hospital under an assumed name in late April 1996 was the wife of the richest person in the world. William Henry Gates III was about to become a father, and this was one event that he did not want the world to know about.

Days earlier, some of the security people who guarded the Gates's home had met with security officers at Overlake Hospital to work out procedures for Melinda Gates's stay in the hospital, from the moment she arrived until she left. She would of course have a private room, with only one nurse to monitor her before delivery and another to take care of her afterward. Both were sworn to secrecy. No one else was to know, not even the nursing supervisors in the maternity ward. "I worked three shifts before I ever learned Melinda was in the hospital. That's how tight security was," said one nursing supervisor. Although she never saw any security people, they were there, out of sight.

At 6:11 P.M. on Friday, April 26, with her husband at her side, Melinda French Gates gave birth to their first child, a girl. They had already picked out a name: Jennifer Katharine Gates. It would be three days before Microsoft officially acknowledged the birth via a short news release. By then, Melinda was home and Gates was back to work at Microsoft.

Some in the computer industry wondered what kind of father the hard-driving Gates would make—with good reason. When Gates was dating Ann Winblad, she had wanted to settle down, get married, and start a family. Hoping to plant the marriage seed in Bill's mind during one of his visits to her cottage on the Outer Banks of North Carolina, Winblad invited Lotus founder Mitch Kapor, his wife, and their year-old baby for a visit. Gates totally ignored the child, preferring to keep his nose in a biography of Henry Ford instead. A few years later, after a personal computer forum in Tucson, Arizona, Gates was having a beer with some industry acquaintances in the lobby of the Westin Hotel when the conversation turned to the number of people in the computer industry who were starting families. Gates was quiet for some time, then suddenly said, "Kids are a problem." Several minutes later, after additional reflection, Gates added another curt assessment: "Babies are a subset," invoking a term used in computer programming.

But he changed his tune when he finally became a father. A few months after his daughter Jennifer was born, he told a *New York Times* reporter that it had been "much more of a thrill than I expected. I thought, 'Well, when the kid starts talking, we'll do things together.' But even a kid who doesn't talk has little triumphs and a personality." Gates would later joke at a Microsoft sales conference that there was something besides Netscape keeping him up at night.

But anyone in the computer industry who for a moment believed that fatherhood would diminish the fire and intensity that Gates had displayed on December 7 when he issued Microsoft's call to arms was badly mistaken. By mid-1996, an army of more than 600 programmers had been shifted to Microsoft's various browser development efforts. The company's Internet Platform and Tools Division, which Gates had created in February under the direction of Brad Silverberg, had swelled to more than 2,500 employees. When Microsoft released its Internet Explorer 3.0 in August 1996, many said it was as good as if not better than the latest version of the Netscape Navigator. And it was free.

Netscape, meanwhile, was asking for help from an old Microsoft foe: the United States Department of Justice. In August, Silicon Valley lawyer Gary Reback, now representing Netscape, filed papers with the department asking to begin an investigation of some of Microsoft's Net-related business practices. Among the complaints was that Microsoft was offering a discount to computer manufacturers who installed Internet Explorer rather than competing browsers. The department later announced that it was investigating the complaint and began asking for documents. That probe was still under way in early 1997, though without Anne Bingaman, who had left for private practice in the fall.

On November 6, 1996, one day after the U.S. presidential election, Microsoft's stock hit a record $144 a share. That put Gates's net worth over the $20 billion milestone. Six days later, Microsoft announced a 2-for-1 stock split, meaning that someone who had purchased $1,000 worth of Microsoft stock in 1986 when the company went public would have a nice little nest egg worth more than $123,000.

By the end of 1996, CompuServe, America Online, and Prodigy had all selected Microsoft's Internet Explorer as the browser of choice for their combined 15 million customers. Netscape still had a commanding lead in market share over Microsoft, though Microsoft was gaining. In February 1997, Jupiter Communications, a research firm, said that Netscape had 58 percent of the browser market, while Microsoft had 38 percent. By the end of the year, the firm predicted that Microsoft's browser would surpass Netscape in market share. But other market research firms said that Netscape would continue to hold a commanding lead over Microsoft.

As analysts began to look more closely at Netscape's future, they saw that its stock had taken a bumpy ride during much of 1996 and had ended the year down more than 50 points.

Microsoft's stock, on the other hand, rose more than 90 percent in 1996. And Gates's personal wealth at the end of the year stood at $23.6 billion.

The Internet World conference held in New York in December 1996 reflected just how much the industry had changed in two years. In 1994, when the conference was held in Washington, D.C., Microsoft was hardly a presence. Netscape and Spyglass were the hot companies then. At the 1996 convention, Microsoft's 32,000-square-foot booth was far bigger than that of any other company.

Although the so-called browser war between Microsoft and Netscape captured the public's imagination during 1996, a potentially much more significant battle ensued over Internet-based computer networks known as intranets. In this corporate market, Microsoft faced serious challenges not only from Netscape but also from its more established foes, Sun and Oracle.

In fact, Sun was emerging from the pack as Microsoft's most formidable competitor. "There are two camps," Sun CEO Scott McNealy told writer Steven Levy for an article in *Time* in late 1996, "those in Redmond, who live on the Death Star, and the rest of us, the rebel forces."

Back in 1990, Bill Joy, one of Sun's founders, had predicted that by 1997 a wonderful new technology would transform the computer industry, and that it would be the undoing of Microsoft's dominance. Joy was right about the technology, but wrong about Microsoft. The company born of the personal computer revolution, had executed in amazing turnabout in response to the next great upheaval—the Internet. Like IBM before it, Microsoft could have been left behind. But driven by Bill Gates, whose burning desire to win and fear of failure compel him not only to beat his competitors, but to destroy them, Microsoft's dominance seems secure for a long time to come.

INDEX

Index

Index

Index

Index

Index

Index

Index

Wetherell, David, 207, 208, 209, 210
White House Office of Science and Technology, 67, 68–69
Whittaker, Sheelagh, 89
Wilson, Sonsini, Goodrich & Rosati, 249
Winblad, Ann, 124–25, 131–32, 135, 139, 248–49, 279, 292
Windows, 55, 96
  America Online sign-up software and, 106
  APIs and, 38–39, 46, 54, 254
  Apple interface similarity to, 97, 153–54
  Chinese reaction to, 173–75
  first program, 121
  Golden Vaporware award, 249
  Microsoft anti-DR DOS campaign, 45
  Microsoft ownership, 8, 34
  multimedia technology and, 81
  positive economic effects of, 51
  sales, 23–25, 29
  and TCP/IP, 105
  tie-in arrangements, 37
  word processing programs, 162
Windows 3.1
  browser proposal, 266, 281, 288
  coded beta version, 45, 111
Windows 95
  and Apple Computer, 254
  and browser package, 207–8, 213, 214, 219–20, 223, 281
  "Chicago" code name, 26, 107–8, 117
  Chinese version, 175
  and competitors' browsers, 276–77
  Internet protocols and, 149
  launch, 1–6, 7, 9–11, 261, 269–70, 271, 273–75
  launch target dates, 107, 111, 114, 118
  MSN bundling with, 26, 106, 109, 114, 117, 118, 211, 224–25, 261, 268, 271
  sales, 279

Slivka and, 207–8
  user complaints, 275–77
Windows for Workgroups, 26
Windows NT, 30, 34, 101, 161, 208, 223, 281
"Windows: The Next Killer Application for the Internet" (Allard memo), 149
Windows Watcher (newsletter), 138
Word for Windows. *See* Microsoft Word
WordPerfect, 43, 46, 47, 55
  Borland merger talks, 163–69
  company background, 161–62
  Lotus merger talks, 163–64, 166–70
  market share, 24
  Novell merger, 7, 159, 161, 163–64, 167, 168–71, 185
  and Quattro Pro price, 169
WordPerfect for Windows, 24, 162
word processing, 159, 163, 164
World Wide Web
  coffeepot and, 117–18
  growth of sites, 206
  Java and, 267–68, 282–86
  Microsoft and, 183, 184, 207, 266, 288
  Mosaic browsers and, 193–94, 195–96
  NCSA request-answer service, 88
  on-line services and, 206–7, 213
  origination, 17, 18, 195, 215
  RealAudio and, 119
  student use of, 148
  See also browsers
Wozniak, Stephen, 85, 126
WP. *See* WordPerfect
Wrigley, William, 128

X-25 network, 110
Xerox, 97, 230
X/Windows interface, 195

Yale University, 85, 86
Yao, Dennis, 50, 53, 57, 64, 65

Printed in the USA
CPSIA information can be obtained
at www.ICGtesting.com
JSHW082151140824
68134JS00014B/178

9 781620 458013